A HISTORY OF
TERROR

Albrecht Dürer's symbolic engraving, *The Knight, Death and the Devil*. Is he chivalrous knight, perpetual pilgrim – or frightened fugitive, pursued by the spectre of mortality?

A HISTORY OF
TERROR

FEAR & DREAD THROUGH THE AGES

PAUL NEWMAN

SUTTON PUBLISHING

First published in the United Kingdom in 2000 by
Sutton Publishing Limited · Phoenix Mill
Thrupp · Stroud · Gloucestershire · GL5 2BU

British Library Cataloguing in Publication Data
A catalogue record for this book is available from the British Library.

ISBN 0-7509-2008-4

Typeset in 11.5/15pt Photina MT.
Typesetting and origination by
Sutton Publishing Limited.
Printed and bound in Great Britain by Biddles Ltd
www.biddles.co.uk

CONTENTS

FOREWORD

COLIN WILSON

It *is* possible to die of fear. A sufficient flow of adrenalin into the bloodstream can cause the heart to stop.

Such a fate may have befallen Joseph Sheridan Le Fanu, one of the finest writers of ghost stories in the nineteenth century. Towards the end of his life – in 1873 – he had recurring nightmares of being in an old house that was about to fall down. And when his doctor noticed the terrified look on the dead man's face, he said: 'That house fell at last.' Le Fanu also demonstrates that something odd has happened to the human sense of fear in the past century or so. We have learned to exploit it.

Paul Newman has described in this book the development of the fear of the supernatural over the ages. And he makes the important point that in the Middle Ages the supernatural was not something that gave people a pleasant frisson on Christmas Eve – as nowadays, when Marley's ghost rattles his chains on television. It was as real as illness and death. If someone had decided to tell a Christmas ghost story eight hundred years ago, it would have ruined everybody's Christmas. Fear was not to be trifled with.

It is true that the Greek and Elizabethan dramatists wrote about tragedy and horror, but their aim was not to frighten their audiences, but (as Aristotle said) to purge them through pity and terror. Le Fanu had no interest in such high-minded ideals. He wanted to scare the reader to death. And he set about it with a cool realism that made his tales twice as frightening.

He was not the first. That dubious honour goes to Matthew Gregory Lewis (1775–1817), who wrote his sadistic fantasy *The*

Monk when he was only nineteen. It became the great bestseller of 1796. And if we wish to understand something of the psychology of horror fiction, we must look more closely at the workings of Lewis's imagination. The 'monk' is the virtuous, high-minded Abbot Ambrosio, whose downfall begins when he discovers that one of his favourite monks is a girl who is in love with him. Finally, when she asks him to feel the beating of her heart, and places his hand on her breast, he can no longer resist. 'Drunk with desire, he pressed his lips to those that sought them . . .'

His contemporaries could have accepted that. What upset them was that when 'his transport was passed . . . and his lust satisfied', and he feels disgusted with himself, she 'twined her arms voluptuously around him and glued her lips to his', and he does it all over again. Moreover, this time 'the fair wanton put every invention of lust in practice, every refinement in the art of pleasure, which might heighten the bliss of her possession, and render her lover's transports still more exquisite. Ambrosio rioted in a delight till then unknown to him. Swift fled the night, and the morning blushed to behold him still clasped in the embraces of Matilda.'

This is what horrified readers like Coleridge – who nevertheless acknowledged Lewis's genius. It was all very well to have a monk succumbing to hopeless passion, but to hint at forbidden sexual delights – which then go on all night – was going too far. Lewis seemed to be trying to debauch the reader.

But Lewis goes further still. Soon bored with the adoring Matilda, Ambrosio lusts after a beautiful penitent named Antonia, and plots to seduce her. And at this point, Matilda reveals that she knows something about black magic, and possesses an enchanted mirror in which she can see anything she likes. Ambrosio borrows it, and sees Antonio getting undressed for a bath. A tame bird settles on her breast and nibbles her nipples. Unable to stand it any more, Ambrosio cries 'I yield, Matilda! Do with me what you will . . .'

He then accompanies her to an underground vault, where she kindles a flame, mutters incantations, and slashes her arm to draw blood. Clouds of smoke ascend to the ceiling, and she shouts 'He comes!' But instead of the demon he is expecting, a beautiful naked youth appears, who finally agrees to grant Ambrosio's desires. Matilda ends by warning the monk that if he wants supernatural assistance again, he must summon the demon himself.

Ambrosio creeps into Antonia's house at midnight, intent on rape. He has a magic charm that will render her unconscious, so he can enjoy her without her knowledge. Unfortunately, her mother interrupts, and Ambrosio is forced to smother her to prevent her from waking the household. The frustrated monk flees back to his monastery.

He is still determined to possess her, even when he hears that Antonia has seen her mother's ghost, and has been told that she will die shortly. The plan is simple. On a visit to the sick Antonia, he slips a powerful drug into her medicine. She appears to die, and is entombed in a vault. The lustful Ambrosio hastens to the cemetery. 'By the side of three putrid half-corrupted bodies lay the sleeping beauty.' Cradled in his arms, she returns to consciousness. At first bewildered, she becomes aware of his intentions and struggles to escape. But 'heedless of her tears, cries and entreaties, he gradually made himself master of her person'.

The rape completed, Matilda rushes into the vault to tell the monk that the townspeople are rioting and everyone is searching for him. Antonia's brother, accompanied by officers of the Holy Inquisition, has cut off his retreat. Since Antonia may betray them with her cries, Matilda tries to stab her. Ambrosio prevents this, then is himself forced to stab her a few minutes later when Antonia's screams alert the soldiers. She dies in her brother's arms. And Ambrosio and Matilda are arrested by the Inquisition.

Most novelists would be contented with all this confusion and chaos. But Lewis is not finished. Ambrosio's torture by the Inquisition is minutely described. Matilda saves herself by selling her soul to the Devil, but Ambrosio refuses to follow her example. But as the soldiers approach to drag him off to the stake, he changes his mind and signs away his soul. The Devil, a huge winged monster, seizes him and soars high into the air, and then hurls him down on to the rocks. And again, we are spared nothing of the torments of Ambrosio's final days as he slowly expires. And when a flooded river carries away his body, the reader finally closes the book with a gasp of relief, and reaches for a handkerchief to wipe the sweat from his forehead . . .

We can see why *The Monk* became one of the most famous novels of its day. But why did Lewis, an upper-class young man whose father was in the government, write such an appalling book? It is true that he had been completely carried away by Ann Radcliffe's *The Mysteries of Udolpho*, and that his favourite reading was witch trials. But the real reason almost certainly lies in Lewis's sexuality. He was a homosexual in an age when it was a hanging offence, and at nineteen must have felt that life had treated him very badly in making it a crime to satisfy his natural urges. So he poured his anger, frustration and contempt into his novel. It was his attempt to hit back at society.

I can recognise a touch of Lewis's temperament in my old friend A.L. Rowse, the historian of Elizabethan England, who was also homosexual, and who usually referred to women as 'the bitches'. Lewis's contemporaries read the scene of the seduction of Ambrosio as the fantasy of an immoral and prurient young man. But as I read it, I can sense the impatience of the author as he describes how easily a demure-looking girl draws a monk into her spider web of sexual enchantment, and then throws off her disguise and becomes a highly experienced seductress who teaches Ambrosio some variations on normal lovemaking. (I can almost hear Leslie Rowse snorting 'The bitch!') And when Ambrosio then completes his damnation by deciding to seduce Antonia, Lewis seems to be muttering 'Serves the idiot right'.

In *The Mysteries of Udolpho*, Ann Radcliffe had created a weird phantasmagoria, but in the end all the supernatural occurrences are explained in natural terms. Lewis obviously felt that this was cowardice and determined to go one step further, so his book is full of genuine ghosts and demons. And that ending, with the monk dying of thirst as birds of prey tear out his eyes, is obviously intended to leave the reader feeling shattered. This is a man shaking his fist at his readers as well as at society.

The authorities were so furious that Lewis and his publisher were indicted, and a new edition had to be expurgated. Yet still it went on selling. And even though, unlike *The Mysteries of Udolpho*, it has failed to become a classic, it still has its devoted admirers, and is periodically reprinted in paperback.

What happened next is, in a sense, even more revealing. 'Monk' Lewis became a literary celebrity. When he was twenty-one, he became a Member of Parliament. His next publication was called *Tales of Terror* (1799), and he went on to become a highly successful playwright, as well as writing more horror fiction. Yet everyone agrees that he wrote nothing else that has the same touch of genius as *The Monk*. His work still has talent – but no more genius.

What happened, clearly, was that the burning frustration disappeared. He was a literary celebrity, and ceased to be sexually frustrated. (His most important love affair was with a fourteen-year-old boy named William Kelly, who caused him some torment with his promiscuity.) But at least he was able to indulge his homosexuality without scandal (his contemporary William Beckford had to flee abroad), and became thoroughly at home in fashionable drawing-rooms.

By all accounts Lewis was a pleasant man, kindly and generous, and became a friend of Byron and Shelley. (He was a guest at the Villa Diodati, where Byron, Shelley, Mary Shelley and Polidori all decided to write horror stories, and where Mary Shelley conceived *Frankenstein*.) Concern over his slaves drew him to his plantations in Jamaica, where he caught yellow fever and died an agonising death, being buried at sea on 14 May 1817.

What *The Monk* teaches us is that to enjoy fear, it is important to only *half* believe in it. More than that would make it a threat to sanity. It was only possible to write *The Monk* a century after Isaac Newton had convinced everyone the universe was a gigantic piece of clockwork.

All this first struck me almost forty years ago, when I wrote a book called *The Strength to Dream*, a study of literature and the imagination. I had been staying overnight in the Dorset farmhouse of an American friend, and I happened to pick up a book called *The Outsider* by H.P. Lovecraft. Since I had written a book by the same title, I took it to bed with me, and read the first few stories. The first was about a gravedigger who comes to a gruesome end after chopping off the feet of a tall corpse to make it fit the coffin. The aim was not only to make the reader feel uneasy, but to make him feel vaguely sick.

It was while pondering the question 'Why *should* a writer make you want to feel sick?' that I realised I had hit upon a subject of endless fascination. In past ages the storyteller was a kind of minstrel, whose business was to entertain, like a fiddler at a wedding. After 1800 his role changed, and as often as not he wanted to tell you about his neuroses and frustrations. Baudelaire observed perceptively of Poe: 'As for the ardour with which Poe often treats horrifying material, I have observed in a number of men that this was often the result of a very large fund of unused vital energy, sometimes the result of an unyielding chastity and of very deep feelings kept repressed.'

In fact, E.T.A. Hoffman (author of the famous *Tales*) was sexually inadequate. So was Gogol, whose weird tales are at once haunting and grotesque – he was so afraid of women that his only sexual experience was onanistic. The stories of M.R. James, with their horrifying physical 'ghosts', are obviously full of *some* kind of repression, although whether it was hetero- or homosexual has never been determined. All these writers achieved their effects by 'riding their own nightmare'. The writers who lack this quality of obsession – and Dorothy L. Sayers' three *Omnibuses of Horror and the Supernatural* have all too many examples – are somehow forgettable.

Let me summarise. The medieval nightmare, which Paul Newman describes so well, evaporated in the age of reason. But the nightmares of 'Monk' Lewis and Sheridan Le Fanu were also unable to withstand the cold light of science, so that both those excellent writers are now museum pieces. In the last decades of the twentieth century, the nightmare has tended to take a more physical form; in the work of Stephen King and Thomas Harris, axe-wielding madmen and serial killers have replaced the ghosts of an earlier epoch. Will the nightmare simply vanish in a future age of computers and space travel? If so, it would be a pity. For, as Paul Newman has shown, nightmares, like dreams, are essential to the health of civilisation.

INTRODUCTION

Through the Jungle very softly flits a shadow and a sigh –
He is Fear, O Little Hunter, he is Fear!
            (*The Song of the Little Hunter*, Rudyard Kipling)

In February 1998 the *Sunday Times* ran a story about a group of scientists who had discovered the seat of fear in the human brain, 'proving that one of the most potent human emotions has a chemical basis and raising the prospect of a new generation of drugs that could make man fearless'. The article was dramatically illustrated by a photograph of soldiers kneeling on a battlefield during the Second World War and praying for courage to face the ordeal.

Apparently the sensation of fear is manufactured in tiny pathways between nerve cells in a small, almond-shaped clump of tissue called the amygdala. Professor Joseph LeDoux – an authority on the emotional brain – commented: 'We have shown that the amygdala is like the hub in the centre of a wheel of fear. If we understand the pathways of fear, it will ultimately lead to better control.' Such information urges a reappraisal of our view of fear. At one time it was seen as something that spread over the body, making the knees shake and the stomach contract, but modern techniques of mind-mapping enable a precise location to be fixed. The recent maps of the brain are not particularly accurate – rather like those sixteenth-century maps of the world where, give or take a continent or two, things are approximately in the right place. But they will no doubt get better and better until perhaps the tiniest of our impulses can be pin-pointed.

The scientist's view is that basically the brain is an elaborate piece of circuitry served by neurotransmitters and that odd behaviour is usually traceable to a malfunction within this assemblage. For instance, a preposterously brave or 'fearless' man could well be suffering from lack of responsiveness in the amygdala. The personality itself – the arena of presence – seems to be stationed in the frontal lobes. Those who lack a sense of personal definition – of agency – may be under-active in that sector. If your frontal lobes are not responding, you may have a deficient sense of being a discrete, fully fledged citizen of the world.

Chemically speaking, fear is close to curiosity – hence many so-called terrors have an eerie attraction. That is why fear can be marketed as entertainment. We start out by being afraid of things – spiders, ghosts, thunderstorms and volcanoes – and end up being immensely well-informed about them. The natural sciences developed out of the study of creatures and objects that once inspired superstition and loathing. In a sense, the Renaissance is the most important watershed in human history, marking the period when curiosity swamped fear. People began to wash the clay of superstition from their eyes and explore the world. Dead bodies were cut open and their organs mapped; stars were observed as they moved in their courses; chemicals were mixed in retorts. The power structure based on Hell and damnation, which had been exploited by the Catholic Church, dissolved and with it went much theological lore that had passed for knowledge. Hence today we find primitive fears are stock sources of amusement: films and other forms of entertainment are devised that mock everything from God and Satan to werewolves and serial killers. Roughly speaking, moving through time, fear expresses itself in four stages, all of which overlap and sometimes run parallel:

(1)   Primal Response
(2)   Superstition
(3)   Frisson
(4)   Satire or Comedy

Take leprosy as an example. This disease loomed as an awful possibility throughout the early medieval period. The primal response was an authentic fear; then, as conditions improved, the threat lessened, but there remained a powerful lingering superstition concerning the curative power of leper's blood. When leprosy became a rare, almost exotic, condition in Western Europe, it started to be employed as a literary device, to add a frisson or pleasurable shiver to a story, such as in the tale *The Silver Man* by Kipling. Finally, when the dreadful affliction became so distanced and so remote, it was recycled as pure farce in buffoonesque comedies set in a Middle Ages peopled by roistering belchers, clanking knights and wimpled floozies.

Though it may seem tangible at times, fear is a protean, shifting sensation, endlessly altering its location and alliance. Down the centuries people feared the wrath of God until scientists assured them that the universe is unlikely to be presided over by a punitive deity. The information did not release them. Many felt oppressed at the idea of being abandoned in a 'godless' universe. Similarly, when the terror of being assaulted at night was allayed by street lighting, people began to fear other things, such as the safety of their property. Insurance policies offered a temporary solution, but as people prospered, more and more personal artefacts needed to be insured – was there enough money to cover these payments? Fear and worry melt constantly and reappear in altered guises. They are part of the intimate life of the individual. In extreme forms, they lead to social paralysis, arrant prejudice and rigidity of outlook.

Fear has been divided into four components: the subjective experience of nervousness or apprehension; physiological changes; outward effects, like trembling or tension; and the tendency to back away from or avoid certain situations. There are morbid anxieties such as the thought of teeth crumbling in the mouth or one's eyes being pecked out by a gull. Other anxieties are not relatable to tangible stimulation but belong to the realm of fantasy: the sky is going to fall or an entity from a UFO will descend and kidnap someone. Then there are inexplicable onslaughts of 'panic' which descend on both men and women and have been linked with the 'numinous' or the threatening silence of God. And there are minor but specific phobias like a dread of spiders, rats or snakes. The latter can be treated by methods of aversion therapy in which, for example, arachnophobes are taught to handle tarantulas and learn about their behaviour, thus quelling fear through knowledge and first-hand experience.

Freud held that many fears arose from conditioning and negative stimuli. If a father regularly beat a child because he upset a drink, then the child, when he grows up, continues to feel the same shrinking terror each time he spills a drop of beer, even though his father is long dead. Then there are fears learned by experience, like a dread of heights, fires, plants and insects that sting. Such fears are educative and necessary for survival. Fear of pain makes people proceed with caution. Fear of being discovered will make a burglar tread less noisily. Fear of fire will make people buy flame-proof furnishings. Fearlessness can be foolishness as well as courage.

Being more contained than horror or revulsion, fear impinges directly on the 'human situation', implicit in which is an almost permanent sense of unease. As one matures it may take on a specific character: old age, the onset of disease, a sense of encroaching isolation or impending catastrophe. Like a stick of rock, each individual is stamped through with mortality, but life demands a focus, a goal, a plan, and the obsessive pattern-making that defines civilisation can be seen as a massive distraction from the primal silence that preceded creation. On the slender foundations of fears withheld and secreted, we build our cities and dreams.

Poets and literary critics often evoked fear in the highly specialised sense of an intense frisson or feeling of awe inspired by the sublimity and wonder of creation. Graham Greene's story *The Ministry of Fear* derives from Wordsworth's expression of gratitude for the sanctimonious 'ministry of fear'. He is aware that he is a guest in an infinite universe whose deeper meaning remains hidden. It is a feeling of reverence tempered by a shiver of unease.

A reflexive manifestation of fear can be found in acts of violence against individuals and races. No one knows what the first uttered word was – but it may have been generated by fear. Consider how many pleasures involve silent communion, such as digging a garden, smelling wild garlic in a wood, or listening to music, and then think how important sound becomes when danger threatens: a shout to warn a child playing in the road of a speeding vehicle, the scream uttered by a drowning woman, the yelp of a frightened animal. The first word might well have been a negative. A cave-man finds himself encircled by enemies who intend to crush him with heavy stone implements. He shrivels and squirms, and utters 'No!' – a pure fusion of sound and terror. In a sense, fear had given birth to a cry, and from that point it can be articulated as part of the shared experience of mankind.

Comparatively little attention has been given in this present work to the reigns of terror imposed by Stalin and Hitler. This is because, psychologically speaking, tyrannies that rule by instant death penalties are similar. In the 1820s the Zulu chieftain Chaka killed around a million people during his wars of conquest. He built his empire on fear. On one occasion he massacred a whole tribe of forty thousand people, including women and children, although some of the more nubile girls were retained for his men's pleasure. After each battle, Chaka ordered his chiefs to 'bring forth the cowards' who were impaled on the spot. A tribesman who coughed, sneezed or irritated him in a minor way was liable to be taken away and beaten to death with sticks. When Chaka's mother died, his men executed around seven thousand out of 'sympathy' for their leader's grief. Chaka's system was arbitrary, erratic, moody. No one knew what would happen – who would die – next. Men were conditioned to a state of unerring cruelty. Instead of being autonomous individuals, they were extensions of their leader's nervous system. To please him, they would volunteer to kill themselves and their own children. The system worked until Chaka was assassinated by his half-brothers in 1828. An attempt was made by his successor to introduce a liberal regime, but the result was a series of tribal rebellions; in order to restore stability, a more moderate 'reign of terror' was installed.

The essence of Chaka's reign was absolute control through a terrifying uncertainty. The ways in which tyrants establish such networks differ, but the generated 'fear' is similar. Hence, to avoid a diet of horror and repetition, large sections of this present work analyse the shapes of fear as they have come down to us through the ages: the Devil, Hell, ghosts, vampires, werewolves, ghouls and little grey men from outer space. People may differ in what they are frightened of, but the same primitive dread lurks behind manifold apparitions. It is the translation in the mind of the perceiver that differs rather than the experience itself.

Anyone glancing through the ensuing chapters may be affronted by disproportions and credulities that beg the question. How can one mention Hiroshima and Nazi death camps alongside frivolities like Fatima, the Angel of Mons and the shenanigans of UFO abductees? Beyond the hard facts of history, there are times when waves of hysteria sweep over groups and nations. Whether these are caused by groundless anxiety or delusive vision, they result in marked changes of attitude. During the Middle Ages, for instance, the prophecies of the *Book of Revelation* triggered dramatic sieges and persecutions – but today, aside from cultic exceptions like Waco, such texts are ignored. Yet men and women are still beset by inner demons, bedevilled by outrageous passions and irrational horrors, and this book, written at the very start of the third millennium, can be sampled as both warning and entertainment.

1

PANIC: THE BIRTH & SPREAD OF TERROR

GREAT PAN IS DEAD

And that dismal cry rose slowly
And sank slowly through the air,
Full of spirits melancholy
And eternity's despair;
And they heard the words it said –
Pan is dead – great Pan is dead,
Pan, Pan is dead.

(A Musical Instrument, Elizabeth Barrett Browning, 1859*)*

In the first century AD, during the reign of Tiberius, a group of travellers were sailing to Italy. It was evening; the wind dropped and the ship drifted near the island of Paxi. The crew and passengers were awake; many had not finished their afternoon dinner wine. Then, from Paxi, a voice was heard calling Thamus, the Egyptian pilot, who was not known to many on board. Twice his name was called but he did not reply. The voice grew loud and impatient, adding 'When you come opposite to Palodes, announce that Great Pan is dead.' All were astonished by this and wondered whether the instructions should be carried out. Thamus said that he would carry out the order, provided the water was navigable. They drew towards the island; there was neither wind nor wave. From the stern, Thamus cried, 'Great Pan is dead!' Before he could finish, a great cry of lamentation arose from all the animals, plants and rocks, mingled with exclamations of dismay and amazement.

This famous passage is taken from Plutarch's *De Oraculorum Defectu*. Christian legend has it that Pan died on the very day Christ was nailed to the cross. The cry came across the water when the agony was over and Christ had left his mortal body to rise into heaven. He had displaced Pan as the ascendant deity. The transfixing symbol of His suffering cowed the old order of nature spirits.

Displaced by Christ

Pan, son of the nymph Penelope, was the shepherd-god from the mountains of Arcadia. He was said to avenge himself on anyone who interrupted his regular nap by appearing before them and paralysing them with horror. From Pan we derive 'panic' or the sudden fear that seizes one alone in the forest. He is that invisible agent who makes cattle and sheep scatter without warning. He is the horned face peering between the leaves, and the god of vegetation. His name has been translated as 'All', for he came to represent every manifestation of nature: the dance of blood along the arteries; the rising sap; sexual desire running amok, and its counterforce, decay and dissolution. This definition leans on scholarship, on the radial nature of language, plucking the goat-god from his forest setting and transforming him into something akin to everything and nothing. But this is exactly what Pan evolved into: the horror of the all-engulfing 'everything' that makes the individual feel he is 'nothing', a spark of identity in a meaningless void.

But to probe deeper into Plutarch's anecdote, why should Pan be displaced by Christ? Is the Saviour of the World the antithesis of Pan? In a manner of speaking, yes. Where Christ attempts to improve or 'better' this world of ours – by streaking its essential violence with notions of morality and duty – Pan stands for anarchy and outrage, the intractable nature of phenomena. For Pan is the rule of nature, embracing all the things we fear, yet see reflected in the world, whether in the crunching rapacity of the food chain or in the mindless destruction wrought by a flood or earthquake. It is nature unredeemed by moral structure or pure idea.

Higher Order of Exultation

If the language of the foregoing is metaphorical and elusive, that is perhaps necessary considering the central subject of this study: fear and dread down the ages. If a theme can be embodied by a name, then Pan is appropriate, being lord of the nightmare and instigator of the 'primal' panic. He is synonymous with the natural world, and nature, as we know, carelessly sacrifices its young and old, starves them, freezes them to death, then leaves them to rot under a sky that remakes itself endlessly.

This is a truth that people accept, grateful to have inherited the mantle of human destiny rather than being born as a gull, an ape or an adder. Yet being non-human has its consolations. For when all the sparrows gather on the rooftops, twitter in an exultant chorus, then lift off and spread themselves across the sky, they may know a wordless ecstasy beyond human ken – a higher order of exultation than was ever felt by saints or mystics. Do they become one massed body of joy – an immense celestial orgasm? Does that sensation outpleasure all human joys of home and hearth? But if their pleasure consists of unison – of flocking together and forming one composite bird – might not their fear be the opposite? When, no longer together, they are a single, isolated, shivering dot of feathers, each dot is threatened by a stabbing beak, a taloned claw, a circle of teeth. Fear of a predator shrivels the locus of one's being. When afraid, you're aware of the tingling perimeters of your skin. You are no longer part of the 'All' but a small, trembling fragment that may be chewed and spat out and left to decay. Was it in such a 'panic' that fear was born? And did it give rise to the first terrified cry?

Vocabulary of Grief

Man's ultimate terror is identified as death – for death governs the 'ministry of fear' which infuses the texture of existence. So what of man's early confrontation with this traditional adversary – when the stark negation of Another forced him to appraise the his own destiny? On this note, let us cite James Hogg (1770–1835), the Ettrick shepherd. A minor figure in English Literature, he was central to the Scottish Calvinist tradition. In *The Black-Faced Sheep and Her Ways*, he describes the gruelling vigil kept by a ewe over her dead lamb, 'so faithfully I think the like was never equalled by any of the woolly race'. Hogg visited her every morning and evening, and always she was there, protecting the small body from the dog who would be chased off twice a day. As the weather grew warm, the dead lamb decayed to a few bones mixed with wisps of wool, 'but still this affectionate and desolate creature kept hanging over the poor remains with an attachment that seemed to be nourished by hopelessness . . . till at length every remnant of her offspring vanished, mixing with the soil, or wafted away by winds'.

Was there a time when human beings felt a similar loss and confusion? Lacking a vocabulary of grief, did the earliest mourners stubbornly cling to the body of their loved ones, visiting it daily, hourly, hoping for a recovery or springtime resurrection with the wild flowers? Did they wait until it was nothing but skull and crumbled bone? Was there a time when, not knowing death for what it is, they burrowed in the desolation?

Today we conceive of death as absolute, a cessation, an irretrievable withdrawal – but this may not always have been so. Thousands of years ago, before the concept of heart-death or brain death had been established, the process was seen as a series of strange transitions. First the body became still and speechless like a tree, a rock, a piece of earth – an unresisting slab. It did not move; the light seemed to have drained from the face and eyes. But there were still apparent signs of activity. In fact, days later it may have appeared 'alive'. For the decompositional process, usually divided into five stages (fresh, bloat, active decay, post or advanced decay, dry or skeletal remains), took on a vigorous, colourful aspect as the skin turned green, the stomach bloated and rank bloodstained fluids seeped from orifices. Putrid blisters sprouted on the skin. The protruding eyeballs burst into hideous bloom. The intestines were pushed out through the vagina and rectum by expanding gases within.

This busy bacterial carnival was an informal prelude to a banquet, in which wolves, rodents, birds and insects all took their share, followed by withering and advanced decomposition. As a climax to this mortal striptease, the resistant kernel – the lean skeleton – made a showing. Here the process, having reached its apogee, abruptly halts. For bones linger down the centuries – that is obviously why a cult sprang up around them. Most resolute of souvenirs, the skull, for instance, resists the changes that consume the soft parts. It hangs around like a grinning parody, haunting men and women by its presence while, paradoxically, reminding them of its soul's absence.

Dispersing the Primal Terror

Appalling yet compulsive, this chemical progression was a major factor in the earliest cultures. The brimming ebullience of putrefaction fascinated prehistoric peoples in the same way it fascinated Baudelaire and Chaim Soutine thousands of years later. But the sight was hardly adequate or satisfying, in that it could not exorcise their grief. It presented a physical spectacle rather than a release of any kind. If these disorderly feelings were to be channelled, it needed to be through a series of actions – a technique of ordering and orchestrating emotion. Thus, when they began to ritualise grief – to articulate it in logical stages – they established a new mastery. The composing of the first funerary chants, the laying and dressing of bodies, the processing along walkways and ceremonial routes, the division and arrangement of bones, tools and shells, the raising of tombs and mortuary houses – all these rituals and accoutrements must have seemed a wonderful way of dispersing primal terror, of creating something solid out of the flux.

Additionally, the making of the first demonic masks – immunising terror by emulating it – represented yet another breakthrough. A loved one may have been taken, yet there had evolved monuments and ceremonies through which loss was transformed into presence. So enthralling and sustaining was this apparent victory over mortality that it directed the prehistoric imagination for centuries. Death, like birth and springtime mating, became an agent of interaction and innovation and was epitomised in barrows, shrines and henges.

Spiritual Delinquents

> Man feels himself isolated in the cosmos because he is no longer
> involved in nature and has lost his emotional 'unconscious
> identity'. . . . Thunder is no longer the voice of an angry god, nor
> is lightning his avenging missile. No river contains a spirit, no
> tree is the life principle of a man, no mountain cave the home of
> a great demon. No voices now speak to man from stones, plants,
> and animals, nor does he speak to them believing they can hear.
> *(Approaching the Unconscious,* Carl Gustav Jung, 1964*)*

In the previous section we examined the prehistoric attitude to death
and funerary rites, the honouring and placation of the dead, but
how did the idea of spirits and demons arise? How did people develop
the idea that the dead are still living – are still, in some mysterious
way, with us?

There is an ambivalence about the issue. Allowing that everything
desires to persist in its own nature, many would prefer to survive
death in some form and derive some comfort from the notion of a
benign, discarnate entity. Furthermore, whenever a companion or
relative passes away, there is a natural gravitation to thinking about
the disrupted bonds of love or friendship, and whether any spectral
vestige lingers.

Not only do the dead crowd our waking thoughts, they come back
in dreams and speak as they did when alive. It was probably through
the medium of the dream that the idea of the disembodied spirit
became implanted. A man dies; his wife attends the funeral, weeping
and placing flowers in his mouth. A week later, while she sleeps, he
appears to her, talking casually, intimately, until the fact that he has
passed over seems irrelevant. But then, remembering, she asks him
where he has gone. He makes a light reply that does not satisfy her.
She repeats the question: 'Where are you now?' His lips make sounds
which never quite shape a point or unlatch a meaning and somehow
he turns over and vanishes. She awakes amazed and tells another
widow in her tribe who says: 'Yes, your husband's spirit has crossed
the bridge of dreams, just as my man's did after the hunting accident.'

Admittedly fanciful, this is nevertheless scarcely over-credulous, for it was in the ceaseless interplay between dreams and waking, life and death, that the twilight realm of magic and superstition came into being, and from which arose notions of gods, demons, angels and spirit entities. It was also an area over which men and women began to claim special authority. In the beginning there was a single priest or 'shaman'. While dreaming or in a trance, he would watch the struggles of his inner life projected in garbled fashion against a background of stars, solstices and seasons. A pattern was perceived, blending the personal and phenomenal, ascribing motivation to events like a failed harvest, a flash flood, an unexpected death. Perhaps a peal of thunder would assume a human voice or the gnarled bark of a tree grimace like a warrior in agony. Voices from the day would blend with visions of rocks, chasms, waterfalls and skies raked by lightning. This enforced the idea of the presence of gods or translatable intentions behind the physical dramas that underpinned daily life.

Gradually each principle was balanced by an opposing one, night by day, fire by water, hot by cold, and things assumed specialised roles, with gods and demons struggling against one another and participating in the cosmic scheme. Shamans were adopted as lucid dreamers, who, having mastered the sensation of fear, were able to anticipate or avert impending calamities. Eventually tribes started to physically act out these struggles: the slaying of summer by the ice-sword of winter, the cloud-dragon blinding the eye of the sun, the rain dancing on dry soil and making it sprout green shoots. Drama and storytelling were thus developed out of the raw material of contrasting natural forces strained through human perception. For storytelling itself is a kind of triumph over fear and terror – a story absorbs and incorporates panic into the body of its being. By presenting the fear of 'another' it relieves our own.

Demons

As for negative spirits or demons, they hark back to the earliest stage of civilisation when tribes were predominantly nomadic and each spring, tree, well and rocky outcrop had a presiding spirit or *genius loci*. Places of violent accident – deep ravines, dangerous swamps, turbulent rapids – gained the reputation of being occupied by a spirit who 'willed' the fatality. Later there came the custom of laying an offering to placate or pre-empt such a possibility; altars or shrines sprang up for the same purpose.

Occurrences that were not traceable to a known cause – an 'attack' of flu or an outbreak of shaking and vomiting – might be attributed to a malign agency. With the spread and acceptance of Christianity, minor spirits of the pagan world were granted an 'evil' specialisation: taunting women, seducing bishops, terrifying animals, spreading contagion. Ten categories of demons were listed by Alphonsus de Spina (1459):

Fates. Some say they have seen Fates, but if so they are not women but demons (and Augustine says the only fate is the will of God).

Poltergeists, commonly called the *duende de casa*, who do little tricks at night, like breaking things, pulling off bedclothes, making the sounds of footsteps overhead. They move little things but do little damage.

Incubi and Succubi. Nuns are especially subject to these devils. When they awake in the morning, they 'find themselves polluted as if they had slept with men'.

Marching hosts, which appear like hordes of men making much tumult.

Familiar demons, who eat and drink with men, in imitation of the angel of Tobit.

Nightmare demons, who terrify men in their dreams.

Demons formed from semen and its odour when men and women copulate. These demons also cause men to dream of women so the demons can 'receive their emission and make therefrom a new spirit'.

Deceptive demons, who sometimes appear as men and sometimes as women.

Clean demons (but really most foul) who assail only holy men.

Demons who deceive old women (called *xorguinae* or *bruxae*) into thinking they fly to sabbats.

Normally demons were shunned but there were circumstances in which magicians were hired to contact them. It was believed force was necessary to activate them and force inevitably aroused their fury. The art of black magic consisted in whipping up the rage of a demon to a malignant brew and ritually deflecting it from oneself to the enemy. This was hazardous, for the demon would try to kill the magician, who had to keep within the circle of protection or risk injury. There is argument about whether a demon physically manifested or appeared merely in the mind of the magician, but this is actually irrelevant since all phenomena ended in mental sensation.

Demons and guardian angels were the handmaidens of magicians. A high god was unlikely to step down from the sky to turn around the affections of a village girl, or cure a butcher of piles, but a lesser spiritual being could be more easily put to work. Hence, by definition, magicians became known as people who trafficked with spirits and demons, and when monotheism became widespread, they were slandered as necromancers who defiled their souls by having intercourse with spirits.

At the name of God demons trembled. Their constitution was perceived as coarser and heavier than that of angels who could command them if desired. Unable to stand strong light, demons hid in the souls of men and animals, causing illness and diseases. In cold and dry surroundings, the gaseous bodies of demons thickened and condensed and, to preserve their proper consistency, they needed to retreat into warm, comforting places: the intestines of animals or humans, holes in the ground, graves or hot steaming baths. Some modern occultists maintain that demons exist in their tens of thousands as inherently destructive forces. Being creators of form, they may entice the magician by taking the form of an innocent, babbling child or a gentle white-bearded grandfather or a beautiful person of either sex. Following the invocation, the demon will make an appearance, first like some strange beast padding around the perimeter of the pentagram and then as a physical materialisation.

Exorcism was seen as a valid procedure for ridding the possessed. Like the legendary Solomon, Jesus was a healer and expeller of unclean spirits. He discharged the demons of a possessed woman into the Gadarene swine; an epileptic boy was cured by the laying on of hands; a blind man had his sight restored by the traditional magical substance of spittle. The use of bodily fluids was in keeping with the occult traditions of Greece and Egypt and it is not always appreciated how fine is the dividing line between magic and religion.

Even the rituals of Christianity, being conducted in secret, were not immune to slander. 'I am told,' wrote Minicius Felix, 'that moved by some foolish urge, they [Christians] consecrate and worship the head of a donkey, the most abject of all animals. Others say that they reverence the genitals of the presiding priest himself, and adore them as though they were their fathers'. As for the initiation of new members, a child, covered in dough to deceive the unwary, is set before the would-be novice. The novice stabs the child to death with invisible blows; indeed he himself, deceived by the coating of dough, thinks his stabs harmless. Then – it's horrible – they hungrily drink the child's blood, and compete with one another as they divide his limbs. Precisely the secrecy of this evil religion proves that all these things, or practically all, are true.'

Until the ironic failure of connective sense, one would scarcely guess that Minicius Felix – an educated Christian of the third century – was satirising rumours that circulated in Greece and Italy. Early Christians reviled the pagan religions, but others perceived Christianity in a similar way. Down the centuries the Church transposed such blood-soaked, sex-ridden pantomimes on to the worshippers of Satan-Lucifer, the rebel angel who, after his expulsion from heaven, infiltrated the world of men, spreading disharmony and corruption even among his own followers.

THE DEVIL

Satan! grand, terrific, revengeful, daring Satan! What terms can express the admiration, the enthusiasm, the grief, the detestation of thy diabolic and tremendous Soul.

(Diary of Benjamin Robert Haydon, 30 August 1813)

As the tendency towards monotheism intensified, the principles of good and evil separated and the notion of a head-demon or presiding evil genius took root in several cultures. In the Christian tradition he was often depicted with a goat's horns and shaggy hindquarters – yet another manifestation of Pan. Known variously as the Devil, Satan, Nick, Old Harry or 'the prince of darkness', he was an evil genius whose duty was to lead men further and further into temptation.

Most religions have their arch-devils, such as Seth in the Egyptian pantheon and Ahriman in the Zoroastrian system. Seth was sometimes depicted as a black pig or serpent and was continually at war with Horus: in different escapades, he trapped the sun-god in a box, tore out his eye and buried it, and attempted to sodomise him. Ahriman had seven arch-fiends under his control – wrongmindedness, heresy, discord, presumption, anarchy, hunger and thirst – and dwelt in a void. His followers were termed 'people of the lie' and he was often likened to a serpent. These theological reprobates may well find their origin in famine, tempest, flood or human discord; in other words, they personified destructive natural forces or mankind in its undesirable or tyrannical aspect.

If the Devil's province is chaos, as is often posited, how can he wield authority? For the whole point of chaos is that no one can direct or control it. So there is a terminological contradiction in being the Lord of Chaos – not unlike a madman being appointed managing director of a lunatic asylum.

However, such confusions and contradictions have never quite dispelled the alluring presence of the Arch-Deceiver. In his guise as Lucifer, the fallen angel, the Devil has inspired some fine pen-portraits – notably the stately lament of Isaiah:

How have you fallen from heaven, bright morning star, felled to the earth, sprawling helpless across the nations! You thought in your own mind, I will scale the heavens . . . yet you shall be brought down to the Sheol, the depths of the Abyss.

During the thirteenth century the Devil was at the height of his influence. Abbot Richalmus wrote a book (*c.* 1270) dealing with the dalliances and persecutions of the Lord of Hell and his swarm of 'impish demons' who placed petty obstacles in his way. Devils made him feel qualmish after he had eaten too much, made him fall asleep over his breviary and his hand feel cold and chapped, even though he hid it under his cloak. 'Once,' he reports, 'when we were gathering stones for building a wall, I heard a devil exclaim, "What tiresome work!" He did it only to tempt us and make us rebellious.'

One does not have to be especially perceptive to notice something rather manipulative and self-congratulatory about the Abbot suggesting that he had been singled out for special torment, presumably because of his outstanding piety and fortitude. But after the Reformation, there was a detectable lessening of superstition and a tendency for the Devil to be internalised.

In her autobiography (1562–8), Saint Teresa recounts being in an oratory when Satan appeared. A huge flame issued from his body, and he spoke with a fearful voice telling her that, though she had escaped, he would lay hold of her again. Terror-struck, she made the sign of the cross; the demonic form vanished, only to reappear twice, being shooed away with holy water. More pleasurable was the occasion when she encountered an angel. He held up a long spear of gold with a little fire on the iron's point. When he thrust it into her entrails, the pain was so great 'that it made me moan; and yet so surpassing was the sweetness of this excessive pain, that I could not wish to be rid of it'.

Did such a sexual onslaught hail from an angel or an evil impersonator? Religious fanatics identified Satan in any encounter that caused carnal pleasure. Neither did they look kindly on those who belittled his dark grandeur. By the time we reach *Pseudodoxoia Epidemica* (1646) by Sir Thomas Browne, Satan has become a guileful double-bluffer who leads men astray by persuading them to doubt his existence: 'Insinuating into men's minds there is no Devil at all . . . he annihilates the blessed Angels and Spirits in the rank of his Creation [and] begets a security of himself.'

The Devil's physical elusiveness proved a vexation to a pragmatically minded workman of Madrid who, at the close of the eighteenth century, was brought before an inquisition for denying the existence of the Arch-Fiend.

'After having suffered every kind of misfortune', he explained, 'to my family, my property and my trade, I lost patience and called in despair on the Devil, begging him to avenge me on my enemies in return for my soul and body. I repeated this day after day; but in vain – no Devil appeared. So I consulted a man who claimed to be a magician, who in turn took me to a woman who he said was more skilled than himself. She told me to go three days running in the hill 'des vitillas', there to call on Lucifer as Angel of Light, offering my soul, renouncing God and the Christian faith. I did so, but saw and heard nothing. She told me to throw away my rosary and all tokens of Christian belief, to renounce my faith in God, and engage myself in Lucifer's service, acknowledging him as the greater divinity. This I did, but still no sign of Lucifer. The old lady advised me to write a covenant in blood, recognizing Lucifer as lord and master, which I should take to the spot and read aloud. I did it, but it was useless. Then I thought to myself: if there are any devils and, if they are really anxious to get hold of human souls, they will never get a more favourable opportunity than I had given them. Since they hadn't taken me up on my sincere offer, it was evident that no such Devils exist.'

Hell

Sir Thomas Browne, quoted earlier, not only held the Devil responsible for any impression of his non-existence but also located Hell in the heart of man: 'I feel sometimes a hell within myself; Lucifer keeps court in my breast.' Contrast this with the Jesuit Father Caussin, the father confessor of Louis XII, who presented several choices: 'What is hell? A silence; for all that which is said of hell is less than hell itself. No just man can think of it without shedding thousands of tears. But do you want to know what hell is? Ask Tertullian. He will tell you that hell is a deep, dark pit of stench in which all the offal of the whole world flows together. Ask Hugo of St Victor. He will answer: Hell is an abyss without a bottom, which opens the gates of despair, and where all hope is abandoned. "It is an eternal pool of fire," says St John the Divine, "its air comes from glowing coals, its lights from flickering flames. The nights of hell are darkness; the places of rest of the damned are serpents and vipers; their hope is despair. O, eternal death! O, life without life! O, misery without end!"'

There are many evocations of Hell, the majority of which combine monotony with sadistic vigour, as they gloatingly evoke molten torture and agony. In *The Historie of the Damnable Life and Deserved Death of Doctor John Faustus* (1592), Hell is styled as a place of utter darkness in which there is a chasm out of which issues thunder, lightning, wind, snow, mist, fog and terrible wailing sounds. Flames of fire and brimstone shoot out of a pool in which all the damned souls are immersed. Ascending from the centre of the abyss, there is a tall ladder, giving the impression of reaching up to heaven, upon which the damned climb, hoping to escape. None ever succeeds. Just before attaining the region of joy and light, they topple back into the heat and darkness. 'And mark Faustus,' Mephistopheles warns, 'hell is the nurse of death, the heat of all fire, the shadow of heaven and earth, the oblivion of all goodness, the pains unspeakable, the griefs unremovable, the dwelling-place of devils, dragons, serpents, adders, toads, crocodiles, and all manner of verminous creatures; the puddle of sin, the stinking fogs ascending from the Stygian lake, brimstone, pitch and all manner of unclean metals, the perpetual and unquenchable fire . . .'.

NATURAL HISTORY OF THE VAMPIRE

'I'm not hungry, Mommy.'
'Shut up, and drink your soup before it clots.'

Agents or manifestations of the Devil were numerous and in prehistoric times fear of the wandering spirit or corpse was commonplace. Precautions were taken to deter the recovery or resurrection of the dead: exhuming the body, scattering the bones, weighing down the coffin with massive stone blocks and pinning down the corpse with stakes. In Juthe Fen, Jutland, there was uncovered in 1839 the body of a fifty-year-old woman, dressed in a cape, skirt and cap, with an apparent look of terror on her face. Her body had been pinned down by stakes driven through the elbows and knees and then covered with heavier branches.

Grauballe Man, likewise recovered from a Jutland bog, had been knocked on the head and slashed across the throat, while Lindow Man from Cheshire, England, had endured the triple death of stabbing, garroting and drowning. He had also suffered a blow on the head – an example of 'overkill' if ever there was. Of bodies interred in such locations Nick Thorpe commented that 'bogs lie outside the domestic world, and for the most part they are trackless wastes, which were perhaps even more effective than burial at a crossroads in confusing any restless spirit – and, indeed, one might well imagine that many of them were believed to be only too keen on revenge, given their treatment before and after death'.

Such violence was sometimes ascribed to the body being that of a 'witch' or 'wizard' – someone of baneful or malign intent – but that hardly satisfies the facts of all Iron Age bog burials. The Kayhausen Boy from Saxony, aged between eight and fourteen, had been stabbed in the throat and left arm and then trussed chicken-fashion. His arms and legs had been bound with cloth, with another strip of cloth going down from his thoat and up between his legs to the back of his neck. The motive could well have been of a propitiatory kind: a young boy sacrificed as an offering to the water deities in order to halt a run of bad luck or ensure a rich crop the following summer.

Down the years, one can imagine this type of custom giving rise to pain, guilt and indignation. Each of those ritually slain belonged to a family, some of whose members probably tried to plea or bargain for the victim's freedom. The choice of 'victim' was possibly biased or arbitrary. So it may well be that, by the nature of the custom itself, the flames of superstition and terror were fanned.

Supplement of Blood

Part of the fear of vampires was connected with the notion of them hovering over graveyards, preparing to enter carcasses and reanimate them. How would a dead person 'start all over again'? The answer is by obtaining nourishment through the gift or supplement of blood. In warfare it is metonymically said the patriot 'gave' his blood for his country – as if the substance stands for the man. Both in folklore and fact, blood is a precious, powerful fluid, the well of life, capable of reviving – through transfusion – the diseased or mortally sick.

Homer illustrates how communication with the dead was attained through blood's restorative power. Following Circe's instructions, Odysseus killed two black sheep and filled the ditch at the threshold of Avernus with their black, steaming blood. Immediately he was encircled by the dead – shadowy, grey and ill-defined, with quivering nostrils and thirsty lips. Eagerly they drank while Odysseus kept his mother and other spirits at bay. The blood briefly revived a flickering, transient vitality.

Another instance of morbid appetite occurs in Philostratus's biography of Apollonius of Tyana. In Corinth the great doctor and philosopher met Menippus, a poor, thin student whose sole possessions were his cloak and handsome bearing. Apollonius learned that Menippus was engaged to be married to a beautiful and rich Phoenician lady who did not care about the difference in their social rank. Apollonius was invited as guest of honour to the wedding banquet where he quickly unmasked the lady as a vampire. Uttering a magical imprecation, he made the plates and utensils fade away and the cooks and the servants fall to dust. Cowed by this act of mastery, the lady confessed she had intended to fatten up Menippus before devouring him, 'for it was her habit to feed upon young and beautiful bodies, because their blood is pure and strong'.

Without blood, presumably, the lady might relapse to dust just as Dracula did, for it is blood that supplies the requisite energy – hence magicians used it when they wished to contact the dead or effect a materialisation. The ladies of the Italian Renaissance, to preserve their complexions, drew over their wrinkles the blood of a freshly killed dove cut down the centre. Countess Bathoria regularly had maidens killed, in order that she should bathe in their blood and stay young and beautiful. 'The primordial substance of blood', wrote Oscar Venceslas de L. Milosz, 'has the power to transmute, for indeed it is none other than the philosopher's stone.'

THE MIDDLE AGES:
THEOLOGICAL NIGHTMARES

CATHARS

> The wicked ministers of Satan have scattered their evil through
> the province of Bourges . . . they have done their work by
> deceiving the shrewd and seducing the simple-minded. They
> seem to be pious but they completely deny all virtue. Their
> sermons are smoother than olive oil; but they are as sharp as
> javelins because their tails sting like scorpions.
>
> *(Letter setting up the Inquisition of the Cathars, 1233,*
>   Pope Gregory IX)

After the spread of Christianity, spirits, demons and vampires were
branded as baneful entities. Anyone who sought to contact the
exhalations and emanations of the dead was labelled a
necromancer. Hence, in a Europe riven with religious dissent,
isolated sects or groups pursuing a spiritual life or set of beliefs at
variance with Catholic orthodoxy were liable to suffer violent
reprisals. If the sect happened to be dualist – maintaining that the
Devil's power equalled God's – that could be seen as arrant
blasphemy. To inflate the stature of the Lord of Darkness in such a
way was akin to an act of homage or worship and such a crime
could be punished only by death.

Such was the ultimate fate of the Cathars or Albigenses who,
historically speaking, were attached to the Languedoc region of
France where their ideas took root in the thirteenth century. The

name deriving from the Greek 'katharos' meaning pure, the Cathars have been traced back to the Orphic cults, the Manichees, the Zorastrians and the Bogomils. In the latter guise they have been called Bulgars, corrupted to 'buggers', for in the view of Catholic Church, heresy is often redolent with sexual perversion.

St Bernard of Clairvaux (1090–1153), who was sent on a preaching mission to restore the Christian faith to the area, conceded in a letter to the Pope that the Cathars were doctrinally in error, but 'if you were to examine their mode of life, you will find nothing more irreproachable'. This moderate judgement did not prevent the first act of European genocide when over 100,000 members of the sect were murdered during the Albigensian Crusade, and an Inquisition was set up for their interrogation and suppression.

Although branded as necromancers, the Cathars pursued a refined asceticism that endured the body rather than enjoyed it. Even in its pristine, youthful state, they saw the body as a physical encumbrance, an obstacle to perfection. Their preoccupation was the visionary experience that took place at death when the soul ascended to heaven and was reunited with the Absolute: 'Have no mercy on the flesh born in corruption, but have mercy on the spirit held in prison.'

Secrecy surrounded their rituals but it is agreed that the Cathars believed in opposing principles eternally at war, Light and Dark, Good and Evil, Pure and Defiled. The Cathars did not touch meat, only fish, thinking the latter did not reproduce sexually. In order that their bodies would stay clean, they ate pure foods – water, milk, bread – and tried to abstain from sexual intercourse. Seeing themselves as mere receptacles in which the spirit was trapped, they paid allegiance to their Father, the Spirit of Light, who created their world, as opposed to the Prince of Darkness, who was responsible for time, gross matter and sin. The Cathars rejected the symbolism of the Cross – a murder weapon – and posited that Jesus was all spirit, posing the awkward question: 'How can a non-corporeal body be nailed to such an instrument?' Because of their rejection of the body, the Cathars did not distinguish between various sexual acts. In their view, buggery or homosexuality was less culpable than normal sexual intercourse which held the risk of conception and filling up the world with more vile bodies:

> Nor do I think the remark of certain heretics that no one can sin from the waist down should be passed over in silence. They called the placing of images in church idolatry; insisted that church bells are trumpets of devils; averred that no one sins more grievously in sleeping with mother or sister than anyone else; and, among the most extreme of heretical follies, they affirmed that if one of the perfected should commit mortal sin (for example, by eating the smallest morsel of meat, cheese, egg, or any other food forbidden to them), all those consoled by him lose the Holy Spirit and must be reconsoled; and they even said that those already saved fall from heaven because of the sin of the one who consoled them.
>
> (*Hystoria Albigensis*, 1213)

The church was well organised and allowed for female ministers. Calling themselves the 'perfecti', they baptised one another without recourse to water, using words only and a book, in a ceremony called the *consolamentum* or consolation. Like certain eastern mystics, it is likely the perfecti emanated an inner rapture that spread serenity and contentment. 'To adore God from love alone', wrote Louis Massignon, 'is the crime of the Manicheans . . . These adore God with a physical love, through the magnetic attraction of iron to iron, and their particles of light are impelled like a magnet back towards the focus of light whence they came.'

The capital of their influence, the ancient province of Languedoc, was a sophisticated melting-pot where Occitan – the medieval language of Oc – was spoken. It drew in the 'feminine' culture of the south with Moorish influences and constituted the heartland of the Cathars or the Albigenses, derived from the town of Albi, a centre of Cathar practices.

The Cathars' popularity and influence in the region enraged Pope Innocent III. So far as he was concerned, this heretical sect of devil-worshippers was spreading and raging like a conflagration of the spirit. Initially he responded by sending missions into Cathar territory – notably one led by the Spanish monk, Dominic Guzmán, who drew large audiences but did not shift the ground of Cathar support. Neither did the threat of force weaken the Cathars' unity and resolve. A letter written in 1170 by Raymond V of St Giles, Count of Toulouse, to the Cistercian General Chapter, decries the impact of the sect: 'Alas and woe! Even those who perform priestly duties are corrupted by the evil of heresy. The ancient places of religious worship, formerly venerated, lie neglected and derelict; baptism is rejected; the eucharist is despised; repentance is held to be of small worth; the doctrine of the creation of man and the resurrection of the flesh is denied and cast out; all the sacraments of the Church are annulled.'

His son and successor Raymond VI of Toulouse was repeatedly rebuked for failing to drive the Cathars out of his domain. He was thought to be in league with the heretics and resented the overbearing attitude of the Church. An attempted reconciliation between the Count and the papal legate Peter of Castelnau took place in January 1208, but ended in a bitter dispute that culminated in the stabbing of Peter later that month. Accusing Raymond VI of complicity in the crime, Pope Innocent ordered that a crusade be launched against the Cathars. Whereupon Count Raymond VI, who did not wish to see his lands overrun, was compelled to make a public penance at St Giles, confessing to the charges and allowing himself to be flogged at the altar of the cathedral.

Meanwhile the lords of northern France were summoned by the papal legate Arnold Aimery, Abbot of Citeaux, to mount the Albigensian Crusade. Enticed by spiritual and financial rewards, not to mention the possibility of annexing vast estates, about 25,000 of them gathered in June 1209 to launch the offensive. Pope Innocent commended 'this affair of peace and faith' as reflecting the will of the Almighty, but the land-grabbing nobles were little concerned with charity. When the army arrived at Béziers, they asked the inhabitants to hand over any Cathars known to the population. The townsfolk refused, and the crusaders started their siege. Knights in chainmail, wielding broadswords and battleaxes, trampled down and hacked to death anyone who got in their path.

'How will we know who to kill?' one knight asked the Abbot of Citeaux. His chilling reply was 'Slay them all – God will recognise his own!' There followed a riot of indiscriminate butchery. Eventually some three thousand inhabitants were herded into the church of St Mary Magdalene and the building was fired by the crusaders with the people trapped inside. Skeletons from the massacre still lie under the floor.

'Our forces spared neither rank nor sex nor age,' the Abbot reported to the Pope. 'About twenty thousand people lost their lives at the point of the sword. The destruction of the enemy was on an enormous scale. The entire city was plundered and put to the torch. Thus did divine vengeance vent its wondrous rage.'

The slaughter spread a ripple of terror followed by instant capitulation. After the fall of Béziers, others towns submitted: Montréal, Mirepoix, Albi and Castres. Of the many anti-Cathar warlords, the most wealthy and formidable was Simon de Montfort the Elder, 4th Earl of Leicester, who was a prestigious secular ally for the Church. With Montfort's banner following behind the Holy Cross, his men destroyed streets and houses, and tortured, blinded and mutilated those they took prisoner. Hundreds of Cathars were consigned to the flames. At the siege of Lavaur Castle, between Albi and Toulouse, Montfort berated the lady of the fortress as 'the worst of heretics' and ordered that she be thrown down a well and then buried under heavy stones.

In the *Chanson de la Crusade* Simon de Montfort was described by William of Tudela as 'a hardy warrior, full of wisdom and experience, a great and gentle knight, gallant, comely, frank and yet soft spoken'. This description can be contrasted with that of an anonymous chronicler who took over from William and set down his assessment after Montfort's burial in 1218:

Those who can read may learn from his epitaph that he is a saint and martyr; that he is bound to rise again to share the heritage, to flourish in the state of unparalleled felicity, to wear a crown and have a place in the Kingdom. But for my part I have heard tell that the matter must stand thus: if one may seek Christ Jesus in the world by killing men and shedding blood; by the destruction of human souls; by setting the torch to great fires; by winning lands through violence . . . by slaughtering women and slitting children's throats – why yes, then he must needs wear a crown and shine replendent in heaven.

There is a vivid report of the massacre at Marmande in June 1219. Prince Louis of France besieged the city, destroying the bridges, smashing the stockades, and burning and slaughtering. The account is told from the angle of the Cathars who sought shelter in the fortress:

> The crusading juggernaut invades the city.
> The massacre begins. Babes in arms, maidens,
> noble ladies, barons, stripped of their clothing,
> are put to the sword, chopped to pieces.
> The ground everywhere is covered with chunks of flesh,
> flowing blood, breasts and brains,
> limbs, bodies, ripped from top to bottom,
> guts, livers, hearts, trunks.
> It looks as though they have fallen from the sky like rain.
> Blood runs in flowing streams right through the town,
> the fields and the rivers. No woman or man
> or child or grandparent escapes.
> No one except perhaps (who knows?) some well-hidden child.
> Now that the carnage is over, they torch Marmande.
> And sire Louis, pious as ever, strikes camp, and takes
> the road to Toulouse . . .

The last refuge of the Cathars was the fortress of Montségur, south-east of Foix, a looming rock-fortress standing over a thousand feet above a valley, as proud and remote as any saint or recluse could wish for. A well-organised attack was launched against this citadel in the summer of 1243 by the Royal Seneschal of Carcassonne, with troops supplied by the Archbishop of Narbonne and the Bishop of Albi. A huge ballistic device – for pounding the fortress with rocks – was dragged up the slope.

Montségur was akin to an island bordered on all sides by steep cliffs, and thus, once heavily surrounded, was difficult to restock with food and water. When the bishops' armies failed to penetrate the stone hide of the fortress, they decided to lay siege to it and wait it out. Nearly a year went by, during which some soldiers actually defected to the Cathar cause, although they must have known it would mean almost certain death. Finally a surprise night attack broke through one of the outer fortifications, giving the crusaders a foothold from which they could complete their overthrow.

In the citadel food stocks dwindled to near-famine level; as morale flagged, the Cathars were forced to yield. Attempts were made at negotiation; the defendants were promised their lives if they repented and rescinded their beliefs before the Inquistion. But no such dispensation was offered to the two hundred or more heretics who met their end on 16 March 1244. They were herded into a wooden stockade in an open field on the lower slopes of the mountain, then a pile of brushwood was heaped in the centre and ignited. The Cathars were dragged and hauled into the flames. Some of them, the chronicles reported, threw themselves ecstatically on the pyre or 'strode into the flames singing'. The site of the holocaust came to be known as *prats dells crematz* (or 'place of burning'). Only a small number of women and children, who had previously been evacuated, were spared. The two *perfecti* who did escape from the fortress were thought to know the whereabouts of the buried treasure of the Cathars.

Pathologies of the Spirit

In the first chapter of this book, Pan was invoked as the deity associated with irrational surges of enthusiasm or alarm. In a more superstitious age the god was held responsible for those uprushes of panic that sometime descend on goats and sheep – making them break into senseless flight or hurl themselves over cliffs. He was also the spirit that sent a panicky terror flooding through armies, securing victory for the side he favoured. This is hardly an adequate analogy for the less predictable facets of human behaviour but neither are the facts as they stand.

One can explain the phenomenon of the crusades in terms of political allegiance, religious intolerance, power politics and zenophobia, but these blanket words barely penetrate the confusion. Names, dates and documentary evidence may appear to fill in the gaps yet fail to tell us why ordinary men – not invariably pious, god-fearing men – were so enfired by a vision that they were prepared to leave home, ride for months through harsh, inhospitable landscapes, endure flu, dysentery and scorching heat, and finally plunge into an orgy of killing, butchering and burning. The objects of their wrath were peoples with whom formerly they had enjoyed little or no contact, nor was there any reason to hate them. In the instance of the Cathars, they were not 'infidels' but sophisticated Europeans. Their only crime was their nonconformism.

'War is like that,' one might say. But we have to go further and acknowledge that history is a process that attempts to find a rationale – sometimes without first acknowledging that humans are profoundly irrational or driven by startling and disturbing pathologies of the spirit. These surges of primal panic, being induced by swift, uncontrollable passions, drown all attempts at justification. Hence the language of history, whether drawn from primary or secondary sources, pays exaggerated attention to the velleities and evasions by which men conceal their hidden, chaotic urges. 'Most men live lives of quiet desperation', Thoreau observed, hinting at dissatisfactions which may one day erupt and take the guise of revolution or reform. It is a much-discussed paradox that Christianity, a religion dedicated to cultivating the passive tendencies of the individual, was capable of unleashing barbaric atrocities upon its opponents. So much murder was conducted under the sign of the cross that it is almost as if the Christians had decided to emulate the cruelty of their Roman predecessors. Did Christ himself order anyone to be burnt alive? Did he starve people to death? Did he punish them for failing to worship him?

After Christianity had become dominant, a high degree of organisation was required to maintain unity and fervour in a Europe that was thick with itinerant preachers, many of them promoting contrasting heresies and outlooks. In each town and city, oratories, abbeys and elaborate churches and cathedrals had been built, and a bureacracy established to preserve and fund such structures. Out of necessity, the Church developed into an economic force, the hub of a power and taxation structure, and the Pope became a mediator between the various cardinals and bishops.

Once such an institution is established, a different outlook comes into being, fostered by the need to defend what has been accrued through centuries of hard effort. Such a strategy consolidates material gain rather than inspires religious fervour. Institutionalised regimes are essentially static: they conserve rather than take things forward. The more cumbersome the structure, the less open it is to progress and change.

The rage against the Cathars was based upon the fact that the Catholic Church believed these passionate upstarts to have rediscovered a spiritual joy similar to that radiated by the early Christians. They had revived an inner-based faith that drew hundreds of new followers daily while the Catholic hierarchy had lost much of its impetus and vision – lost it in reams of paperwork, doctrinal disputes, papal bulls, administrative hubbub, useless crusades and the bills and demands of clerks and masons. When a new spiritual force challenges an established one, anger is the counter-reaction. How dare they appropriate God for themselves? In persecuting the Cathars, the Pope was stamping out all traces of a faith that had the temerity to be more inspiring than his own.

SUFFERING WITCHES

The wife of Knertz, the butcher
The infant daughter of Dr Schultz
A blind girl
Schwartz, canon at Hach
Ehling, a vicar
A student who knew many languages, an excellent musician
The tailor's fat wife
Bernhard Mark, vicar in the Cathedral
A stranger
A strange woman

A knife grinder
A little girl, nine or ten years old
A younger girl, her little sister
  (From the records of witch burnings in Würzburg in the sixteenth
                               and seventeenth centuries)

In 1628 Johannes Junius, burgomaster of Bamberg in Franconia, lay
in the town dungeon condemned to death for attending a witches'
Sabbath. Denounced by the Chancellor of the principality, who was
himself subsequently burned for a 'suspicious leniency' towards
suspects, he had confessed to riding to a Sabbath on a black dog and
having been seduced by a succubus who demanded that he kill his
daughters and youngest boy. Before he was burned at the stake,
Junius smuggled out a long confession, addressed to his daughter
Veronica. It concluded:

> Now my dearest child, here you have all my acts and confessions, for
> which I must die. And it is all sheer lies and inventions, so help me
> God. For all this I was forced to say through dread or torture beyond
> what I had already endured. For they never cease the torture till one
> confessed something; be he ever so pious, he must be a witch.
> Nobody escapes, though he be an earl. If God send no means of
> bringing truth to light, our whole kindred will be burned . . . Dear
> child, keep this letter secret, so that people shall not find it, else
> I shall be tortured most piteously and the jailers will be beheaded . . .
> Goodnight, for your father Johannes Junius will never see you more.

The letter is a painful document, tragic and appalling; the phrases
reel under the enormity of the injustice. It shows an individual
caught in the wheel of a remorseless mechanism. If the purpose of
the court had been to establish whether a witch existed, the result
might have been different. But that supposition was an axiom. No
sceptical voices spoke up or asked why, if witches truly possessed the
amazing powers credited to them, they did not use their skills to
escape torture and burning? A body of men was appointed to root
out witches rather than question the evidence.

Junius's testimony stands as an example of the classic confession, intensely elaborate, with all the proper demonic trappings, climaxing in his attendance at a Sabbath. The confession was oiled by the application of thumbscrews and 'urgent persuasion'. After repeated attacks on his body, Junius's executioner implored, 'Sir, I beg you, for God's sake, confess something, whether it be true or not. Invent something, for you cannot endure the torture which you will be put to; and even if you bear it all, yet you will not escape, not even if you were an earl, but one torture will follow another until you say you are a witch. Not before that will they let you go, as you may see by all their trials, for one is just like another.'

Under Prince-Bishop Johann George II (1622–33), Bamberg was notorious for the zeal and savagery of its witch-hunts. At least six hundred suspects were burned alive, including the Chancellor and five of the burgomasters of the principality. An official of the law court at Rheinbach, Hermann Loher, observed two savage waves of persecution in 1631 and 1636. 'To fall in the hand of a witch judge,' he wrote, 'is just as if a condemned person were forced to fight with lions, bears, and wolves for his life, and were prevented from protecting himself, since he is deprived of weapons of every description.' Loher noted the methods by which a judge tried to extract a confession: 'You apostate, you witch, you dumb dog! Confess your sin of witchery; reveal the names of your accomplices! You filthy whore, you devil's wanton, you sackcloth-maker, you dumb toad! Speak and confess in God's name! Swallow the holy salt! Drink the holy water! Tell us who it was that taught you witchcraft, and whom you saw and recognised at the witches' sabbat. Then you will not be tortured any more but have eternal life.'

Little sympathy was expressed for the condemned. One inquisitor boasted that he could make the Pope himself admit to being a wizard. Any show of finesse or virginal reserve on the part of the victim was twisted into perversity or diabolic pride. In his study of evil angels and demons (1612), De Lancre reports with astonishment that a witch called Detsail refused the 'kiss of pardon' offered by a handsome young hangman: 'She did not wish to profane her lovely lips,' he exclaims, 'which yet had so often kissed the devil's back.'

As the executions increased, so did the number of men and women involved in their stage management. Local economies absorbed the apparatus and bureaucracy of witch-hunting; there arose a demand for more judges, jailers, torturers, wood-choppers, carpenters, clerks and demonologists. Itinerant teams of witch-finders would arrive, be put up at village inns and consume large amounts of bread, meat and wine. Hangmen and executioners became well-paid citizens, able to swank around in carriages and parade their wives and daughters in silken finery. Around the stake or gallows area, stalls and makeshift shops were set up, selling crosses, rosaries and tracts along with hot food and drink. The varied schedule of burnings, duckings and hangings became social occasions. People met, flirted and exchanged gossip before the solemn drama was enacted; afterwards they would weigh up the outcome, declare those they thought guilty or innocent or merely feeble-minded.

To lend the ceremony added pomp and credence, viewing platforms were erected for local notaries and members of the inquisition and a special box was provided for the judge to mount to issue his sentence. Neither was costume omitted, for the witches appeared in symbolic garb. In Spain, for instance, they wore a sulphur-yellow shirt and a cardboard tiara adorned with painted devils, flames and a human head resting upon burning faggots. Naturally all witches had been forced to name their 'accomplices', and thus each burning prepared the way for others. The persecution upon which numerous livelihoods depended had been set in motion and it gathered momentum. Denying the truth of witchcraft was akin to subverting the status of those who thrived by its manias and rulings.

The Sabbath

The gala event for witches was the Sabbath. Traditionally it took place after midnight on Friday at least once a year in remote, deserted places, high moorlands or mountains like the Brocken in the Harz Mountains. The Devil favoured a site where four roads met or in the neighbourhood of a lake. After an infernal celebration, no grass was said to grow again on the spot, which had been poisoned by the hot feet of demons. If any witches or wizards failed to attend, the Devil would lash them with a rod of serpents or scorpions. The essential course of a Sabbath gathering comprised the assembly followed by homage (to the Devil), banqueting and festivities, especially dancing, climaxing in indiscriminate intercourse.

In the shape of a he-goat, the Devil took his place upon a throne. Arriving at the spot by various methods of supernatural conveyance, the witches paid homage to the Dark Lord, offering him gifts such as pitch-black candles or infants' navel cords, and kissing him upon the buttocks. Having completed the opening courtesies, those witches who had not yet received the Devil's mark – a burn, mole, wart or birthmark in the shape of a hare, a spider or toad's foot – were properly branded. Next came the celebration. The congregation would start singing and dancing in a wild, abandoned manner. This would continue, loud and ecstatic, until a newcomer arrived, requesting to be allowed to join the company. To qualify for acceptance, the newcomer was obliged to deny salvation, spit on the Bible and swear obedience to the Devil. Having passed this test, he would be admitted. The frenzied celebration might start up again, broken perhaps by a conference or meeting, in which the congregation recited their felonies and misdeeds, eager to impress the Lord of Darkness with their diligence and conscientiousness.

By this time, there was little else to do save round off the proceedings with an orgy in which the witches and wizards freely copulated and offered themselves to the carnally demanding Devil, who liked to take beautiful women from the front and ugly ones from the rear. From a female viewpoint, Satan was not the ideal lover, as sixteen-year-old Jeanette d'Abadie testified, for 'his member was scaly and caused extreme pain; furthermore his semen was extremely cold, so cold that she had never become pregnant by him . . .'.

For those interested in comparative anatomy, Nicholas Remy (1595) cited Alexia Drigie, a witch who reported that the devil's erect penis was as long as a certain kitchen utensil but there was nothing where the scrotum and testicles should be hanging. Others claimed that his member was of two parts, half of iron, half of flesh, and that it was as cold as ice. The latter was only to be expected, explained Henry More (1653), for the bodies of devils, 'being nothing but coagulated air, should be cold . . . and should have the more keen a piercing sensation . . . and therefore more fit to insinuate, and more accurately and strikingly touch the nerves'.

One inquisitor, trading off the testimony of Sister Madeleine de Demandoix, introduced the refinement of a lascivious calendar, claiming that Sundays were reserved for copulation with succubi and incubi, Thursdays for sodomy, Saturdays for 'abominable bestiality', while on the other days witches were allowed freedom of choice.

Supercharged with Meaning

Various explanations are given for the lurid, voluptuous superstitions concerning devilish forces that reached their apogee in the sixteenth century. First, it has been suggested that the depredations of the Black Death caused many to question the Christian religion. Who could trust a God that killed alike rich and poor, innocent and debauched, young and old? If that was the best Christianity could offer, it might be better to revert to the pagan gods. Secondly, there are those who maintain that the prosecutions acted as a useful weapon in sectarian rivalries – for instance, a lone Protestant in Catholic territory might lay himself open to accusation: 'Whenever the missionaries of one church are recovering a society from their rivals, "witchcraft" is discovered beneath the thin surface of heresy.' Thirdly the witch-hunts have been ascribed to psychological tensions reaching bursting-point, 'when people find that they ought to feel well-disposed to others but do not'; instead of donating charity and assistance, they deflect their rage on a particular trait or tendency. The victims are dubbed 'witches' because it exonerates others from social responsibility, just as dubbing a person a 'Jew' in the Third Reich freed German citizens from moral obligation. Fourthly the trials can be seen as a method of exerting social control: 'In a Europe racked by religious disagreements which often spilled over into war, the preservation of popular obedience and loyalty was of urgent concern to states and churches alike, and no measures were spared to secure a religious conformity that seemed to many to be an essential bulwark against social disintegration.'

Certainly the 'evidence' of the inquisitors amounts to little more than denunciations of orgies and diabolic drolleries. It is an old adage that coiled springs, once released, are liable to rebound with added force. Suppress the pleasure of the senses, harden into a pillar of theological exactitude, and there's a chance that, after an interval of adjustment, the will may slacken and be replaced by a restless imp of perversity. At first this irritation – like a slightly aggrieved ripple of boredom – has no object upon which to fix, but when it seizes upon a quarry, the very Devil that is despised moves in and completes the circle of delusion.

'What the inquisitors were doing,' suggested Colin Wilson, 'was to create a body of myths and symbols that were supercharged with meaning and that consequently exercised an overwhelming gravitational pull on the imagination. The Devil literally finds work for idle hands and idle minds.' It is appropriate to add that the myths were 'supercharged' with meaning because they drew their potency from that heady cocktail of fascination and revulsion which sexual desire traditionally arouses in Puritan countries. Considered coolly, events at a Sabbath stray little beyond the commonplaces of bawdy sensualism. The sexual specifics – kissing buttocks, applying greasy salves, leaving bite-marks on skin – are not demonic. Rather they are dark fictions projected on others – a map of unexplored carnal possibilities, a lurid pornography of repression. Indeed, it is obvious that such orgiastic diversions were lodged in the minds of the inquisitors even before the persecutions began.

Instructive, too, is the casually employed designation 'the witchcraft craze', as though the persecutions were a fad or passing whim. The irony is instructive, for a 'craze' is like a 'panic' – an outburst of enthusiasm or fear which manifests itself and abruptly vanishes. No one refers to the 'Cathar craze' although parallels have been drawn between the persecution and burning of the Cathars and those accused of witchcraft over three hundred years later. Both sects were seen as consorting with the powers of darkness and both admitted female priests. But the Cathars were well organised, possessing an efficient, effective bureaucracy, while it has never been established that witchcraft was a 'religion' in the strict sense at all. However, the Cathars and the witches provoked an extraordinary rage and retribution, and although attempts have been made to reconstruct both sets of belief the central mystery of their *raison d'être* persists.

The Heart of Man

In the same year (1628) that Johannes Junius languished in a dungeon, accused of witchcraft, the English doctor William Harvey, the eldest of seven sons of a yeoman farmer, published a treatise dedicated to Charles I and entitled *An Anatomical Disquisition Concerning the Motion of the Heart and the Blood in Animals.* 'The heart of animals [it declared] is the foundation of their life, the sum of everything within them, the sun of their microcosm, that upon which all growth depends and power proceeds. The King, in like manner, is the foundation of his kingdom; the sun of the world around him, the heart of the republic, the fountain whence all power, all grace doth flow . . .'.

Harvey became convinced that, owing to the beating of the heart, the blood flowed through the body in a 'circular manner' using a one-way system of valves. Arteries did not secrete blood. Rather, the fluid was always on the move, activated by the heart, a muscle not unlike a pump. Harvey's approach was only partly Aristotelian. He extolled the traditional harmonies, arguing that the circle is an ideal form, while conceding that the heart was basically a functional organ. The de-mythologising of the human body, with the emphasis on mechanics rather than metaphysics, was dislodging the 'ghost in the machine' and making way for the 'Modern Prometheus' or Frankenstein-style scientist who could assemble a person from assorted bits like a jigsaw puzzle. After Harvey, other discoveries were made concerning the hydraulics of being human: the levers and pulleys of the body were charted down to the smallest hinge and ligature.

Is there any significance between the confluence of these two events, Junius's execution and Harvey's discovery? Many would say without hesitation 'None whatsover' – but perhaps that would be too dismissive. For the climax of the witch persecutions coincided with the height of the Renaissance, an age of observation and experiment, when a methodology for acquiring and testing knowledge was steadily being developed and people stopped being afraid and started to become interested. Curiosity became the dominant emotion and the searching lens of the microscope replaced the all-seeing eye of God. In a sense, the witchcraft trials can be seen as religion's last stand before the spread of scientific learning. It was akin to a hysterical distraction from the historical process that would eventually whittle down the stature of faith – a final attempt to reinstate the old Hebrew monotheism before the spread of learning. None of the persecutors could actively prove the reality of God. So what they did, in fact, was argue backwards by projecting the phantasm of Satan on various 'outsiders' and 'suspect' women and men. In other word, because witches exist, so does the Devil who consorts with them and the God who opposes them. It is hardly coincidental that from all the trials, little emerges save repression: repression of knowledge, of necessary evidence, of generosity and compassion.

WEREWOLF

> The wind sweeps through and the hunched wolf shivers.
> It howls you cannot say whether out of agony or joy.
> *(The Howling of Wolves*, Ted Hughes, 1967)*

Over a thousand years ago packs of wolves roamed the forests, mountains and moors of Europe. Many place-names in Britain perpetuate their memory: Wolfscrag in Sussex, Wolfstones in Lancashire, Wolferlow in Herefordshire, Wolfscotes in Derbyshire – there is even a Bleeding Wolf Inn in Cheshire, recording the hunting and wounding of such a creature. Hearing such names, we dream of a Dark Ages of the mind, a countryside rich with hazard and alarm. The landscape is rockier, starker, more thickly wooded than the chequered fields and grazing meadows of subsequent centuries. We view Saxon England as a landscape that had not yet been curbed and cowed. Man had established ascendancy, yes, but nature could always bite back and, when it did, it was often with wolves' teeth.

Wolves were largely exterminated in Wales during the reign of Edgar, King of England. His army laid waste large areas of North Wales in 965; this was, ostensibly, an exercise in humiliation. Writing of this, Powel tells us how,

> in the year 965 the country of North Wales was cruelly wasted by the army of Edgar; the occasion of which was the non-payment of the tribute that the king of Aberffraw, by the laws of Hywel Dda, was obliged to pay to the king of London. But at length a peace was concluded upon these conditions, that the king of North Wales, instead of money, should pay to the king of England the tribute of 300 wolves yearly; which creature was then very pernicious and destructive to England and Wales. This tribute being duly performed for two years; the third year there was none to be found in any part of the island, so that afterwards the prince of North Wales became exempt from paying any acknowledgement to the King of England.

The wolves that escaped the hunters survived in the remoter parts of England until the reign of Henry VII, and in Scotland the last wolf was alleged to have been slain in the wilds of Lochaber as late as 1680 by Cameron of Lochiel, a famous chieftain who was knighted by Charles II for his support for the royalist cause. Nearly 140 years later Cameron's trophy found its way to a London museum auction catalogue (1818): 'Lot 832: Wolf – a noble animal in a large glass case.' The designation 'noble' might have been queried by the villagers of Ederachillis, on the coast of Sutherland, who were forced to shift their burial-ground in order to prevent hungry wolves from digging up their graves:

On Ederachillis shore
The grey wolf lies in wait,
Woe to the broken door,
Woe to the loosened gate,
And the groping wretch who sleety fogs
On the trackless moor belate.

The lean and hungry wolf,
With his fangs so sharp and white,
His starveling body pinched
By the frost of a northern night,
And his pitiless eyes that scare the dark
With their green and threatening light.

He climbeth the guarding dyke,
He leapeth the hurdle bars,
He steals the sheep from the pen,
And the fish from the boat-house spars;
And he digs the dead from out the sod,
And gnaws them under the stars.

(*A Book of Highland Minstrelsy*, Mrs D. Ogilvy, 1860)

Wolves became synonymous with nature in its least desirable aspect. No pity was meted out to them. They were ravagers of the countryside, known for the keenness of their hungers, for their passionate, detailed voracity. January was called 'Wolf Month' by the Anglo-Saxons, for it was then – at the coldest time of the year – that they seemed most threatening. Tradition has it that the battlefield of Hastings was cleansed by hungry wolves feasting on fallen warriors. Men waged a constant war against wolves, for hungry packs were a menace to travellers, cattle and poultry. Any human who voluntarily associated himself with a wolf or claimed, in a state of affliction, to be a werewolf, was liable to be treated as brutally as the animal itself.

But werewolves were never punished on the scale of witches, there being less scope to draw credible testimony. Usually the suspect suffered from a disease or aberration – mimicking a wolf suggests compulsion rather than motive. The transformation, too, raised a problem. If one casually identified a wolf that picked off poultry as one's next door neighbour, magistrates would not be invariably convinced. Neither did a wolf radiate the potent sexual charge of a witch who had enjoyed intercourse with the Devil, so the handful of werewolf cases stand as gruesome curiosities rather than large-scale social problems.

Jean Grenier

A startling encounter took place in 1603 on the coastal fringe of Gascony. Some village girls tending their sheep came across a pale-complexioned boy of about fourteen seated morosely on a log. He had tawny red hair, small grey eyes in a narrow face and olive skin. His teeth were white and canine, protruding over the lower lip, and his expression was flat, vacant, save for a watchful ferocity in his glance. He was clothed in shreds and tatters. The girls clustered round the boy, who showed no sign of alarm.

'Well, my maidens,' he said, 'which of you is the prettiest?'

'Why do you want to know?' one asked.

'Because I have decided that I will marry the prettiest.'

One of the girls, Jeanne Barboriant, told the boy that the issue did not lie in his hands and, besides, they had never seen him before. The boy told them that he was the bastard of a local priest.

'Is that why you look so dingy and black?' he was asked.

'No, I am dark-coloured because I wear a wolf-skin,' he replied. 'It was given to me by a Pierre Labourant. Do you know who he is? He's a man with an iron chain about his neck which he constantly gnaws. Do you want to know where he lives? Ha, in a place of gloom and fire, where there are many others, some seated on iron chairs, some on glowing beds, but all burning, burning. Some of them take up men and cast them on the flames or thrust them in cauldrons of liquid fire!'

The girls let out squeals of incredulity and the boy continued: 'You want to hear about my wolf-skin cape. The man gave me that. He wraps it round me. Every Monday, Friday and Sunday, and, for an hour about dusk every day, I am a werewolf. I have killed dogs and drunk their blood. But little girls taste better – their flesh is tender and sweet, their blood rich and warm. I have eaten many a maiden, as I have been on my raids, together with my nine companions. I am a werewolf! Ah ha! – if the sun were to set, I would soon fall on you and have you for my supper.'

He burst into a paroxysm of laughter. The girls fled. Happenings in the area accorded with the boy's account of his exploits. Near the village of St Antoine de Pizon thirteen-year-old Margaret Poirier was in the habit of tending her sheep with the same boy that Jeanne Baboriant and her friends had encountered. Margaret, too, had listened while he regaled her with tales of bloodthirsty cavortings. She complained to her parents who did not take the matter seriously until she returned home one evening in a fit of terror, saying that she had been attacked while looking after her sheep. A wild beast had sprung out of the bushes and torn her clothes with its fangs. Using her shepherd's crook, she had hit back and driven the creature away, whereupon it had seated itself on its hindlegs like a dog, only a few feet from her, and regarded her with a look of intense rage. She had fled but recalled that it resembled a wolf, save it was shorter and stouter, with red hair and stumpy tail and a smaller head.

This statement caused a surge of fear in the parish. Several small girls had recently vanished and their parents suspected Jean Grenier. The boy was brought before the district attorney of Roche Chalès who referred the matter to a local judge. Perplexed and appalled by the gory evidence the boy enthusiastically proffered, the judge had the case transferred to a higher authority, the judge at Coutras, who ordered a search of the Grenier's house in order to recover magic salves or wolf trappings.

The evidence that emerged was extraordinary. Jean Grenier, son of a poor labourer from St Antoine de Pizon, had left home and worked under several masters as he travelled the countryside, begging and taking charge of flocks. Inclined to be negligent in his duties, he had been dismissed by several farmers, but his life took a different turn when he reached the age of ten or eleven. It was then that his neighbour, Duthillaire, took him into the depths of the forest and introduced him to the Master of the Forest, 'a black man, who signed me with his nail, and then gave me and Duthillaire a salve and a wolf-skin. From that time, I have run about the country as a wolf.'

At the command of the Master of the Forest, he went out hunting for children, first smearing himself with the salve to effect the transformation. He stored the substance in a small pot and his clothes in a thicket. Usually he ran his course for two hours in the day, when the moon was on the wane, but often he'd go out on nightly hunts. On one occasion, he had run with Duthillaire but neither had killed anyone. He told the court he had once, on entering an empty house, found a baby in a cradle, dragged it out and devoured it. What remained he had given to a wolf. In the parish of St Antoine de Pizon he had attacked a little girl whose name he did not know and later another child, near the stone bridge.

His father, too, he claimed, had a wolf-skin and had accompanied him on at least one of his excursions, when he attacked and ate a girl in the village of Grilland, who had been tending a flock of geese. His stepmother was separated from his father, he believed, because she once saw him vomit up the paws of a dog and the fingers of a child. He added that the Lord of the Forest had strictly forbidden him to bite the thumb-nail of his left hand, which nail was thicker and longer than the others, so long as he was in werewolf disguise.

Duthillaire was arrested, and the father of Jean Grenier was called as a witness. The elder Grenier denied his son's allegations but was able to confirm many of the details related by Jean. He admitted that both he and the neighbour had procured village girls, but for natural pleasure rather than consumption. People from the localities where children had gone missing found that the dates were consistent with Jean's account of his predations. The wounds were also in the right places.

Margaret Poirier was brought to testify. Jean pointed to the gashes in her neck and confirmed that he had made them and had been beaten off by a stick. Furthermore he described an attack he had made on a small boy, whom he would have certainly eaten had not a man come to the rescue saying, 'I'll have you presently.' This man, the boy's uncle, was produced and confirmed that he had indeed made that remark.

After much deliberation, Grenier was found guilty and sentenced to be burnt. But the execution did not proceed. The case had prompted so much speculation that it was reviewed by the Parlement of Bordeaux. Again they pored over the evidence, retracing the route of Jean's murderous exploits, but gathering little additional information, save that Jean knew the neighbourhood intimately, was constantly seen roaming around and liked boasting of his grisly exploits. Although he showed a detailed knowledge of the murders, no one had seen him change into a werewolf and no salves or skins had been recovered. It is indeed possible that Jean had attacked and eaten some children. But his naïve, almost exuberant honesty, coupled with an obvious lack of discretion, left many in a state of doubt. So appallingly graphic was his evidence that at times it overstepped the fine line between horror and hilarity. He described chasing an old woman only to find her flesh 'tough as leather' and snatching up a baby from a cot who 'shrieked so loud that it almost deafened me', suggesting an element of performance – almost clowning – in his testimony.

The evidence was assessed by President Dassis who showed an untypical compassion when he delivered his verdict in September 1603. 'Consider the age of the child,' he reasoned. 'Why, although he's fourteen, he's so stunted and undernourished physically and intellectually that a seven-year old shows more sense. Look at his sickly appearance – those rags he's got on – think what a sorry tale they tell! Neither of his parents lavished on him care or affection. Not only was he driven out by his own father, he was treated cruelly by his stepmother. They sent him out to wander the fields, friendless, begging for bread. The only way he could secure attention was by concocting stories. Magic salves, wolf-skins, the Master of the Forest – members of the court, I am impelled to dismiss such nonsense. If only someone had taken an interest in this boy – given him a proper education – instead of filling his head with devilish babble! Such talk is proof of his backwardness. Lycanthropy and Kuanthropy are hallucinations. They cannot be punished because they do not take place. My verdict is this: life has been harsh enough on this boy. He does not need further punishment, but firm moral instruction and a regular routine. Let him be sent to a monastery where he can take daily religious instruction and do menial duties until he throws off this unfortunate and evil delusion.'

Jean Grenier was sent to a religious house to do chores for the monks, but he had only been there a few days before he was running round the grounds on all fours; finding a heap of bloody offal, he set upon it and wolfed it down. Delancre, a judge responsible for burning over six hundred witches, visited him after seven years. Jean was still small, shy and incapable of looking anyone straight in the face. His eyes were deep-set and restless, his teeth long and protruding, his nails black and in places worn away, his mind completely blank. He told Delancre he still craved human flesh, especially little girls, and that the Lord of the Forest had visited him twice while at the monastery – but he had driven him off with the sign of the cross. He did not vary any of his original statements nor relent or dispute the accounts of his crimes. He died shortly after Delancre's visit.

WHERE THE WILD THINGS ARE

> Niagara Falls is simply a vast, unnecessary amount of water
> going the wrong way and then falling over unnecessary rocks.
>   (Oscar Wilde, 1854–1900)

Jean Grenier died at the age of twenty-one. Although descriptions of him are unappealing, his honesty and naïve buffoonery come over as almost likeable. There is some literary embroidery in the retelling by Baring Gould. Jean is described as blank-minded, near-imbecilic – yet he is introduced as having a quick and ready tongue, quipping about marriage and gastronomic extravaganzas like a Restoration rake. Grenier was feared not because of his savagery or because of popular credulity about werewolves, but because he transgressed the conceptual divide between man and beast. A profound – and

dangerous – distinction came about when men ceased to hunt and
began to herd and husband animals. Transitional creatures, like rats,
snakes, coyotes and wolves, lost their magic and mystery; they
became invisible enemies, unuseful to man, outlaws and banditti of
the animal world.

In *Feudal Society* Marc Bloch remarked that 'wild animals that now
only haunt our nursery tales – bears and, above all, wolves –
prowled in every wilderness, and even amongst cultivated fields'.
Animals were liable to be designated according to the extent to
which they threatened men and livestock, combined with whatever
traditional moral blemishes were assigned to their character. In the
realm of the bird kingdom, robins bore the crest of hellfire on their
breasts. Kingfishers were symbols of pride and calm weather. Crows
and ravens had a predilection for feasting on corpses. Female
pelicans were saintly and self-sacrificing, for they pecked out their
breasts, so that their young should feed off their blood. As for the
mammals, they slotted into the stereotypical patterns of the
bestiaries. Lambs were meek, lions brave, foxes cunning, apes
lecherous and wolves untamedly vicious. And then there was the
ensemble of superstitions, such as toads sucking the milk from cows
at night, or black cats consorting with witches, or the belief that
finding a ladybird with seven spots brought good luck.

In the Middle Ages nature was seen as an arena of fear and
exposure. Alliances with untamed beasts were frowned upon, as
were the uncouth, ragged landscapes that sheltered them. The
notion of 'scenery' did not exist; there were only such stark contrasts
as 'fertile' as opposed to 'barren' land. Mountains were portrayed as
'hideous', discomforting regions where naked rock constantly peeped
through, like bones through the tattered coat of a pauper. The upper
air was considered damp and unhealthy, promoting colds, agues and
goitres. In the gloomy recesses of tarns dwelt devious and dark water
sprites. Upland forests played host to wolves and bears, while
strange, unaccountable electrical phenomena – ball lightning or
violent electric storms – could be observed higher up. Furthermore,
on the peaks of mountains, weird spectral phenomena might be
seen, like the Brocken Spectre. Here, a man's shadow, radiating

weird purple rings of light, was magnified to titanic dimensions and stretched across the face of a cloud.

This attitude is prevalent right down to the eighteenth century. In his *Tour Through the Whole Island of Great Britain* (1723), Daniel Defoe spoke of Westmorland as 'a county eminent for only being the wildest, most barren and frightful of any that I have passed over in England, or even in Wales; the west side, which borders on Cumberland, is indeed bounded by a chain of almost unpassable mountains, which, in the language of the country, are called Fells . . .'.

The classical writers had, of course, led the way. Some had experienced the violent drama of mountains: lightning-lashed storms, rumbling avalanches and all-engulfing torrents that washed away villages and farms. Or volcanic eruptions, like that of Vesuvius on 24 August AD 79, when the the ground trembled and the sea seemed to roll back on itself as a huge ascending cloud blackened the sky. Pliny the Younger described the stampeding crowds and the awful night that followed. It was like a normal night without moon or stars, but terrifyingly dark – such as you remember as a child when you are shut in a small room and all the lights put out. And through that dark could be heard the shrieks of women calling for their children, wives for their husbands, small boys for their mothers. Some lamented their fate; others wept for their family. Then there were those who wished to die and cursed the gods for deserting them. After a while it grew lighter and the refugees welcomed the return of the day, but shortly after a thick fall of ashes doused the world in thick darkness again. 'I might boast,' Pliny recalled, 'that, during all this scene of horror, not a sign or expression of fear escaped me, had not my support been grounded in that miserable, though mighty consolation that all mankind were involved in the same calamity, and that I was perishing with the world itself.'

Animalising the Enemy

Volcanic eruptions were seen as symptons of divine rage. Nature was both approved of as God's handiwork and rebuked for its disregard of moral or religious matters. This was in contrast to the attitude of prehistoric man who did not consider himself superior – nor did he question the divinity of flora and fauna. No man was as strong as a tiger, or could swim underwater like fish, or run as fast as a deer, or burrow in the earth like a snake. Such abilities attested a special knowledge – hence deer, serpents, bears and wolves were singled out as objects to imitate, worship and imbue with magical properties.

But as vast areas of forest were cleared and people established a network of settlements over the globe, the domain of the farmer increased proportionately and nature was translated in terms of practical usefulness: the metals that could be mined, the animals that could be flayed and eaten, the plants that were most nourishing and the ground on which they might best be cultivated. Ascendancy over the animal kingdom was established and language started to reflect this dominance until the word 'beast' came to be used in a pejorative way. Cowed, penned and stabled, animals were demoted to a lower order of being and, finally, when 'man and beast', 'tame and wild' became equated with 'good and evil' or 'pure and impure', the gulf became unbridgeable.

The final stage of this transference was its imposition upon races and nations in order to validate mass extermination. First animalise the enemy, and then you will be able to kill or punish him with impunity. After securing the surrender of Calais, Edward III demanded that seven of the chief burgesses of the besieged town should be delivered to him bare-footed, bare-headed, in their shirts and with halters about their necks. These wealthy merchants had to assume the meekness of oxen in order to placate the conquering monarch. This humiliation is repeated in country customs down the ages: bridles, horse's collars, cow's tails, stag's horns – all have been used to degrade prisoners and felons.

By the time Christianity had triumphed, the creed of man's dominion over wild creatures was dogma and imitative festivities were frowned upon. 'If anyone at the Kalends of January,' warned Archbishop Theodore (668–90) in the *Liber Potentalis*, 'goes about as a stag or a bull – that is making himself up as a wild animal and dressing in the skin of a wild animal, and putting on the head of a beast – those who in such wise transform themselves into the appearance of a wild animal, penance for three years because this is devilish.'

It is at this juncture, this point of cleavage, that the image of the dragon – the hybrid all-purpose monster – becomes imbued with special meaning. The devil-dragon came to stand for the undesirable qualities of the animal world which were liable to surface in the human personality. In many ways the image was detrimental to the spiritual growth of the Church, harking as it did on antagonism and conflict. Pointing an accusing finger at a heretic became a substitute for religious emotion or political expediency, and a similar impulse may be discerned in the genocides of the present century.

In the Wilderness

Etymologically speaking, the word wild derives from 'willed' – an animal in the grip of its own self-willed nature, unruly and out of control. The Spanish phrase *falta de cultura* means a place where one is lost or be-wild-ered. In the Bible men were cast into the wilderness as a punishment, much as criminals were sent to Siberia or Australia. To dwell in the wilderness and feed upon honey and locusts like John the Baptist was to put oneself beyond human ken. Saints and anchorites went there to slim down their bodies and fatten their spirits. They went there to suffer the chill of separation and, in so doing, plumb spiritual depths that they had never previously attained. A letter of St Jerome to the virgin Eustochium well conveys the experience of an eremite:

> Alas! how often, when living in the desert, in that dreary sunburnt loneliness, which serves as a habitation to the monks, did I believe myself revelling in the pleasures of Rome. I sat lonely, my soul filled with affliction, clothed in wretched rags, my skin sunburnt like an Ethiopian's. No day passed without tears and sighs, and when sleep overcame me I had to lie on the naked ground. I do not mention eating and drinking, for the monks drink, even if sick, only water, and regard cooking as a luxury. And if I, who had condemned myself from fear of hell to such a life, without any other society than scorpions and wild beasts, often imagined myself surrounded by dancing girls, my face was pale from fasting, but in the cold body the soul was burning with desires, and in a man whose flesh was dead the flames of lust were kindled.

So far as Jerome is concerned, the desert is a negation, an absence of being. Whatever diversity it offers – cacti, vultures, rodents, jackals – is smeared by the brush of a self-punitive theology. To his way of thinking, one can do nothing in such a place but be haunted by memory-pictures and images of lust and longing. Instead of yielding to the texture and breath of the landscape, he reads it like a blasphemous text. His only choice is to sink into the darkness of the soul and, in that darkness, temptations fester and breed – temptations that Christ may help him overcome. No doubt the dancing-girls were emissaries of Satan and the scorpions loathly denizens of the underworld.

Desert and forest were twin aspects of the wilderness, the first offering an expanse of uninterrupted space, the second an enclosed, shadowy silence. In the forest you were liable to encounter outlaws who would rob and kill for the paltry change stored in the pocket. Then there were those who had succumbed to the law of the wild or whose character was irredeemably linked to that of the animals: the hairy outcasts whose protuberant features, bracketed by foliage, grimaced out of a darkness of looming oak spires and babbled uncouth nonsense in a tongue like the wind seething between the leaves.

Ancestral Bogeymen

Consider – exactly who was this Master of the Forest who converted Jean Grenier to wolfdom and later visited him at the monastery? Apparently he was a black man, a woodland deity who interceded between the human and natural worlds. Being Master of the Forest, he was presumably lord of the animals, a shamanistic figure who could issue the desiring with a magic salve and a wolf's skin. He was the official outfitter of the possessed and the action of signing or blood-marking Jean with his nail is obviously akin to signing a devilish pact.

Attitudes to strong-muscled, primitive beings have always wavered between reverence and contempt. In one breath the 'noble savage' is held up as an exemplar; in the next he is dismissed as an 'uncouth barbarian'. Neanderthal man, who first appeared about eighty thousand years ago, was traditionally disparaged by historians; they depicted him as 'a crouching, stooping, squat and brutal creature, with huge jaws and little or no forehead, and a low grade of intelligence'. Even open-minded thinkers like H.G. Wells perpetuated such a myth – 'an extreme hairiness, an ugliness, or a repulsive strangeness in his appearance over and above his low forehead, his beetle brows, his ape neck and inferior stature . . .'

In popular imagination, civilisation had passed them by. Shambling, uncouth and threatening, they confront the disdainful historian much like the Wild Man or woodwose of medieval lore – a hairy hominid who wielded a club and lurked in the depths of the forest. His significance was that of a 'frightener' or ancestral bogeyman who wore no clothes and bowed to no rule of law. He stood for man in his natural state, before the Church and education had tamed and tutored him.

Similar to the Wild Man was the vegetation spirit or forest demon known as the Green Man, found on the roof bosses of numerous churches, usually depicted as a leaf-entwined head, the mouth sprouting vines or shoots. Not only was green redolent of death and decay, but also of springtime growth and resurrection, and the Green Man reconciled these opposites. In *Sir Gawain and the Green Knight* – a manuscript dating from the late fourteenth century – we meet a possible descendant of this strange being, an attractive mixture of boaster and supernatural antagonist. He is excessively hairy and, when roused, presents rolling furious eyes before Arthur's court:

> Yes, garbed all in green was the gallant rider,
> And the hair of his head was the same hue as his horse,
> And floated finely like a fan round his shoulders,
> And a great bushy beard on his breast floating down,
> With the heavy hair hanging from his head,
> Was shorn below the shoulder, sheared right round,
> So that half his arms were under the encircling hair,
> Covered as by a king's cape, that closes at the neck.

Another supernatural being, sacred to the forest of Windsor Park, was Herne the Hunter, memorably evoked by Shakespeare in *The Merry Wives of Windsor*:

> There is an old tale that goes that Herne the Hunter
> Sometimes a keeper in Windsor Forest,
> Doth all winter time, at still midnight,
> Walk around the oak with great ragged horns.

Herne was another species of wild man, possessing only a slight resemblance to a human being, clad in the skin of a deer and wearing on his head a kind of helmet, formed from the skull of a stag, and from which branched a handsome pair of antlers. Tradition states that Herne would be seen standing or crouching near his favourite tree, as if about to spring on a victim, or otherwise galloping round the trunk, festooned with chains and accompanied by a pack of howling dogs.

THE FOURTH HORSEMAN

> Upon this path, stepping forth from the margin of the wood, a white figure now appeared. It paused a little and seemed to look about; and then, at a slow pace, and bent almost double, it began to draw near across the heath. At every step the bell clanked. Face, it had none; a white hood, not even pierced with eyeholes, veiled the head; and as the creature moved, it seemed to feel its way with the tapping of a stick. Fear fell upon the lads, as cold as death. 'A leper,' said Dick hoarsely. 'His touch is death,' said Matcham. 'Let us run.'
>
> (*The Black Arrow*, Robert Louis Stevenson, 1884)

Whatever powers are invoked by men, whatever crazes, flushes and arousals they incite, whatever institutions they create, other agents are at work that fly in the face of individual destiny and resolve. Cathars and heretics, witches and werewolves – though feared and despised – were seen as tangible fixtures of reality who could be located and dispatched, unlike those mysterious contagions that seemingly came from nowhere and vanished just as mysteriously. Non-human, bearing neither grievance nor discernible motive, they were capable of effecting horrific asymmetries, making humans grotesque, misshapen, incapable of breath or speech. They changed the colour of the skin and made rank fluids seep from orifices. Once they had destroyed the flesh that hosted them, they themselves starved away from the repletion of their virulence. They were pure, selfish agencies to whom death meant nothing.

Dead to the World

The man stood, head bowed, in the freshly dug grave, holding a candle. A black veil covered his face as he heard the mass being recited. The priest, letting drop three spadefuls of earth on his fissured head, intoned, 'Be dead to the world, reborn to God.' From his hole in the earth the man replied: 'O Jesus, my redeemer, you formed me out of the earth, you dress me in the body; let me be reborn in the final day.' The small congregation of friends sang *Libera me, Domine* and, at the close of mass, the priest read a set of formal instructions to the man. No more church-going, no drinking in taverns, no eating from dishes or cups save his own, no handling goods for bargaining or buying; no touching of children, no drinking from public wells, no drinking and eating in company, no love-making and no travelling without the right clothes or appurtenances.

Following the acceptance of such proscriptions, the man, whose name was Jean Bodel, was made to dress in appropriate garments: a long black or grey robe embroidered with a red letter L and a rattle or castanet to warn others of his approach. Hurriedly he put these on and was escorted to a place of retreat – a shabby hut situated in an open field outside of town. 'This retreat is mine,' he announced. 'I will live here because I have chosen it.'

Tragedy had befallen Jean Bodel, a poet and municipal worker of Arras. He had exposed himself to leprosy, a disease men were more prone to catch than women, for they ran the majority of errands through the garbage- and stool-splattered streets. At first he found hard spots and swellings arising on his body and visited a doctor who carefully shaved him and greased his body with mercury ointments but the disease was already well advanced. When all attempts at concealment became useless, Bodel realised that he would have to publicly announce his condition.

So in 1202 he wrote a *Conges*, a letter setting out the reasons for his withdrawal from the world, for a cast-out leper hardly ever saw his parents or friends. Writing a long, reflective and sorrowful missive was the most satisfactory way of laying the ghost of kinship. 'My sadness surpasses all others,' he wrote. Not only was he forced to face the fact of his physical death but also to live with the knowledge of his social burial. 'The world excluded me and prosecuted me,' wrote Bodel. 'The disease which torments my body, for which society rejects me, causes everyone to avoid me.'

He then partook in the service described and, the formal vows of separation being complete, set out to find suitable lodgings. Too poor to buy a room in a decent leper house, Bodel camped in a wretched spot downwind of Arras. He asked his former employers for money, arguing that he had caught the disease while in their service: 'Messeigneurs, before I leave you, I ask at this crisis, in the name of God and our birthplace, that you get up a subscription among you to put an end to this difficulty, for which each one of you ought to have pity.'

Bodel lived on until 1210. He died among lepers, believing as did others that the departure of his mortal soul would finally release him from the snares of his body.

Because medieval descriptions of leprosy were rarely precise, it is by no means certain how many of the outcasts were true lepers and how many actually suffered from severe skin disorders. It is likely that Bodel had contracted bacterial leprosy, a variant which destroys skin sensitivity, attacks the upper lip and nose, and spreads to the larynx, making the voice harsh and rasping. Dubbed 'leonine' leprosy after the lion-like face it produces, it harks back to the Graeco-Roman elephantiasis which, in its early stages, was known as 'leontiasis', and produced an offensive skin odour, flushed cheeks, thickened lips and swollen eyebrows. The dominant emotion provoked by such symptons was fear – fear of infection and fear of becoming a fellow outcast.

In a funeral sermon delivered by St Gregory of Nazianus in 379, lepers are portrayed as a race dead to the world. With their festering bodies and insensible limbs, they are driven from market-place, village and fountain. They cannot break bread with others nor partake of fresh water with them. They are the living dead, objects of terror and loathing, wandering around by night and day, shunned and detested by fathers, mothers, relatives, spouses and children. No comfort can be given them in their present lives, save that offered by their own kind. The fate of such men speaks for itself. But it did not arouse the compassion that might have been expected. Theologically speaking, lepers provoked the question: did they deserve their disease? Those who did not believe in ill-luck or the caprices of fate argued that lepers had been singled out for their indulgence in sins of the flesh. They were being punished for their lechery, pride, cupidity and absence of faith. Such a startling, terrible taint could not be randomly dispensed among the just and unjust.

Or perhaps a leper was akin to Job being tested by God? This consolatory crumb was tossed to the afflicted by doctors and priests along with the parable of Lazarus. In the life beyond, the leper's diseased body will be transfigured into a glorious whole. Leprosy was a worldly blight, a purgatory of the soul, but finally the sufferer will attain paradise 'where there is neither disease nor adversity, but all are pure and spotless, without filth and without any stain of filth, more resplendent than the sun, where you will go, if you please God'.

This beatific vision offered more consolation than did the treatment meted out by certain highly placed lepraphobes. Philip V of France and Henry II of England preferred to disregard the mournful formalities of religious exile and instituted their own draconian rites. The French king decreed that the leper be strapped to a post and set alight, while Henry, keeping more closely to the letter of the ecumenical decree, had him led down to the cemetery and buried alive.

However, acts of compassion do shine out of the repressive gloom. When famine struck Constantinople in the fourth century, the common people protested that, while they were going hungry, the rich leper Zodicus was feeding the inmates of the leper hospital he had founded. The crowd cited the Bible: God was angry with Zodicus for sheltering sinners and had sent the famine. Finally

Zodicus was arrested by the Emperor Constantine who demanded that he surrender all his jewels. Zodicus agreed and Constantine himself went to the leper house where all the inmates, including the emperor's own daughter, were assembled. They greeted the potentate, holding up lighted candles. 'Here are my jewels,' declared Zodicus. The emperor, furious, ordered that Zodicus be torn apart by wild mules and his own daughter drowned in the Bosphorus. But afterwards he relented, donating money to the hospital which became a celebrated, long-surviving fixture of the city.

The issue of leprosy highlights our addiction to surfaces – our fear of the secret processes that threaten the *personae*. Lepers like Bodel were forced to create their own brotherhoods of the excluded. If a man's body generates revulsion, rarely does one seek the metaphysical riches of his soul. Look beneath the surface, we are told; observe the inner being. But this piece of advice is inscrutable, as the only evidence for the inner is what is made visible and articulate. Furthermore it is a disconcerting fact that, in present-day society, those with conventionally pleasing or symmetrical features are liable to have more love lavished on them as babies, more pocket money as teenagers, better jobs in later life, lighter prison sentences and more help and good turns done to them by others. If beauty is skin-deep, surely too are love, hate and that panoply of reactions determining what is known as 'character'. Professors of aesthetics, who try to establish the rules by which a person or object is deemed beautiful, seldom produce a watertight, coherent theory, only descriptions of what they find agreeable or disgusting.

The Black Death

In Russia they tell the story of a peasant sitting under a larch tree and spying a large woman in billowing robes who approaches him. Before he can run, the Pest Maiden grabs him by the neck: 'Do you know the Pest?' she hisses. 'I am she. Carry me all over Russia, and I will do you no harm. Miss no village for I must visit all.' The peasant carries out her order, taking the Pest Maiden from village to village, where the dogs howl as she shakes her robes, unleashing death on thousands until the streets are thickly piled with coffins and bodies. Eventually they reach the village where the peasant lives with his wife, children and aged parents. In horror he turns upon the maiden, throwing her into the river and drowning himself in the process. But the Pest Maiden survives, climbing out of the water and taking cover in the forest, where she bides her time before spreading the next outbreak.

The story personifies the arbitrary, awful swiftness of certain epidemics, how they come in death-dealing waves, lie low and then erupt again like a long-simmering grudge. Although leprosy altered Europe's civil structure – resulting in the creation of thousands of specialist hospitals or lazar houses – its impact was less ferocious than bubonic plague. The latter, caused by fleas that lived on the backs of rats, spread its infection from rat to human, ultimately killing both, then finding another animal or human host on which to batten. The plague, thought to have originated in the region of the Himalayas, spread across the Chinese Borderland, Central Asia and the Roman Empire, causing sporadic outbreaks throughout history.

Its most dramatic depredations were seen during the fourteenth century. After taking root in Sicily in 1347, it spread to the port of Messina and within a few days it was overrunning the city. The citizens blamed the sailors whose galleys had recently docked in the harbour and tried to drive foreign ships away – but such measures were fruitless. Hundreds were already dying in the streets. Hoping for a miracle cure, the Messinese appealed to the Patriarch Archbishop of Catania to allow the relics of St Agatha to be transferred from Catania to Messina. The citizens of Catania protested; they would rather die than forfeit their relics. The Patriarch acceded to the Catanian mob. As a compassionate concession, he promised to dip the relics in holy water and take the precious liquid to the citizens of Messina. The Archbishop duly landed at Messina carrying the holy water and processed around the town. The crowds followed him, chanting litanies, but their devotions were broken up by a pack of demons who had been 'transfigured into the shape of dogs', one of whom, bearing a drawn sword in its paws, rushed in among them, breaking the silver vessels, lamps and candlesticks on the altars, casting them hither and thither . . .

Panic-induced hallucinations of this kind were commonplace, as above the cities and towns of Europe flocks of crows and vultures freckled the skies, like a celestial contagion, before settling and feasting on the dead. Wolves invaded the streets of Paris and fought with dogs, pigs and cats over the litter of unburied carcasses. Vengeful mobs, aroused by vindictive preachers, set upon wealthy Jews as scapegoats. Dragged out of their houses, they were tortured, fried, nailed down and sealed in wine casks and pushed into rivers. Huge purifying bonfires were lit in the streets, garnished with orange leaves, camphor and sage, around which commoners and soothsayers congregated, talking of the vanity of possessions and the transience of life.

In 1349 the plague reached England, behind a wave of horror. Three months before the pandemic struck, William Edendon, Bishop of Winchester, had written: 'A voice in Rama has been heard, much weeping and crying has sounded throughout the various countries of the globe. Nations, deprived of their children in the abyss of an unheard-of plague, refused to be consoled . . . Every joy has ceased in them; pleasant sounds are hushed and every note of gladness is banished. They have become abodes of horror and a very wilderness; fruitful country places without the tillers, thus carried off, are deserts and abandoned to barrenness.'

The Bishop goes on to say how he cherished a terrible fear that the plague might strike the diocese, for it was already ravaging the coast. In the past God had devised various punishments for mankind – but he hoped that men's base, sensual natures had not provoked wrath of this magnitude. Accordingly the Bishop exhorted his clergy to impress it upon their flocks to attend church. They should make atonements, too, on Sundays, Wednesdays and Fridays, reciting the seven penitential psalms and the greater litany while processing barefoot around the market-place. Despite these measures, the plague struck Winchester and almost half the beneficed clergy died. In March and April the pestilence spread through Wales. The poet

Jeuan Gethin, who witnessed it at first hand, spoke of seeing death 'coming into our midst like black smoke, a plague which cuts off the young, a rootless phantom which has no mercy for fair countenance. . . . It is of the form of an apple, like the head of an onion, a small boil that spares no one.'

The after-effects of the plague have been much debated. Social unrest, high prices, declining standards of craftsmanship, profiteering, luxury, expenditure, debauchery and religious hysteria – all have been linked with the disaster. But if the plague reaped benefit to some in material terms, it increased the burden of gloom and pessimism that weighed down the spirits of men and women in the Middle Ages. The skeletal figure of death – cavorting on graves, tormenting men, riding oxen – became a ubiquitous motif in art and recreation. How people responded to the pervasive *miseria* depended on individual outlook or circumstances. The plague gnawed at the 'moral stamina' of Europe, leaving tithes unpaid, manorial coffers empty and fields unattended. Those who survived were more sceptical and tolerant of extremes, but still desired a spiritual anchorage on which they could base their recovery. Most pieced together the bits of their lives and resumed their trades and vocations. Others retired to shrines of healing, prayed devoutly or tried to 'lash' themselves out of their sinfulness. And a third group succumbed to messianic personalities, such as Thomas Munzer and John of Leyden, hoping that the ashes of their lives might be enfired by visions of glory.

SOCIOLOGY OF THE LOST SOUL

The secret horror of the last is inseparable from a thinking being, whose life is limited, and to whom death is dreadful. We always make a secret comparison between a part and a whole; the termination of any period of life reminds us that life itself has likewise its termination; when we have done anything for the last time we involuntarily reflect that a part of the days allotted to us is past, and that as more is past there is less remaining.

(*The Idler*, Samuel Johnson, 1758–60)

In *The Triumph of Death* by Pierre Breughel the Elder, the Reaper is shown on his pale horse, brandishing his scythe and leading an army of skeletons. Neither love nor chivalry nor piety can withstand his advances. Behind him, a skeleton riding a starved horse pulls a cart filled with skulls and bones. Despite its unfestive subject matter, the painting is not unappealing; from the rich brown-orange colours and the ebullience of detail radiates an insect-like vitality. One would scarcely venture the word 'engaging' in the context of a grim visual sermon, but the sheer exuberant mayhem does succeed in swamping the macabre subject matter and conveying an attitude that might be termed as robust.

Because of the prevalence of leprosy, plague, starvation and catastrophe, the monks of the Middle Ages recognised there was no denying or fleeing from death. It had to be accepted – some might say embraced – and a pathos surrounds the ritual emollients that attempt to 'soften' its obdurate ascendancy. In countries that had become used to plague, a dance of death was performed by mummers in the streets, each dressed to represent a different trade, for no occupation was excluded from the grand finale. It began in France during the late thirteenth century and its earliest known illustration – formerly in the cemetery of Les Innocents in Paris – showed the hierarchy of Church and State dancing with skeletons or corpses who escort them to their graves.

To assist the dying were special texts that listed their symptoms as irritability, vanity, pride, greed and morbid concern with worldly attachments. All these were manifestations of the Devil who might seize a dying miser's moneybags or taunt a conceited high-ranking burgher. Counteracting the Devil's baneful devices were visions of heaven, the gardens of paradise over which angels hovered and from which heavenly music played. The pursuit of material goals was fruitless, for these would perish along with the flesh, leaving only the spirit for divine appraisal.

Death was an agent by which people were frightened into belief. Transience was broadcast from each pulpit, painting and sculpture. This inculcated a sense of solemn worldly obligation and, to flesh out the negation, death was personified engaged in activities such as riding, jousting, dancing, courting and fornicating. The hyperactive skeleton became a vital presence, a dark counterfoil to the radiant Christ who triumphed over him by the resurrection of the body.

Hence the message: follow Christ in order to defeat death. This is repeated in the thousands of church monuments wherein knights and noblemen are shown praying devoutly or reclining on table tombs with serene expressions and feet resting on small dogs. Sometimes angels are incorporated into an elaborate tableau, clasping their newly released souls or joining in their prayers, as if entry into paradise had always been a foregone conclusion. And beyond the conventions of artistic portrayal, numerous superstitions invoked death's presence. A star falling above a peasant's house might presage a visitation; a white flower blooming out of season; a ringing in the ears; a bay tree rotting in a garden; a candle burning blue; an inexplicable shivering of the body; crows or magpies fluttering round a person; being cut by a razor that had been used to shave a corpse; a black beetle scrambling over a shoe; stumbling into an open grave; hearing one's name uttered by a dying man – a myriad connections spelt out the same message. With so many possible harbingers of death, what chance did a man have of living a long, contented life? Obviously there was fallibility in such observations, and out of such beliefs, finally, was bred scepticism and mockery. The philosophy behind such superstitions translates everything as meaningful – a phenomenal world perpetually intent on delivering gloomy warnings.

Remembering the Dead

In such a climate, men and women became imbued with an intimate, despairing sense of cessation. Human life seemed fragile and quick-dissolving and naturally post-mortal welfare was an issue seriously debated. This gave rise to superstition and malign rumour concerning spirits and apparitions. What happened to those who passed over? Did God gather in their immortal souls? Or did they unhappily linger around deathbeds and graveyards? No doubt many people had seen 'ghosts' – but were they authentic apparitions?

Could they not as easily be diabolic simulations? How could an apparition be vetted and authenticated?

With this in mind, we may consider how many tales of ghosts emerged from a specific social matrix, embodying the historic attitudes, beliefs and prejudices that various factions once held dear and were, in many instances, able to profit from. Considerable sums of money passed between laity and priest in order that the dead should be honoured at the right period of the month. Furthermore, if the dead were presented as desiring or spiritually benefiting from that service, the role of the priest would be consolidated.

Conversing with people who have 'seen' ghosts of deceased loved ones, it becomes apparent that in many instances the visitation came not long after the funeral. In the Middle Ages this was recognised as the time of memoria when the dead were still 'warm in the mind'. If a testator had so specified, masses were regularly performed to ease the spirit's transition to the afterlife and to offer solace to the grieving relatives. Literally the services enacted a rite of passage, a ceremonial bridge. The anniversary of the death was a popular time for ghosts; the apparitions might appear, thank their loved ones for their kindly intercession, testify to the efficacy of their suffrage before passing again beyond mortal eye or hearing.

Frequently it was monks who were the scribes and confidants of supernatural happenings. This was common throughout the Middle Ages. A small literate segment elected themselves as guardians and filtrators of truth. Drawing upon a corpus of traditional pagan terrors, such as fear of malicious spirits, they invoked supernatural scenes to reinforce the authority of religion. They contrasted the blood-chilling spectacles generated by devils with blessed miracles, visions of descending angels and glimpses of joyful souls basking in the gardens of Paradise. Elements of folklore might be adapted or refashioned into a sermon, a narrative or exempla, drawing attention to a debt unpaid, a sin unshriven. For instance, during a pilgrimage to Santiago, Richard Rountre saw a company of dead men. Among them was a newborn baby who left the troop and rolled to his feet in a stocking. The little spirit spoke. 'I am the son you aborted,' he told Richard. 'The midwives buried me in my mother's stocking without first baptising me.' Richard was moved. Invoking the Holy Trinity, he clothed the child in his own shirt and gave him a name. The baby immediately jumped up, full of joy that his father had recognised him and kinship had been established.

Such stories both enforced guilt and at the same time offered healing and reconciliation by pointing out that sinners could redeem themselves by acts of kindness and generosity. In another common type of tale, the ghost of a dead father appears to his son saying he is in purgatory and adding: 'Pray for me, I implore you. I am enduring terrible torments for the sins I have committed. But listen – you can hasten my liberation. What you must do is attend the masses, make regular prayers and almsgiving.' Invariably messages cast in this form hinted that the church or monastery desired to promote the commissioning of such services.

Crossing the Gobi

Not all tales of ghostly happenings conformed to a clerical pattern or were constructed around the needs of a particular lost soul. While crossing the Gobi Desert on horseback, Marco Polo (*c.* 1273) wrote of strange sensations that afflicted the traveller during the night and made him loiter and lose touch with his companions. He overheard spirits talking, assuming the voices of his companions – sometimes hailing him by name. 'Often,' he went on, 'these voices make him stray from the path, so that he never finds it again. And in this way many travellers have been lost and have perished. And sometimes in the night they are conscious of a noise like the clatter of a great cavalcade of riders away from the road; and, believing that these are some of their own company, they go where they hear the noise and, when day breaks, find they are victims of an illusion . . .'.

A psychologist might say that here we have a typical account of a traveller whose brain, starved of the usual auditory stimulation, appears to be supplying a medley of sounds absent from the gloomy, monotonous terrain. In other words, silence generates the effect of sound, just as too much noise makes one long for silence. But medieval readers would have a different view. They would see Marco Polo as crossing a wild domain, the outlands of civilisation, where mischievous spirits, who also happen to be masters of disguise, gather and weave their wiles, mimicking the human voice, deceiving and leading off track the doomed travellers.

Legions of the Lost

The spirits overheard or imagined by Marco Polo hark back to a pagan world of mischievous, drifting entities. They have little or no theological purpose compared with the ensemble recorded by the monk Orderic Vitalis at the close of the eleventh century. Orderic was an ecclesiastical historian of Normandy who included in his chronicles the testimony of a young priest called Walchelin.

On 1 January 1091 Walchelin was returning home after visiting a sick parishioner. He heard the din of an approaching army which he assumed to be that of the local warlord, Robert of Bellême, en route for the siege of Courcy. The priest hid behind a group of medlar trees and waited for the soldiers to pass – but what he saw was a troupe of lost and tortured souls. First the lay folk, on foot, weighed down by terrible burdens; then the clergy, bishops as well as monks, all black-cowled and weeping – followed by a black-clad, fiery army of knights, storming past on black chargers. All these dead souls were suffering horrible tortures: the women especially, for they were mounted on saddles of burning nails; they would be ejected in the air by an unceasing wind and then plummeted down again on the sharp points. This cavalcade of agony was known as Hellequin's Hunt: the lost, perpetually tortured legions of the lord of the dead on their procession through the world of men.

Thinking no one would believe the ghastly sight he had seen unless he was able to offer proof, Walchelin left his hiding place and tried to catch and mount one of the riderless horses – but the stirrup burned his foot and the reins froze his hand. Four knights bore down on him, accusing him of making away with their property, but then one of them, William of Glos, son of the deceased Barnon Glos, asked of him a favour. Apparently he had fraudulently acquired a mill and now wished it to be returned to the legitimate heirs. Walchelin refused – he did not care to run messages for a felon. In a fit of rage, William of Glos grabbed the priest by the neck, burning an indelible mark, the signum of the damned. Fifteen years later Walchelin still bore this same scorchmark, which he showed to Orderic, impressing on him how the dead retain their guilty consciences.

Many of the damned Walchelin had recognised – murderers, wantons, renegades – but there were also many he was surprised to see: those thought to have lived exemplary lives. Several tried to speak to him, requesting his intercession or influence to lessen their suffering. His own brother Robert, son of Ralph the Fair, stepped out of the throng, reproaching Walchelin for forgetting him and begging for his prayers, so that he might be released from the penance of carrying a flaming sword eternally back and forth. Walchelin asked Robert why his spurs were covered in a mass of congealed blood; his brother replied that it was not blood but fire that weighed heavier to him than Mont Saint Michel. This was in perpetual remembrance of all the blood he had spilled during his lifetime.

Why were such tales of terror devised? One of the problems the church faced was controlling the unruly barons and warlords who might take over whole towns and act entirely outside the law. They were overbearing and oblivious to finger-wagging lectures by priests or bishops. They lived by action and plunder – violence stirred their blood like strong wine. Only one thing made them flinch: the prospect of eternal incineration as thundered from the pulpit. As they could not live harmoniously within an ordered social regime, the problem was how to divert their jostling rivalry and go-getting aggression. It was partly solved by sticking a spiritual seal on their savagery and making them warriors of Christ. Hence Christian orders like the Knights Templar were formed, partly to introduce self-discipline and piety among the military, so that their hitherto unruly energies might be channelled into crusades rather than perpetrating bloodshed and rapine on their own doorsteps. Stories like Walchelin's threatened an afterlife of unremitting agony for those who soldiered and slew for material gain.

Malicious Spirits

Not all ghosts, however, were roasting in hell, freezing in purgatory or stampeding pointlessly over the countryside with their damned companions. Nor were they fawning supporters of the status quo, begging relatives to pray for them or inaugurate masses. Some were literally 'free spirits' who behaved as impulsively and selfishly as any grudge-bearing demon.

Around 1400 a monk of Byland Abbey set down an account of a particularly grisly haunting that took place in Yorkshire. Generally the spirits took human form but they could assume animal guise as well. A mercenary from Rielvaux appeared in the form of a horse that reared up, then as a haystack with a light in its middle, and then in the shape of a man who proposed that the villager carry his sack of beans (Pythagoreans maintained that the souls of the dead dwelt in beans which, through their flatulent properties, caused evil dreams and nightmares) but not beyond the waterfall. The waterfall marked a threshold or boundary beyond which the spirit dared not venture. Another dead man came to the tailor Snowball in the form of crow flying and shooting out sparks. It slammed into him, wounding him and making him fall from his horse. The crow-spirit reappeared as a dog with a chain around its neck, but still it managed to speak, begging Snowball to request the suffrage of a priest on its behalf. When it materialised a third time, it had changed to a goat that groaned, 'Ah, ah, ah!' Two other spirits taunted the ghost-ridden Snowball: one was his wife's murderer, resembling a steer without eyes, mouth or ears; the other a hunter sounding a horn and purporting to be a dead religious figure.

In Kilburn the spirit of Robert, son of Robert of Bolterbi, escaped from the cemetery and terrorised the neighbourhood; the spirit of the former curate at Kirkby, Jacques Tankerlay, returned one night to gouge out the eyes of one of his former mistresses. A spirit from Ampleforth pursued William of Bradforth for four nights, crying out in a terrible voice that resonated like an echo in the mountains.

Notable about these northern ghosts is their crude aggression. They threaten, barter and seek vengeance in the manner of the primitive ghouls and vampires of legend. It was possibly such a view that prompted prehistoric peoples to make sure the dead were securely walled in their tombs and their bones scattered and mixed –

sometimes ground to powder – in the belief that dispersion might deter violent haunting.

Secrets of Others

A common problem stems from modern man's attempt to 'read' the Middle Ages in the open-minded way one might read a fax instruction manual or telephone directory. Such dramatic reports as Walchelin's may be first encountered in sundry works on the paranormal. Usually the source material is not 'framed' contextually, so one reads it as an isolated tale of wonder – an inexplicable intrusion of the miraculous – not as part of a compendium selected and organised with a degree of guile and forethought. Just as many Christians are uneasy about commentaries tracing mythic echoes or patent borrowings in the Bible, ardent supernaturalists do not care to acknowledge that their favourite hair-raisers have been 'assembled' and elaborated over a long period.

It is demonstrable that legends of the wandering, restless troupes of souls pre-date the eleventh century. They were invoked over broad areas of Western Europe. In the Scandinavian tradition, Odin headed the soul-ravening hunt astride his eight-legged stallion Sleipnir, but there were variants invoking other representatives of the irredeemably damned: Cain, the Devil or regional malefactors like Tregeagle in Cornwall. An *Anglo-Saxon Chronicle* entry of AD 1127 contains an account of the Wild Hunt storming through the park of Peterborough: 'They straddled black horses and black bucks while their hounds were pitch black with staring hideous eyes . . . All through the night monks heard them sounding and winding their horns.'

Aside from a corpus of 'pagan' legends centred upon tortured souls and hungry ghouls, the material out of which ghost stories arose was often the troubled, grieving testimonies of friends and relatives. If one becomes sensitive to distinctions, one may view them not as spiritual revelations but as human documents in which widowers and despairing parents set down encounters with lost spouses and offspring that took place during waking vision or grim nightmare. Sometimes the living love the dead too much; the sombre narratives plough deep furrows of sadness and regret. But is it the dead who haunt or the empty spaces they bequeath? The eternal echo of their absence? 'What haunts are not the dead,' wrote Nicholas Abraham, 'but the gaps left within us by the secrets of others.'

SHADOW OF THE ANTICHRIST

The coming of Antichrist was even more tensely awaited. Generation after generation lived in constant expectation of the all-destroying demon whose reign was indeed to be lawless chaos, an age given over to rapine, torture and massacre, but was also to be the prelude to the longed-for consummation, the Second Coming and the Kingdom of the Saints.

(*The Pursuit of the Millennium,* Norman Cohn, 1957)

The vengeful spirits evoked by Marco Polo and Orderic Vitalis thrived in the wilder principalities of Europe during the sixteenth century. Their existence was acknowledged by monks and scholars and frequently incorporated into their chronicles. Martin Luther (1483–1546) hailed from remote Thuringia where old German paganism blended with Christianity. Werewolves, elves, gnomes and fairies flitted through the forests of the province, just as water sprites darted and splashed in the rivers and lakes. Peevish devils, it was believed, unleashed storm, flood and pestilence; they depleted the vitality of mankind by dispersing melancholia and sickness on the wind. Luther's mother thought them able to steal things like eggs, butter and milk from the dairy. 'Many regions', he remarked, 'are inhabited by devils. Prussia is full of them, and Lapland of witches. In my native country on top of a high mountain called the Pubelsberg is a lake into which if a stone is thrown a tempest will arise over the whole region because the waters are the abode of captive demons.'

This is a telling comment from the moving spiritual light of the age. Luther emerges as an animist in the almost pagan sense. Spiritual confrontations of a melodramatic kind enlivened much of his career, and it was only after an encounter with death that he resolved to enter the cloister. On a sultry July day in 1505 he was returning to school when a flash of lightning felled him. In that explosion of radiance, he saw a vision of God the all-terrible and Christ the inexorable. There was also a cluster of leering fiends springing up from pond and wood – he sensed them seizing him by his shock of curly hair and flinging him into Hell. He cried out to his father's patron, 'St Anne help me! I will become a monk!'

Combing through his voluminous writings, it seems that what Luther feared was not so much Satan as God. There was too much horror, too much wayward cruelty and physical disaster in the world for the Creator to be compassionate and even-handed. One *could* ascribe plagues, wars and floods to Satan – but that would make him seem all-powerful. Yet to ascribe them to God would be like imputing Him with malign intentions. Hence Luther conceived God as a rumbling, raging deity, stronger on punishment than humour, who liked mankind to follow meekly at heel. Basically he was just – but too harsh and unpredictable to allow more than a moment's pleasure or relaxation.

Sorting out which phenomena were God's and which the Devil's could not have been easy, for the latter might adopt an angelic disguise. Luther tended to hold the Devil responsible for the life's minor vexations and ailments, including his own stubborn bowel movements. His tortured evacuations were a way of ejecting Satan from his body. 'But if that is not enough for you, you Devil,' he wrote, 'I have also shit and pissed. Wipe your mouth on that and take a hearty bite.' This is childishly smutty – one senses the priest had recourse to the Devil as light relief after the ferocious gravity of God. Satan was wicked and devious, yes, but at least you could rile and poke your tongue out at him without being guilty of blasphemy.

Did They Literally Believe?

One question about the medieval world certainly needs attention: did the average man and woman literally believe in the Devil, Hell and Eternal Damnation? At the beginning of the twenty-first century, for instance, millions of people watch horror films in which demons perpetrate every type of assault and slimy transformation, but unless they are Christian fundamentalists, or earnest students of the occult, most do not take it seriously. Perhaps the people of the Middle Ages were the same? Are we being patronising when we portray them as lumpen yokels who believed the Devil to be lurking in dirty corners of the kitchen?

In tackling such a question, picture a country like Germany five hundred years ago, where forests spread dark shawls over the shoulders of mountains that loom over lakes, deep-shadowed and fed by numerous streams. In the hilltops and spring-lines of settlement are crag-perched castles and walled towns enclosing a medley of thatched hovels, the timber-beamed houses of wealthy burghers and intricate church spires rising up like jewelled fingers. Narrow streets are scarred by the passage of creaking carts and plodding hooves. Where the thoroughfares end stretch oppressive acres of green over which a ceaseless wind wanders, stirring smoke from isolated farmsteads, taking the smell of midden, sty, charcoal burner, to other nostrils, other lives. In these ample spaces mist and clouds gather – sometimes blotting out the landscape for miles. When heavy rain falls, nothing can penetrate the grey screen of moisture that seeps under doors and through rooftops. In the deep silence, broken only by the bells of cattle and monastery, night will descend stealthily. Within the solitary farmhouse, a candle provides comfort – but it is only a fragile, transitory gleam. If a lightning bolt strikes during the small hours, who can prove that it is not an enraged deity? If the farm dog contracts rabies the next day, who can doubt that a snarling demon has taken over a once-friendly pet? If the milk is found to be bad a second after a raven has perched on the churn, why not blame the contamination on the Evil One in feathered guise?

It was not a question of men and women being stupider than their modern counterparts, but of there being more fear and hazard in the world, and only one set of explanations – a theological one – to account for them. What we are talking about is a landscape of fear. In Luther's views there can be found little glorious assurance. The only certain facts are gloomy and grim: that men are born and will die. As for salvation, that rests purely on God's whim.

One may read this in the art of the Middle Ages. Consider the symbolic engraving by Albrecht Dürer, *Knight, Death and the Devil*. The knight is riding, his hound following with meek, trusting eagerness. A leering goat-headed devil ambles behind. Beside the knight, also on horseback, is the hoary figure of Death, with a serpent encircling his neck and an hourglass in his right hand. The way is prickly, menaced by thorn and thicket, and through a gap one can see a village with dainty spires and timber-framed merchants' houses. It is situated on a hill, so one only attains it after an effort. Yet it's worth it, for it's a place in which a man could live, marry and spread out his network of loyalties and allegiances until sickness or old age lays him low. To the knight, however, it's only a passing-place, for he's a perpetual pilgrim. One sees that in his frown of resolve, that rocklike fixity of purpose. But then an unsettling thought occurs: has he a destination? Is there a Holy Land to be freed or a dragon to be dispatched? Suppose he's not pursuing a gallant errand but fleeing those very forces, Death and the Devil, that shadow his steps? In other words, the knight is no rescuer or redeemer, but a frightened, foredoomed fugitive, pursued by the spectre of mortality.

Prophecy of the Convulsion

Luther's lifetime turned out stormy and unsettled, rife with plague, portent and uprising. Signs of impending upheaval were picked up in the autumn of 1524 when the planets occupied the constellation of Pisces. Over fifty astrological tracts were printed on the 'Prophecy of the Convulsion', a huge celestial disturbance thought to be imminent. A woodcut of the time shows an immense fish poised in the heavens with the peasants holding banners and flails to one side and the emperor, Pope and ecclesiastics on the other.

Naturally there were murmurs of Apocalypse – of the imminent end of the world. The apprehension was a familiar one. In a sense the world – being perceived by millions of single souls – ends each instant for countless numbers as they sink into oblivion or extension. Yet there is a yearning in many for a shared destiny, a sky-cracking finality, a wrenching apart of the mineral fabric, followed by the disclosure of some starry marvel or unearthly presence. In the past, such signs inspired penitents and pilgrims to pack their robes and relics and make off to some pre-ordained site. There, armed with staves, holy texts and rosaries, they would wait, open-mouthed and trembling, for the loudest and most tumultuous of curtain-calls.

At the close of the tenth century (999), many believed Satan's banishment was over. Soon he would appear with his son, the Antichrist, to preside over Armageddon, while Jesus Christ returned to judge mankind – predictions confirmed in reports of falling stars, meteors and sunspots. The thought of all this dramatic activity set Christendom in panic. Those who believed, those who feared and those who did not want to miss something big packed their bags and headed for the Second Coming. Armed with staffs, mules and ponies, thousands of men, women and children embarked on the long trek, praying as they trudged. The road to Jerusalem became so crowded with beggars, penitents and doom-brokers that the monasteries en route, the great almsgivers, were forced to deny them sustenance – hence many experienced the end, so to speak, prematurely from starvation. The remainder continued with their pilgrimage, drinking from roadside wells, picking berries and olives by the verges.

When they arrived at the Holy City, the pilgrims found the Turks in control. Having ousted the moderate, hospitable caliphs of Baghdad, they resented the intrusion of hordes of Christian infidels and kept them waiting at the gates of the city for months. Once admitted, the pilgrims were liable to be beaten, robbed and humiliated. Time passed. Steadily it dawned on the bands of the faithful that either they had got the date wrong or God had decided to suspend the proceedings.

Despite the inability of the world to end punctually, these panics persisted down to Luther's age, with scholars and agitators still attempting to decode the future through *Revelation*. Together with the *Book of Daniel*, it served as primary fuel to feed millennial fire or the doctrine of the 'last days' before the Second Coming of Christ, who would incarnate and establish a kingdom on earth over which

He would reign for a thousand years. Today *Revelation* is regarded as an eccentric text, florid, overblown and slightly crazy; interpreting it has become very much a pastime of cranks. '*Revelation* either finds a man mad or leaves him so,' the saying goes. But this was not a medieval reaction. To those who could not support or protect themselves and their families, *Revelation* offered hope and the possibility of change. It was a text crammed with marvels, exaltations and reversals of the conventional order:

> And I saw a new heaven and a new earth: for the first heaven and first earth were passed away; and there was no more sea. And I John saw the holy city, the New Jerusalem, coming down from God out of heaven, prepared as a bride adorned for her husband.

Oppressed peasants found in *Revelation* an uplifting vision of the defeat of the Antichrist and the Second Coming, when the poor would be released from their travail, and a New Jerusalem established. Charismatic preachers touted visions of this kind. To those who owned nothing or had nothing to lose, they stood as powerful inducements. Throbbing oratory, backed up by choice phrases from the holy book, sent their brains spinning: 'You will be released from your chains,' they were promised. 'Christ will exalt the poor and righteous among you, just as he will crush the strong and sinful. You shall be rich as kings and eat off plates of gold and silver. No longer need you fear disease or suffering – no longer will women in childbirth feel pain. They will conceive their offspring immaculately, just as Mary, Mother of God, conceived our Blessed Saviour.'

In the early Middle Ages there was little sense of history as a progressional mechanism. History was intimately wrapped up with theology, and theology was deeply preoccupied with the catastrophes and visions contained in the Bible. The holy book contained men's past and their future, and the religious-minded, who were the majority, measured events by their correspondence with scriptural predictions. If a cruel Turkish ruler arose, he might be identified as the Antichrist, just as were the Pope and Martin Luther. Any clashing of mighty armies invoked Armageddon. As for sweeping pestilences, they decimated the population of Europe as effectively as the Egyptians in the Old Testament.

Flagellants and Anabaptists

The end of the world was often proclaimed after outbreaks of plague and social turbulence. Out of the collective sense of foreboding, various 'panic cults' would arise. Identifying God with disease-and-famine-riddled reality, many tried to conciliate their Creator by scourging their bodies. With such an aim 'The Brotherhood of the Flagellants' was formed. They are said to have originated in Eastern Europe – headed by 'gigantic women from Hungary' – and rapidly spread throughout Europe. Their performances proved a stirring if profoundly disturbing spectacle. The Flagellants processed in a long crocodile, in groups of two or three hundred, the men segregated from the women, at their head a Master and two lieutenants bearing banners of purple velvet and a cloth of gold.

Led by a hermit from Perugia, an early wave of Flagellants sprang up in 1260 in Italy and rapidly spread south to Rome. Usually led by a band of priests, carrying banners and burning candles, they tramped from town to town and were greeted with rapture and applause. So energetically and devoutly did they flog themselves that robbers handed back their loot, sinners confessed, feuds were patched up and usurers returned their interest. Convinced of their influence, they mantrically chanted as they struck their bloody skins: 'Holy Virgin, take pity on us! Beg Jesus to spare us!' And so they burnt out the candle of their agonising day, lashing and lamenting until, hours after they had lain down exhausted, the fields and mountains still vibrated with their implorations, drowning all musical instruments and songs of love.

Steadily the Flagellant groups became more organised, devising special uniforms, chants and prayers. The movement entered Germany where it gathered thousands of new adherents, many of a revolutionary persuasion. Word would go ahead of their approach and, when they reached the town church or market-place, a large circle would be formed and the worshippers would strip down, retaining only a linen cloth or skirt that reached to their ankles. These outer garments would be piled in the centre of the circle and the Flagellants marched around until, at a signal from their Master, they threw themselves on the ground. Moving among the spreadeagled bodies, the Master would thrash anyone who raised a hand or who indicated they had particular sin on their conscience or who had offended in some way against the Brotherhood.

After this came the collective whippings wherein the Flagellants, carrying heavy scourges with three or four leather thongs tipped with metal studs, began rhythmically to beat their backs and breasts. Three of the Brothers, acting as cheerleaders, led the movement from the centre of the circle, urging them on to greater intensities of agony. Chanting the hymn of the Flagellants, the Brothers quickened the pace of the scourging, throwing themselves on the floor, trying to outdo each other in self-punitive fervour, while around them the townsfolk roared, shook, sobbed, screamed and applauded.

It seems a strange, almost pitiable cult. Yet before dismissing it as witless credulity, one must remember the depths of fear that inspired it. By self-inflicted punishment, the Flagellants believed they were pre-empting the wrath of the same God who had sown the seeds of pestilence. The Flagellants sought to mimic the pitiless savagery of the Creator – to flatter Him by degrading themselves.

As their following spread, their behaviour graduated to sado-masochistic sex orgies and claims that the rich would be forced to marry the poor as soon as the world ended. To scotch further developments, a Papal Bull was issued in 1349, denouncing their practices as unauthorised by the Catholic Church. In devising rituals and expiations of their own, they had taken blasphemous liberties with God. But many would find no objection in such a criticism. God only mattered in so far as He spoke to the inner man or woman. That was what the crowd-rousing preacher Thomas Muntzer believed – he was spurred by thoughts of a new spiritual imperative wherein the common man, hearing the voice of God, rises against the institutions that dominate him, overthrows them and stamps out residual figures of authority like priests, monks and godless rulers.

Muntzer came from Zwickau and combined deep learning with a captivating personality. He rejected baptism and cast doubt on the letter of the scriptures. 'Bible, Babel, bubble!' he cried. Like Luther, Muntzer wished to translate the word of God, but unlike the former he was not prepared to acknowledge the authority of tradition. Although drawn to *Revelation* with its talk of wars and a Second Coming, he did not lean too heavily on texts and citations. After all, the Bible meant nothing to the Turks, he argued, and the men who wrote the Bible had no religious authority, save that the spirit of God inspired them. What mattered was what God was saying to men now. This doctrine freed Muntzer from having to chain his actions to a particular creed. It gave him the freedom to whip up strong passions and ascribe to them a divine purpose.

After a period of wandering, Muntzer settled and became curé at the small Saxon town of Allstedt in the province of Thuringia. Here he married and created the first liturgy in the German language. His reputation as a charismatic preacher spread; soon peasants from the surrounding countryside were flocking to his sermons, particularly the copper-miners of Mansfield. 'Let my sufferings be a model for you,' he urged. 'The living God is sharpening his scythe in me, so that later I can cut down the red poppies and the blue cornflowers.'

Muntzer evokes the sharpening of tools, the flourishing of swords, the honing of scythes and sickles. It is as if he is eager for conflict. The poor were enthralled by this muscular stance. They were made to believe – if they stood together – that they could be God's agents of change. So much support and enthusiasm did Muntzer arouse among miners, field-workers and artisans that he was able to form the 'League of the Elect', a body of mainly uneducated people who, despising scholarship and pedantry, held that spiritual illumination was the only goal worth attaining.

Muntzer soon clashed with the civil authorities. Uneasy at the reports he had heard, Duke John of Saxony visited Allstedt and asked Muntzer to preach a sermon. He did – a florid, bellicose tirade stating that the millennium was at hand and the last of the world-empires was nearing its end, and that the Saxon princes had better decide whether to be servants of God or the Devil. Priests, monks and godless rulers must all perish: 'If they resist, let them be slaughtered without mercy . . . At the harvest-time one must pluck out the weeds from God's vineyard.'

Duke John, finding the sermon rousing rather than reassuring, was not inclined to throw in his lot with this spiritual incendiary. But Muntzer continued to incite open defiance until the time came when the peasants revolted and joined ranks under different leaders. They attacked monasteries and nunneries and skirmished with the armies of local princes. Muntzer seemed a natural leader – a scholarly agitator who wished to topple the princes and prelates from their high perches. By May 1525 he was commanding a peasant army, with his own Elect at the core, set on leading them to victory. By now he was convinced that he was a Messiah, divinely ordained to usher his followers into a new millennium of spiritual freedom.

Duke John entreated the aid of the military commander Philip of Hesse to help quell the uprising. On 15 May Muntzer gathered his army to meet their opponents. The sides were ill-matched. Philip had a skilled, well-trained army, equipped with swords, pikes and armour, whereas Muntzer's shambling peasants had clubs and farming tools. Appraising this pitiful mob, Philip conferred with the other leaders, some of whom were eager to enter the fray, while others were inclined to caution. Eventually it was decided to offer them pardon if they would hand over Muntzer. Gazing at the formidable array waiting to crush them, the peasants were tempted to betray their cause, but Muntzer stepped in with rousing, inspiring oratory, promising easy victory and invoking David's triumph over Goliath. 'I will catch their cannonballs on my sleeve,' he boasted.

At that moment a rainbow appeared in the sky – Muntzer's own symbol – which the peasants interpreted as divine affirmation. They hurried forward to confront their enemy, whereupon Philip fired his cannons into their midst. Hundreds promptly dropped dead and the rest started to scatter in panic. The trained army bore down upon the mob and utterly routed them. Over five thousand peasants were butchered but Muntzer managed to escape to Frankenhausen. When Philip's army overran the town, he was found hiding in a cellar, from where he was taken, tortured and beheaded.

John of Leyden

Despite victory in the Peasants' War, the princes of Germany did not subsequently enjoy a period of peace and consolidation. Poor harvests and rising prices continued to oppress the population and another outbreak of the Black Death (1529) killed thousands and fanned rumours that the Day of Judgement was at hand.

In Munster, the capital of Westphalia, a peaceable man called Hoffman had taken over the Anabaptists' spiritual initiative. (Anabaptists believed that Christians should be re-baptised on reaching adulthood, renewing their sacred pact.) But Hoffman was less of an insurrectionist than Thomas Muntzer – he advised his followers to await passively the dawning of the millennium. Despite a willingness to compromise, Hoffman overstepped the mark when he announced in 1533 that Strasbourg was the New Jerusalem and the Last Trump was about to sound. When the year passed without anything apocalyptic happening, Hoffman was arrested by the town council and declared a false prophet. He was placed in a metal cage, hung up and left to starve to death.

Meanwhile in Munster a new leader had arisen – an Anabaptist prophet called Bernard Rothmann. Backed by his father-in-law, the rich businessman Bernard Knipperdollinck, he inveighed against Catholicism and the improper use of money. The two men, dashing through the streets, babbled about marvels, malevolences and divine interventions. They urged everyone to repent their sins and prepare for the final judgement. Such was their effect that nuns left nunneries and began pursuing them. Women cast themselves on the ground, writhed, frothed and reported visions of saints and angels. All this transcendental agitation drew in more and more converts, including the followers of the Dutch prophet Jan Matthyson. Droves of them poured into Munster, declaring the town to be the New Jerusalem; among them was a tall, handsome, bearded man called Jan Bockelson, who later became known as John of Leyden.

Soon the leader himself joined his disciples. Jan Matthyson arrived in Munster accompanied by his beautiful wife, an ex-nun. Charismatic and commanding, in flowing robes and holding two tablets under his arms, he told a rapt audience that God had singled out their city as the New Jerusalem. The citizens applauded. The place was soon awash with religious ecstasy. There were vision of Christ and the Virgin Mary. People danced and spoke in tongues. There was sexual frenzy, too, for God is Love, and when the spirit moves one to physical rapture, surely the expression should not be barred? By 1534 the Anabaptists had proved so popular that some had been elected to the town council. In that same year they became virtual rulers of the city and turned on their rivals. They drove out the Catholics and ransacked their churches and homes. In the midst of a whirling snowstorm, crowds of the 'godless' were herded together and beaten out of the town. The Anabaptists mocked their appalling plight. Many died, frostbitten, naked and starved, outside the city walls.

But there were counter-measures that checked the so-far unimpeded progress of John Matthyson and the Anabaptists. Bishop von Waldeck ordered his soldiers to surround the city. But the Anabaptists were not cowed; they believed that God was on their side and would hurry to their aid. At Easter the prophet Matthyson announced that, with God's help, he could raise the siege. Accordingly, accompanied by twenty men, he marched out beyond the city walls. There he was cut down by the opposition, who mounted his head on a pike where his supporters could see it.

Now the journeyman tailor, John of Leyden, became leader of the Anabaptists. To establish his pre-eminence, he ran naked through the town and later lapsed into a silent ecstasy. Three days later, he summoned the population and announced that God had spoken to him, saying that the old man-made constitution of the town had to be replaced by one based on God's plan. In this way, John of Leyden made himself mayor and appointed twelve Elders and other subordinates to serve him. Apportioning labour in a strict, inflexible way, he devised a new legal code, conferring on the council absolute authority in matters spiritual, financial and judicial. For anyone who objected or did not comply, the death penalty was automatic. It was left to this new council to solve the problem of the social imbalance created by the sizeable number of wives and daughters left behind in

Munster by the Catholic refugees. Formerly sexual intercourse had been subject to strict rules. It was permitted between two Anabaptists – but adultery and fornication were capital offences. Either to allay the frustrations of the numerous unattached women or to satisfy the natural desires of his supporters, Leyden reversed his original strictures. 'Increase and multiply,' he proclaimed, instating polygamy and making marriage compulsory for all women over a certain age. Both as a symbol of continuity and as an initiatory gesture, Leyden took as his bride Divara, the alluring widow of Jan Matthyson. When his stock of admirers proved too large to resist, he picked out additional partners, finally presiding over a harem of fifteen wives.

One day, in the main square, arrived a goldsmith called Dusentschur, who claimed the gift of prophecy. He declared that God had told him that Leyden was destined to become king of the whole world. Hearing this, Leyden fell on his face, protesting his unworthiness, yet admitting he had little choice but to follow the divine command. 'In like manner,' he said, 'was David, a humble shepherd, anointed by the prophet, at God's command, as King of Israel. God often acts in this way; and whoever resists the will of God calls down God's wrath upon himself. Now I am given power over all nations of the earth, and the right to use the sword to the confusion of the wicked and in defence of the righteous. So let none in this town stain himself with crime or resist the will of God, or else he shall without delay be put to death by the sword.' During this period Bernard Rothman produced two gloomy tracts, *Restitution* and *Announcement of Vengeance*. Hanging over the throbbing prose is the grim 'Sword of Justice' wielded by the spectre of a fanatical God who looks forward to the 'great killing' or cleansing.

For the elect few – the rest had to adopt a more ascetic mode – the New Jerusalem proved a garden of earthly delights. John Leyden was its strutting, handsome Messiah. Draped in the trappings of luxury – silken robes, rings, chains and spurs – he requisitioned stocks of money and food for himself and his inner circle. He told those who had been deprived that such things meant less than mud and stones to him – for he was dead to sensual comforts. However, if they maintained their loyalty, they too might be raised up. They too might sit on silver chairs and eat the choicest food. They too, like the saints and martyrs, might triumph over death and pain.

The summer of 1534 was an idyll of unimpeded sex and consumption. A throne was set up in the market-place draped with a cloth of gold; arranged below it were benches occupied by Leyden's councillors and subordinates. Heralded by a fanfare of trumpets, the king, surrounded by a core of bodyguards, would process on horseback around the town. Wearing a crown and carrying his sceptre, he announced new ordinances and innovations. Extravagantly the Anabaptists consumed some twelve hundred oxen and mountains of fish and cheese. Endless processions and banquets kept the population in high spirits. Money was abolished but medallions were struck with the head of John of Leyden encircled by the motto: The Word Made Flesh.

From the exultant swell of megalomania ebbs a dark undertow – a dread of one's mortality being trapped or exposed. This fear gnaws at the breast of a false messiah and finds its reflex in acts of draconian self-assertion. Doubts must be annulled through the agency of terror. A few days after Dusentschur had proclaimed Leyden a vessel or vassal of Almighty God, he declared that all sinners – all doubters, deviants and miscreants – must be punished by death. The first victims were women. One was beheaded for denying her husband his marital rights, a second for bigamy (for sexual initiatives of any sort were strictly a male prerogative), and a third for insulting a preacher.

Beyond the city wall, the Bishop's army gathered, intent on winning back the town. But John's supporters, who numbered some 1,700, managed to repel the attacks and maintain a high morale. But as autumn gave way to winter, other princes from the Upper and Lower Rhine joined the Bishop's army and food supplies started to run low in the city. Troops and equipment continued to pour in until Munster was sealed off by trenches and blockhouses and a double line of cavalry and infantry. During the summer of love the Anabaptists had overgorged themselves with meat and fish and now had to stave off hunger with dogs, cats, rats and dead horses.

Hundreds died from starvation; the spirits of those remaining sank fast, but still John of Leyden's oratory managed to rally them. He proclaimed that God was merely trying to test them and victory would soon be theirs. Success had swelled his self-image and led to paranoiac exaltations and subsequent glooms. When Bernard Knipperdollinck's mistress tried to leave the city, he killed her with his own hands.

Gradually starvation whittled the Anabaptists' bodies to skeletons. Those desperate to survive consumed grass, moss, old shoes, whitewash on walls, excrement. Many more died and their bodies accumulated in corners of the town. Spirits dropped so low that Leyden, desperately inventive as ever, promised them that God would turn the hard cobblestones to bread rather than let his children starve. When no such miracle was effected, they gazed at the hard unappetising slabs and wept.

John of Leyden tried to distract his people from these appalling conditions by staging theatrical shows, parodies of the Mass and a play based on Dives and Lazarus. There was even a day devoted to racing, dancing and athletics. As conditions worsened and unrest grew, he declared that those who wished could leave the city. Accordingly many parents left, taking their children outside the walls. There the army waited – but the Bishop refused them food or mercy. He put the able-bodied men to the sword, and refused to allow the women and children to move beyond the blockhouses. If they reached the lower ranks of soldiers he feared that they might enlist support or sympathy. For five weeks they pleaded, crawled about, grazed grass like animals until their dying bodies littered the ground.

Inside the walls, the stink of rotting flesh made Munster an unpleasant location. Rebellion started to ferment. Two of John of Leyden's followers slipped out beyond the walls and contacted the generals of the Bishop's army, advising them how they might enter the city unobserved. On Midsummer Eve, 24 June 1535, four hundred soldiers crept into Munster after dark. The next morning they were discovered; fierce fighting ensued and it looked as though the soldiers were about to be massacred. But then the Bishop's forces

Pan (right) playing his pipes in his classic furry-legged manifestation. This shows him in his elfin aspect, dispensing other-worldly music to those with the ability to hear. This not unfriendly image is replicated by Kenneth Grahame in *The Wind in the Willows*, where Pan appears as the Piper at the Gates of Dawn, a disturbing importation in such a quintessentially English setting. Rat and Mole are searching for a lost baby otter and one of them, raising his head, 'saw the backward sweep

of curved horns, gleaming in the growing daylight, saw the stern, hooked nose between the kindly eyes looking down on them humorously . . . saw the rippling muscles on the arm . . . the long supple hand still holding the pan-pipes only just fallen from the parted lips; saw the splendid curve of the shaggy limbs disposed in majestic ease on the sward; saw, last of all, nestling between his very hooves, sleeping soundly in entire peace and contentment, the little, round, podgy childish form of the baby otter. . . . Then the two animals, crouching to the earth, bowed their heads and did worship.'

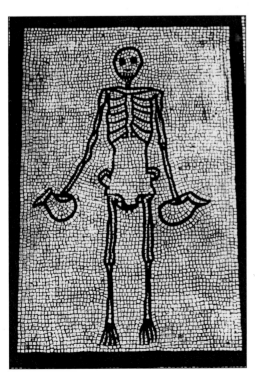

This Roman mosaic from a dining-room floor in Naples shows a utensil-bearing skeleton. It seems a disturbing image to live with and walk around, but the Romans had a hard, easygoing attitude to extinction, preferring brisk nameplate tombs, identifying the occupant but not indulging in elaborate panegyrics. The typical Roman epitaph is: 'I was what you are. You will be what I am.' With such a forthright attitude, one sees why the Romans had such a strongly developed sense of pleasure: wine, food and sex were there to be enjoyed. One should 'seize the day' for tomorrow might bring the skeleton knocking at the door.

Describing the religious customs of the Celtic tribes, Caesar provides a gruelling description of how they construct 'figures of vast size, formed of osiers, [which] they fill with living men; which, being set on fire, the men perish enveloped in the flames'. Strabo, reporting the same custom, added that the figures were filled with 'wood for fuel, cattle and several kinds of wild beast'. The image of the 'wicker man' or basket idol, crammed with sacrificial victims, has haunted men down the ages, featuring in the poems of Wordsworth and other visionaries. Such holocausts are not unusual – in fact they seem to attach themselves to the more fanatical religious sects who see their gods as relentless and punitive. Many secular messiahs, such as David Koresh, are prepared to

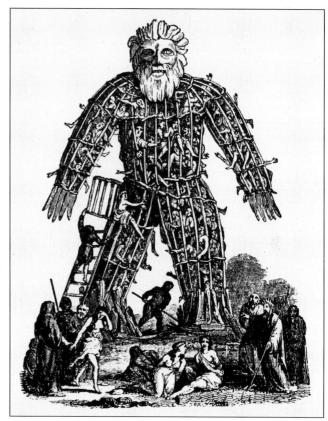

sacrifice, or demand the death of, their disciples. *The Wicker Man* (1973) was also the title of a cult film about extraordinary antics on an ordinary Scottish island, starring Christopher Lee, Edward Woodward and Britt Ekland. Traditionally fire and bale-burning rites were enacted at the Christmas solstice, Beltane and Midsummer Eve (the festival of St John), all turning-points of decay and cyclical renewal. Ash was used as a fertilising or renewing agent – out of its black nothingness sprang healthy crops.

Images of women in repose or dreaming have always attracted artists. Hundreds of years before Freud, sleep was recognised as a time when sealed-up desires and fantasies were liable to come out to sport and gambol. This nineteenth-century drawing shows an incubus floating above the body of a sleeping woman. He is horned, vaguely mischievous, long-tailed – yet there is something almost 'foetal' and undeveloped in his aspect – does this skinniness hint that she is starving her own desires? Probably not, but her leg is raised provocatively as if preparing for coitus.

In this 1850s sketch of the Parcelly Hay cairn, by the excavator Thomas Bateman, the skeleton is sitting upright, almost as if alive, the customary burial method in many early cultures. Layers of heavy stone seal him down for, unlike Christians, prehistoric peoples did not always see the resurrection of the body as a boon. It was dangerous to have contact with the dead, who had become transfigured through putrefaction and burial. If they arose from the tomb, like the ghost in the winding sheet (right), it was to haunt or seek revenge on those who did them ill in their previous lives. Modern interpretations of ghosts see them as manifestations of dread and anguish; the dead do not step out of tombs but out of the minds of individuals who harbour guilty secrets. Ghosts are exiled facets of the personality; they haunt because they are denied their natural habitat. Hence, you do not drive out a ghost but integrate it – an explanation that is only partly satisfactory, for there are manifestations which appear to relate to historical events and poltergeists which create disturbances whatever the disposition of the perceiver.

Not only is the Devil an eater of souls but also an excreter of souls, as it seems from the fresco of the Last Judgement (left) in the Campo Santa at Pisa. We see him in all his serpent-entwined, horrific glory, with horns, scales and claws. He is Satan the Devourer of Souls, quite unlike the decadent and dandified figure who was to surface during the diabolic revival of the 1890s. The image of the dragon-devil (below) depicts an almost identical conception. It is taken from a German woodcut of the Reformation, and presumably is supposed to terrify the doubter into belief, for surely no fate could be worse than being offered as a repast to this horrific consumer who knows nothing at all about not eating when his mouth is full.

(*Opposite*) Albrecht Dürer's depiction of the four witches is actually a copy of an engraving by Israel van Mechelen. The witches are getting ready to set off to their sabbath and presumably have smeared themselves with ritual ointment in preparation for flight. The drawing is impressive, having a robust, matter-of-fact quality, with a strong undercurrent of the erotic – note the sturdy healthiness of the breasts and buttocks, and the provocative skirt-raising posture of the young witch on the right. Earlier Leonardo had drawn a portrait of a witch who utilised a magic mirror, and one of the drawings by Hans Baldung (1514) depicts a witch riding through the air on a billy goat and carrying a forked pole which clasps a baneful brew. There are many other illustrations marking the juncture at which witchcraft becomes a branch of sexual pathology. Witches are shown consorting physically with the Devil, offering their bodies to him in a variety of postures and vomiting toads, bats and adders. (British Museum)

In the drawing (left) the werewolf does not seem perturbed by the spear piercing his hide – he is intent on ravaging and eating the young woman in his jaws. Such legends may be attributable to monsters like the Wild Beast of the Gevaudan (1764–5), who rampaged through the Languedoc region – and ate more than twenty people before it was killed and dissected. The surgeon thought it was more hyena than wolf. In the lower illustration we are shown how, in 1685, in the margraviate of Ansbach, a wolf that had attacked citizens was taken, after it had been killed, and hanged in human clothing, complete with mask and wig. The population read in the features of this wolf the face of an unpopular and hated burgomaster who had died shortly before its appearance.

The Cuillins of Skye have long been famous for the sublime, almost intimidating quality of their scenery. The same earth movement that pushed up the Alps created them and their basalt or 'gabbro' makes excellent rock-climbing material. The winding inlet of Loch Coruisk (top) narrows until steep mountains enclose the sombre lake. 'This the peerless loch,' one observer wrote, 'whose stillness and solitude poets have sung, as though no other spot on earth could show such leaden-hued waters, embosomed in such a wilderness of rugged rock mountains, whose black pinnacles seem to pierce the heavens, towering far above the masses of floating clouds which forever hang around their summits.' In the second engraving (below) the Cuillins are seen from a less claustrophobic vantage, but are still massive and forbidding in appearance. With the advent of colour photography, guidebooks show them as far more colourful, the dark peaks framed by blue skies, green shores and fleecy clouds. Nowadays, walkers flock to their misty altitudes to aerate their city-soiled souls.

The Day of Wrath by Albrecht Dürer shows earthquake, horror and lamentation. Kings and princes, great men and rich men, and the chief captains of the world huddle in their dens to hide from the wrath of the Lamb. Usually Dürer's illustrations carry a singular conviction but in this instance – to modern eyes at least – the marvels and disruptions are formally, almost symmetrically balanced. The problem of crowding all the horror and glory into a single composition has forced Dürer to parcel it up a little too thriftily. Intensely aware of theological controversy, his outlook was formally pietistic and he loathed Erasmus of Rotterdam and the Protestant cause: 'I have seen them return from a sermon as if inspired by an evil spirit.' The scene is from *Revelation*: 'And lo, there was a great earthquake; and the sun became black as sackcloth of hair, and the moon became as blood; and the stars of the heaven fell upon the earth . . .'. (British Museum)

assailed the walls, selecting the weak, unmanned points. The fighting lasted all day but the Anabaptists, feeble with starvation, proved no match for the army and on 25 June Munster fell to the invaders. John of Leyden, Bernard Knipperdollinck and another leader named Krechting were dragged before the Bishop and humiliated. The mistresses or 'queens' of John and Bernard were beheaded. The Bishop challenged John of Leyden to a debate – he found his opponent wily and well versed in the scriptures. When the Bishop said the Pope had conferred on him his authority, Leyden replied that his own authority came direct from God.

For the following six months, the three Anabaptists were dragged through the streets and public places of the neighbouring towns. In January 1536 Leyden was chained to a stake and his flesh was torn out with red-hot pincers. He did not let out a cry while this was happening. When the pain became too great, he finally begged for mercy; the Bishop smiled and ordered Leyden's tongue to be pulled out. Then his heart was stabbed with a red-hot dagger.

Knipperdollinck had tried to beat his brains out by striking his head against a wall, but the executioner took him away with Krechting and tortured them both to death, while the Bishop watched from the window opposite. Their torn and burnt bodies were hung from the tower of St Lambert's Church, where Bernard Rothman had originally declared the coming of the millennium.

3

ELIZABETHANS: DISORDER IN THE KINGDOM

ALL THE QUEEN'S ENEMIES

Fain would I climb, yet I fear to fall.
(Line written on a window pane by Sir Walter Raleigh, 1552–1618)

During Lent in 1597, when Elizabeth I was sixty-three, the Bishop of Rudd preached before her at Richmond, taking his text from the 90th Psalm: 'So teach us to number our days, that we may apply our hearts unto wisdom.' The sermon skated over the mystic significance of numbers: three standing for the Trinity and seven for the Sabbath, while seven times nine was the 'Great Climacterical Year'. The last reference angered the Queen, for she took it to refer to her age. The Bishop hastily shifted his pitch to the Beast 666 (none other than the Pope!) and the year 88 when the Queen's enemies had predicted she would be overthrown, but which turned out to be the year of her victory over the Armada. But Elizabeth, far from mollified, told him that he'd best keep his arithmetic to himself and that the best of clerks do not make the wisest of men.

The aptness of her reply was typical. Elizabeth showed guile and diplomacy throughout her reign. She could be equally quick to forgive or to dispatch her enemies, the most formidable being Mary Queen of Scots. On 8 February 1587 Mary met her death in the great hall of Fotheringay Castle where a wooden stage had been erected in the centre. Three hundred spectators were gathered, along with the Earls of Shrewsbury and Kent. The evening before, Mary had completed her correspondence and handed over her will. She had distributed purses to her servants, thanking them for their loyalty and bidding them farewell.

At about 9.30 a.m. the tall figure emerged, stately and composed, and was escorted to the platform. She was dressed in black save for her veil and peaked head-dress. She refused the administration of the Dean of Peterborough: 'Mr Dean, I am settled in the ancient Catholic Roman religion', she told him, 'and mind to spend my blood in defence of it.' After prayers, as was the convention, she forgave her executioner and then was helped to undress down to her red petticoat and satin bodice with a neckline cut low down the back. Laying her head on the block, she started praying, and the axe descended. The first blow missed the neck; a second was required to complete the severance. The executioner snatched it up, holding it aloft and crying 'God save the Queen!'

The head fell from his grasp, leaving him clutching an auburn wig. Mary's true hair, now revealed, was grey and short-cropped. And then, from under her petticoat, snuffled out her little Skye terrier, faithful to the end.

'So perish all the Queen's enemies,' commented the Dean but others were too moved to speak.

Mary had been found guilty of plotting with French Catholics against the Queen of England. Lord Walsingham, who had engaged a Catholic exile, Robert Gifford, to incriminate her, had largely contrived the conspiracy, but after arriving in England as a fugitive, Mary had tactlessly allied herself with those who wished to usurp the throne of her cousin and fellow-queen. After Gifford had been found carrying a letter of introduction to Mary, he was persuaded by Walsingham to collude in a plot. First he told the French embassy that he had a foolproof way of conveying information to the royal prisoner. He was believed; the messages were passed between Tutbury Castle, where Mary was imprisoned, and the embassy, culminating in a letter outlining a plan for the assassination of Elizabeth. Although more interested in her own release than in her cousin's downfall, Mary wrote back, endorsing the scheme, and saying that she would prefer Elizabeth's assassination to precede her rescue. Under the 1585 Act covering the Queen's safety, Parliament was provided with the necessary evidence to execute Mary. Her death stemmed from the fear that, were she allowed to live, she might well end up in power and able to pass sentence on those who had plotted against her. In other words, like Macbeth, one gradually extends one's radius of killing in order to preserve one's skin.

The Prince

In the age of Elizabeth, and in subsequent centuries, a general lessening of supersition and the secularisation of ancient dreads and anxieties allowed people to fear what was going on around them more than spirits or irksome elementals. What was embodied in the flesh was seen as more dangerous than the Devil, Hell or Damnation, and one principal royal fear revolved around conspiracy or insurrection. Of early Tudor England a Venetian visitor noted that 'three Princes of the blood, four Dukes, forty Earls, and more than three hundred other persons, have died by violent death'.

In such an atmosphere it was necessary to protect oneself by identifying and removing enemies. Conspiracies are networks of deceit by which one power is removed and another substituted. If one enters the thick of a conspiracy and emerges successful, one acquires a certain low cunning – a familiarity with lies and labyrinths. But one also inherits the disconcerting insight that the processes that worked upon the enemy may one day be turned against oneself. This breeds a fear of the world, a karmic dread of natural justice waiting to spring.

Some Elizabethan plays and texts, including *The Jew of Malta*, contain defamatory references to a guileful Italian who examined the workings of power politics under despotic or autocratic regimes with skill and authority. Born in Florence in 1469, Niccolo Machiavelli entered the Florentine Chancery in 1498, serving as secretary to the republic under Piero Soderini until 1512. His masterpiece *The Prince* created a shudder of revulsion by mapping out plainly the methods by which an autocratic regime might sustain its health and vigour. Rendered in prose of reptilian delicacy, the advice has an uplifting astringence, the cynicism sterilised by the clarity of its articulation. Even on matters of common gratitude, Machiavelli is wary, advising the prince that, should anyone befriend and assist him into a position of pre-eminence, on attaining that authority it would be wise to 'remove' the former helper, for otherwise he will almost certainly use his knowledge to extract favours and manipulate his own self-advancement.

The Prince was criticised for its lack of idealism and sharp separation of political and moral concerns. Machiavelli did not address the question of how a prince should behave in order to secure a tenure in Paradise. Instead he observed the methods by which the most effective leaders of past ages stayed in power – how they justified the means by the ends. Christian morality was irrelevant to the business of maintaining a solid, stable state. When first published, *The Prince* was branded the work of the Devil and confirmed Italy's reputation as a citadel of high corruption. This was hardly fair; the prince's policies had been practised by monarchs and emperors down the centuries. But although they might have acted in such a manner, they had at least gilded their ruthlessness with a veneer of high intentions. Machiavelli did not hide behind euphemisms – instead he exposed *realpolitik* with magisterial composure. The strategies his exemplar is forced to consider demonstrate that individual lives count little; preserving authority is paramount.

He tackles such issues as 'Cruelty and Mercy', and 'Whether It Is Better to Be Loved or Feared or the Contrary' and concludes that the prince should not put 'the reproach of cruelty' before such overwhelming issues as political unity. If he were cruel to a few, the impact will have greater effect than the summary dispersal of mercy. Too much mercy is liable to encourage disorder and revolt, 'from which arise murder and plundering', and so, in the long run, cruelty is justified; the stricter control it brings about saves lives. As for the question of the prince's personal standing among his people, it is better he be feared than loved, for men, generally speaking, 'are ungrateful, fickle, simulators and deceivers, avoiders of danger, greedy for gain; and while you work for their good they are completely yours, offering you their blood, their property, their lives, and their sons . . . when danger is far away; but when it comes nearer to you, they turn away.'

So, in Machiavelli's view, men are base, capricious and perpetually biddable and fear is the social cement that keeps them that way. Whether manuals of statesmanship such as *The Prince* serve as useful correctives or whether they enforce malpractice is a moot point. Probably both: effective communication has the potential of both stimulus and deterrent.

The Paris Garden

Despite their verbal sophistication and political guile, the Elizabethans did not show an equivalent subtlety when it came to street entertainments. Using beasts that inspired fear and superstition during the Middle Ages, they staged confrontations in which they were abased and humiliated. In London both aristocrat and commoner would flock to watch the pleasures offered in the Paris Garden, not far from Shakespeare's Globe Theatre, where Hunks and Sackerson, the most famous bears of the period, were kept penned by their warders and brought out for regular baiting. 'Here come few,' wrote Donald Lupton (1632), 'that neither regard their credit or loss of time: the swaggering roarer, the cunning cheater, the rotten bawd, the swearing drunkard and the bloody butcher have their rendezvous here and of chief place and respect. There are as many civil religious men here as there are saints in hell.'

A fanfare of trumpets would announce the start of the entertainment. The first item might be an old brown bear straining at a stake. His teeth have been broken off, so that he cannot bite deep, but his claws and feet are able to crush and claw. About three mastiffs are loosed; they leap at the bear's throat, sinking in their fangs and wrenching at his hide, but the bear clouts them down, sometimes actually breaking their skulls 'like rotten apples' but more often wounding them. This happens repeatedly – an appalling drone fills the arena – until the dogs are scarred and bleeding and the bear broken-spirited.

The second 'show' would be heralded by the entry of an old blind bear who staggers round the arena pursued by a team of small boys who slash it with canes. Besieged and helpless, the animal lunges and lashes out. Eventually one small boy gets incautious and comes too close. The bear's claws hook into his head; he bleeds profusely and falls at the animal's feet. Now a warder advances with a huge stick and holds the bear at bay, while the crying boy attempts to run for safety and the others continue to torment the animal. The audience reacts with increasing tension, some sympathising with the boy, others saying he had it coming, but all pleased, the glimpse of blood having heightened the tension.

The third part opens on a big white bull who is bound to the stake. Four mastiffs are released and charge at it. The bulls uses its horns as defence, goring and lunging, sometimes impaling the dogs, other times tossing them back into the arena, where their fall might be broken by watchful attendants standing by with cradles made of pliant canes. Although death heightened the spectacle, the owners of the Garden preferred a token mortality rather than a massacre, as the latter might entail costly replacements.

The last display is something worthy of a Roman emperor or an English queen. An ape, placed astride a stallion, is let loose into the arena pursued by barking dogs. The ape gibbers and shrieks as the dogs fly at the horse's heels, getting smashed by hooves and suffering dreadful wounds. Eventually the ape falls off the horse and the dogs tear him to pieces, drawing out a steaming mess of entrails for the delectation of the hysterically applauding audience. This cleared up, the people repair to a tavern to refresh themselves.

Being akin to 'mirrors' or intermediaries, animals are a means by which people measure their humanity. Snatching them from their forest and mountain habitats and torturing or antagonising them was 'natural' to the Elizabethans who, in a sense, were avenging themselves on a natural world that had once posed a threat. 'As flies to wanton boys are we to the gods; they kill us for their sport,' goes the line in *King Lear*. Truly this is the philosophy of the Paris Garden, where men have relapsed into wanton boys and fear has been anaesthetised into spectacle. Ironically, a number of those who watched such sights wrote enamelled verses about the perfection of the world and how each bird and flower had a definite place in the jewel-like intricacy of creation. These poems were often exquisitely chased and finished – perfect, brittle, hard, like the best of Hillyard's miniatures.

Besides, bears and dogs were not the only recipients of such treatment. On their way to the Paris Garden, the audience might see a gibbeted corpse at Tyburn or a body floating in the Thames being pecked and dissembled by hungry gulls. Human life, so ennobled by sonnet and song, was held cheap and replaceable. No doubt, if Sade had been an Elizabethan and written a tract extolling the sensual gratification derived from such sights, he would have been beheaded or dismembered for propagating blasphemous, obscene fancies.

But Elizabethan England was positively Sadean in its imaginings. Shakespeare's prentice work *Titus Andronicus* was summed up as 'like some broken-down cart, laden with bleeding corpses from a scaffold, and driven by an executioner from Bedlam dressed in cap and bells'. Similarly, Stephen Gosson criticised Elizabethan drama in 1579 as being obsessed with 'wrath, cruelty, incest, injury, murder, either violent by sword or voluntary by poison'. The technique was to render injury and outrage as pasteboard and gesture: an attempt to regulate terror by containing it within a wooden frame and drawing it from the audience into the actor.

Terror of Consequences

If Machiavelli had identified a method by which political terror could be made effective, there was another type of dread or foreboding examined at length by Shakespeare, part-political, part-moral, almost a fusion of the two: a kind of guilty terror that arises in the gap between Machiavellian opportunism and Christian morality. D.H. Lawrence remarked how the English 'are paralysed by fear, obsessed. That is what thwarts and distorts the Anglo-Saxon existence . . . Nothing could be more lovely and fearless than Chaucer. But already Shakespeare is morbid with fear, fear of consequences. That is the strange phenomenon of the English Renaissance: the mystic terror of the consequences, the consequences of action.' Lawrence is presumably referring to plays like *Hamlet* wherein the hero's balancing act between reflection and action, delusion and reality, are more gripping than the sword-fights. Hamlet's frowning deliberations make a drama of the mind. But it is *Macbeth* that is Shakespeare's great drama of fear. Macbeth is a formidable warrior; he values honour and courage above all other qualities. After he has fought bravely against the Norwegians, the elderly King Duncan rewards him by making him Thane of Cawdor. Macbeth's prosperity seems assured. Unity and joy irradiate the kingdom of Scotland which is likened to a family of bright stars. Macbeth and his wife are shown glowing in the armour of their new prestige and standing. However, such brightness searches out the corners of the soul until it locates a vein of black ore:

> Stars, hide your fires;
> Let me not see my black and deep desires;
> The eye winks at the hand; yet let that be,
> Which the eye fears, when it is done, to see.

Despite these intimations, Macbeth hesitates to kill Duncan who has treated him like a son. But Lady Macbeth upbraids him, saying he is a weakling who wants power but is too timid and scrupulous to grasp it. The fearless warrior is 'frightened' of committing a truly terrible crime. Repeatedly taunted, he gives way, murders Duncan and the grooms, and later Banquo, who appears before him as a ghost. Eventually, in the mechanical repetition of bloody deeds, he loses all sense of fear. He moves into a zone beyond ordinary definition, a no-man's-land of the soul.

In the opening scenes, Macbeth is shown basking in hospitality, kinship, wine and feasting; in committing murder, he substitutes the warm assurances of community for a nightmare realm of air-drawn daggers, blood-stained ghosts, witless sleepwalking, sombre apparitions and cackling midnight hags. He has offended nature and the play is characterised by its emphasis on unnaturalness. The witches are nature's abortions who feast upon foul, inedible things. The 'horrible shadow' of Banquo's ghost arises and attends the banquet, denying Macbeth the joy of celebration. There is no sleep – 'Macbeth hath murdered sleep' – nor joy, nor warmth. Even the courage he retains is meaningless, for he has effaced the moral values that gave it definition. In a sense, he dies by the hand of ghost, Macduff, who from his mother's womb was 'untimely ripped'.

Macbeth dislodged the natural order by murdering the king who had divine right, and from that point he inhabits a terrible parenthesis, a hell in which moral values give way to demonic opportunism and baseless ambition. Similarly King Lear, by quixotically apportioning his kingdom to his daughters, donated what was never his to give. In surrendering his throne and lands, not only was he rebuking destiny, but creating political disarray and upsetting the balance of the cosmological system.

The Bonny Halls of Bedlam

While it is Macbeth who sees the ghost of the murdered Banquo, it is Lady Macbeth, the instigator of the original murder, who succumbs to insanity as the compassion she thought she had expunged returns and ravages her conscience. The descent into madness was a great theme of Elizabethan drama: the king or prince who cannot cope seeks refuge by abandoning control. Hamlet's mind steadily warps and cracks under the pressure of indecision; in utter despair, Lear lets the lord of chaos take him over. Neither dares succumb to the primitive 'panic' which might have served as a kind of orgiastic relief. Being men of high position, they are bound to maintain self-possession and authority. Their escape is to embrace, fully and permanently, insanity.

Elizabethan ideas about madness tended to be muddled because those afflicted rarely showed consistent symptoms. The theory of humours, with its astrological components, was invoked. One of Europe's leading doctors, Denys Fontanon (1549), attributed the mania to 'stinging and warm humours, such as yellow bile, attacking the brain and stimulating it along with its membranes. It sometimes even originates in incorrupt blood which may even be temperate but which harms the brain by its quantity alone.'

Excess of blood stimulated an excess of sexuality. According to Felix Plater (1650), a younger contemporary of Fontanon, those afflicted 'express their mental impulse in a wild expression and in word and deed . . . Some of them intensely seek sexual satisfaction. I saw this happen to a certain noble matron, who was in every other way most honourable, but who invited by the basest words and gestures men and dogs to have intercourse with her.'

In London the sanctuary for the mad was the asylum or 'bedlam', a name derived from the priory of St Mary of Bethlehem, founded in 1247 by Simon FitzMary, Sheriff of London. It started to receive lunatics in 1377 and Henry VIII donated it and all its revenues to the City of London as a hospital for the insane. By 1675, transferred to Moorfields, it had become one of the tourist sights of London; for twopence anyone might stare at the lunatics and bait them. It was also a pick-up spot, a place of assignations, double-dealing and low life. 'All that I can say of Bedlam,' wrote Ned Ward in *The London Spy* (1698), 'is this; 'tis an almshouse for madmen, a showing room for harlots, a sure-market for lechers, a dry walk for loiterers.' In *The Ballad of Tom O'Bedlam*, the madman is romanticised as one who chases dreams, fancies, lost loves. Essentially gentle-natured, he does not balk at dirt or roguery but rides out and basks in the horror and glory of existence:

> From the hag and hungry goblin
> That into rags would rend ye,
> The spirit that stands by the naked man
> In the Book of Moons defend ye,
> That of your five sound senses
> You never be forsaken
> Nor wander with yourselves, with Tom.
> Abroad to be your bacon.

In his moonstruck world of phantoms and imaginings, Tom is lord of his own destiny:

> With an host of furious fancies
> Whereof I am commander,
> With a burning spear and a horse of air
> To the wilderness I wander.
> By a knight of ghosts and shadows,
> I summoned am to tourney,
> Ten leagues beyond the world's wide end –
> Methinks it is no journey.

Tom's madness allows him to range over vast areas of sensation – there are no bounds to his fancies. He is a knight, a beggar, an outcast, a visionary, while being, paradoxically, impotent. For despite the splendour of Tom's full-sailed rhetoric, Bedlam framed the madman as a zoological type. He epitomised 'man as wild beast', who had forfeited his allegiance with human kind, an object of mockery and derision. If possessed of adequate ferocity, he might well have provided entertainment for the habitués of the Paris Garden.

Madness was feared because of its implicit disorder. Lunatics were hot-brained and full-blooded and under physical provocation were liable to strip naked, cry like children, spout vehement nonsense or unleash their desires on whatever creature or object appeared available. Hinting at the possibility of unbounded chaos, their behaviour undermined the world view that granted each facet of creation a pre-ordained function. It subverted the orderly theology to which men like Thomas Starkey, chaplain to Henry VIII, subscribed. The body of the realm needed to be kept healthy, Starkey argued, with the King and Parliament operating the brain, their under-officers the eyes and ears, the craftsmen and warriors the arms, and the ploughmen and tillers of the ground the feet. These well-chosen analogies acted as sealants of the status quo – but random, unpredictable madness brought this cool Platonic pyramid tumbling down.

Blazing Starres and Secret Plotters

Even John Donne (1572–1631), whose sermons solemnly brood on the perishability of all living matter, bowed to this attitude. He acclaimed the predictable and constant, against which timely precautions could be taken, but warned against that which appeared without signal or warning. 'No Almanack', he pointed out, 'tells us when a blazing starre will break out, the matter is carried up in secret, no Astrologer tells us when the effects will be accomplished . . . and that which is most secret, is most dangerous.' The poet twists his analogy to accommodate enemies of the government and sundry plotters whose behaviour is as morally poisonous as any bodily contagion: 'Twentie rebellious drums make not so dangerous a noise, as a few whisperers and secret plotters in corners. The Canon doth not so much hurt against a wall, as a Mine under the wall; nor a thousand enemies that threaten, so much as a few who take an oath to say nothing.'

Unpredictable phenomena tended to be viewed as evil, for it bred confusion and subterfuge and defied the shapely concentricity accredited to the spiritual universe by hermeticists. In theory, the entire elaborate system was governed by Providence, for God's will percolated and echoed through the tiniest action. If someone committed a dastardly murder, Providence caught and punished him. If someone was rewarded with gold or riches, this was Providence conferring bounty on the deserving. However, Providence is a large, solemn word that may well apply to planetary conjunctions or the punishment of brutal tyrants – but what of the smaller things? For instance, a droplet falling off the tip of an old man's nose at a certain time and place – is Providence responsible? Is Providence directing each sneeze, each belch, each bowel evacuation?

The lapsed monk and hermeticist Giordano Bruno, who died at the hands of the Inquisition in 1600, was mockingly aware of the implications of such a philosophy. If each phenomenon was part of a master-plan, then millions of seemingly flimsy, self-negating gestures had to be quantified and taken seriously. In a satire written during his English exile and called *La spaccio de la bestia trionfante* ('The expulsion of the triumphant beast'), he applied *reductio absurdum* to the idea of divine purpose. It features an account of how Jove minutely orchestrates each single event in the causal chain, from providing for a melon patch to making a precise itinerary of the cuckoo's song and flight. Furthermore, it is ordained that 'twelve bedbugs should crawl out of the board of Constantino's bed and make for the pillow: seven of these being quite large, four quite small, and one of medium size – and what will become of them this evening at candlelight we will provide; and that Ambruoggio will interrupt his transactions with his wife after the hundred-and-twelfth thrust, and that he will not impregnate her on this occasion, but at some other time with the semen produced by the leek stew which he is now eating with millet bread . . .'.

Marlowe the Overreacher

Although the Elizabethans retained an essentially Aristotelian view, they had already begun to dissect and explore processes that would overturn the traditional notions of a perfect divine order and ever-descending hierarchies of angels and demons. They had learned things about the cosmos and the human body that would shake such preconceptions. In 1543, a few weeks after his death, the heliocentric theory of Nicholas Copernicus was published. It stated that the earth moved round the sun, and that any appearance to the contrary was caused by the earth's rotation on its own axis.

That same year the groundwork of modern anatomy was laid with the appearance of *De Humani Corporis Fabrica* ('Of the Fabric of the Human Body') by Andreas Vesalius, a Flemish professor of anatomy at the University of Padua. The detailed drawings showed a man's musculature with a frankness that some thought impious. They invoked a cool methodology of inspection, liberating to the scientifically minded, unnerving to the tenaciously devout. Even if the body was God's sacred handiwork, it had a structure conforming to mechanical principles which might be understood and duplicated by means of pulleys, levers and wires. Copernicus had displaced the Earth from the centre of the cosmos to the periphery. Knowledge – the spirit of exploration – was opening up the world like one of Vesalius's cadavers. What would come next? Would a cartographer produce a star-chart of heaven or an artist capture the likeness of Almighty God? Fear and fascination lay at the heart of such enquiries – of finding out if there was a limit to man's powers.

Spurred on by a curiosity tinged by self-aggrandisement, certain Elizabethans could be seen as overreachers. One such was the playwright Christopher ('Kit') Marlowe, who was a member of an atheistical college called 'The School of Night'. At one point in his life – after his sojourn at Cambridge – he considered going into the ministry. He was interested in theology but from a revisionist point of view. In London, he tended to spend time drinking, gambling and writing. He had pederastic leanings and openly said that they were fools who did not like boys and tobacco. His religious views had a subversive piquancy that many found startling. He dismissed Moses as a mere juggler and Christ as a bastard and sodomite who enjoyed an affair with his beloved disciple John. Furthermore the Virgin Mary was 'dishonest', the miracles were 'naught' and religion was devised only 'to keep men in awe'. His firebrand opinions might have resulted in his arrest had he not been fatally stabbed by Ingram Frizer – an agent of Thomas Walsingham – after a quarrel in Eleanor Bull's tavern.

Marlowe's sombrely effective play *The Tragical History of Dr Faustus* (1604) shows how overreaching knowledge can both empower and destroy. It is the work of someone who resents the presence of a powerful controlling God yet is thrilled by the idea of rebellion and subsequent damnation and hellfire. In a sense Marlowe needs God like a child with a catapult needs a target. His hero is a magician – here an important distinction should be borne in mind. Whereas a priest prays to a spiritual being, a magician seeks to command it. One is passive; the other active. The latter was more in keeping with the Renaissance hero, who saw himself as bold, learned and fearless.

Faustus is a Promethean figure, a man who exceeds the boundaries of learning, spurred on by a dream of limitless power. Arrogant and unrelenting, he barters his soul to the Devil in order that he may enjoy years of pleasure and authority. Mephistopheles, the servant-devil whom Faustus conjures, turns out to be a likeable and fair-minded consort of Satan, possessed of a self-torturing intelligence and air of jaded honesty. At one point he explains that Hell is no more than 'separation from God' and has no geographical location:

> Hell hath no limits, nor is circumscrib'd
> In one self place, but where we are is hell,
> And where hell is, there must we ever be;
> And, to be short, when all the world dissolves
> And every creature shall be purify'd,
> All places shall be hell that is not heaven.

After a splendidly sombre passage of blank verse, Faustus is carried off to Hell and punished for his overweening pride, like Lucifer his master. Despite allegations of atheism, the play has a sound moral: Faustus sins; he is punished and dispatched before his time – 'Cut is the branch that might have grown full straight.'

Contacting the Diabolic Fraternity

Sceptical Elizabethans, including Shakespeare, had observed that drownings, hangings and violent fates were the lot of blasphemers and Christians alike and the Bible admitted diverse interpretations. Whatever devils one cocked a snook at or cultivated by way of pentagram and invocation, one's fate could scarcely be worse than that of the dissenter who met the Queen's justice at Tyburn or elsewhere.

As Christopher Marlowe demonstrated, Elizabeth's reign retained much of the occult lore of the Middle Ages. The pagan notion of the air being filled with discarnate spirits was still held by many. Thomas Nashe (1567–c. 1600) maintained that the atmosphere comprised a fog of elementals, imps and demons, whose malign influence might be inhaled by ordinary men and women in the same way one might take in a blast of droplets sneezed by a victim of the plague. 'Infinite millions of them will hang swarming,' he states in *Discourse of Apparitions*, 'about a worm-eaten nose. Don Lucifer, their grand Capitano, asketh no better throne than a blear eye to set up his state in. Upon a hair they will sit like a nit and overdredge a bald pate like a white scurf. The wrinkles in old witches visages they eat out to entrench themselves in.'

Such 'presences' were Satan's microcosmic manifestations that witches utilised in order to effect changes in the weather, in the affections and health of men and women, in the running of farms and households. Robert Burton (1577–1640) included a chapter in *Anatomy* wherein he listed each demon and its speciality like a register of unruly pupils at a minor public school. Similarly, when St Thomas Aquinas (c. 1225–74) discussed the attributes and standing of various angels and devils, he introduced hierarchies of spiritual specialisation; in other words, he was creating order. Now once order has been created, fear has been diminished and the second stage – designing a procedure by which such beings are contacted – comes into being. And thus it is no surprise that Elizabethan magicians felt able to contact these lesser manifestations of Christ and the Devil. The door had been left ajar by so much theologising.

Practical magic, like capitalism, allowed for a variety of transactions. Purchase the right equipment, select the appropriate deity or demon, make sure the correspondences are in sympathy, perform the spell and wait for the money, love, sex, brand-new chariot or spacious mansion to come rolling in. If you want love, perform a ritual to Venus; if luck in battle, Mars; if success in trading, Mercury; if a safe sea voyage, Neptune; if a fertile orchard, Priapus. It was this bustling free-market aspect of magic that caused offence. If there is one God, then all other deities are blasphemies and falsehoods. No order and spiritual authority can exist in a world where minds are led astray by a prodigality of dubious spiritual beings, all at war with one another. You may achieve mastery like the Romans by ruling with brute force while allowing every conceivable sect to flourish under your nose, but in order to serve Christ, you must convert people from diverse deities to the One True God.

Such convictions did not deter knowledge-seekers from exploring the shadowy by-ways of belief. Despite the courageous scepticism of writers like Reginald Scot (1584), who dubbed superstition as 'godless religion, devout impiety' and attributed ghosts to melancholy and poor-sightedness, a renewed interest in alchemy and magic had resulted in the issuing of many grimoires or 'black books' for those who wished to include the diabolic fraternity in their circle of acquaintances. In addressing demons, craven verbs such as 'beg' were used to create a subordinate effect. *Le véritable dragon rouge* (1521) has a selection of rites and spells in which the basics of conjuration are spelt out: 'If you wish to make contact with hell, you must first decide whom you want to call.'

Having selected your demon, procure a bloodstone and two 'blessed' wax candles; two days before the conjuration, cut a slender bough from a wild hazel tree with a new knife. For the rite, select a lonely, neglected place – an old ruined castle or deserted mansion – for spirits feed off the reek of mustiness or decay. In the chosen location draw a triangle with the bloodstone, setting candles at the sides, writing the holy letters IHS at the bottom of the triangle flanked by two crosses. Then, grasping the hazel wand, summon the spirit with firmness: 'Emperor Lucifer, master of the rebellious spirits, I beg you to be favourable to me, when I call for your minister, the great Lucifuge Rofocale, as I desire to sign a contract with him. I beg also that Prince Beelzebub may protect my enterprise. O Astaroth, great count be favourable likewise, and make it possible for the great Lucifuge to appear before me in human form, without bad odour, and that he grant me, by the agreement by which I am ready to sign with him, all the riches that I need. . . .'

All this decorum and formality was superficial, for if the demon failed to respond promptly, the magician threatened to 'torment' him by the powerful words of the key: 'Aglon Tetagram Vaycheon Stimulamathon Erohares Retragsammathon Clyoran Icion Esition Existien Eryona Onera Erasyn Moyn Meffias Soter Emmanuel Sabaoth Adomai, I call you, Amen.' One can imagine that hearing out such a cacophony required fortitude.

By establishing his mastery and forging a pact, the magician is able to step out of his magic circle and follow the evil spirit to where the riches are buried, after which he will dismiss the elemental: 'O great Lucifuge, I am satisfied with you, for now I will leave you, go in peace, and I permit you to retire wherever you desire, but without noise or stench.' The business-like quality of these transactions does not lack an element of bathos. After the sycophantic serenade comes the brisk command 'Take me to the cash' – hinting that magicians saw the spiritual underworld in much the same way as criminals saw their underworld: a short cut to a quick profit.

Talking with Angels

The most renowned practical magician of Elizabethan England was the Welsh-born mathematician, geographer, navigator, alchemist and court astrologer, Dr John Dee (1527–1608) who selected 14 January 1559 as the most auspicious date for the Queen's coronation. Once his reputation emanated a frisson of necromancy, but today he is mentioned in the same breath as Paracelsus and

Bruno, for he tried to devise a methodology for contacting spirits. After leaving the Chantry School at Chelmsford, at the age of fifteen he went to St John's College, Cambridge, where he studied intensely, allowing himself only four hours' sleep a night, and by nineteen he was made an under-reader in Greek and fellow of the newest college,Trinity. His academic skills took him abroad to the great European universities where he picked up any information he could pertaining to magic and the occult. In 1552 he met Jerome Cardan, the physician and astrologer of Padua, who was staying at the house of Sir John Cheke. It was through Cardan that Dee became interested in spirits as a means of acquiring knowledge and riches.

His scientific accomplishments and mystical scholarship brought him into the court of Queen Elizabeth whose accession he had predicted. Aside from issuing prophecies and astrological tracts, Dee went on spying errands on behalf of the Queen and her councillors. This took him abroad, to many important centres of learning, but skulduggery was not altogether in keeping with his studious nature. Back in England he made a bid to establish a more settled way of life when he married a young woman whose name has not been recorded. It turned out to be a short-lived union: a year later, in March 1575, his wife died. On the very same day Queen Elizabeth called to see his 'magic mirror', but superstitiously refused to enter on hearing of the recent death. Two years later, Dee married Jane Fremond, lady in waiting to Lady Howard of Effingham, then moved into his mother's house at Mortlake. Children followed from this union – some eight in all. At Mortlake, Dee cast horoscopes, drew maps for the Queen and made geographical and military calculations. Furthermore he was becoming increasingly immersed in occult matters – keeping a spiritual diary in which dreams, visions and insights were set down.

In 1582, convinced that knowledge awaited those who mastered the art of scrying, he enlisted a youth called Barnabas Saul as his seer, but the young man got embroiled with the law and denounced Dee. Two days after Saul's dismissal or withdrawal, Dee answered a knock on his door and admitted a tall, swarthy, handsome young man called Edward Kelley, twenty-eight years his junior, whom he employed as his scryer or interpreter of the 'shewstone' or magic crystal. Kelley's reputation was tainted. He had been held in various prisons and penitentiaries and his ears had been cropped for forging – a defect he concealed beneath a skullcap. Moody, irascible and unstable, even the spirits criticised Kelley by telling Dee he was 'a youngling but old sinner' – yet he did possess second sight. Within a short time, Dee was enthused by Kelley's scrying skills and asked him to stay at his house and become his assistant.

When the young man agreed, a procedure was developed wherein Kelley would gaze into the doctor's shewstone or magic crystal (an angel was said to have brought it to Dee through a window) and describe the activities and appearances of the spirits. Through Kelley's mediumship, much esoteric knowledge was acquired, including how to make a protective talisman and how to translate 'Enochian' – the 'language of the angels' – that enables access to the various domains or 'Watchtowers' of the spirit world.

In 1583 Dee and Kelley were introduced to the wealthy Count Laski, for whom they guilefully produced a series of fantastic, flattering prophecies. Securing the patronage of this Polish nobleman, an active servant of Henry III of France, they were able to take their skills further afield. Travelling though Europe, they arrived at Cracow in 1587, where they persisted in their search for the philosopher's stone. At a séance in the city, the angels urged Dee and Kelley to perform a wife-swapping exercise, which they did despite Jane Kelley's disinclination. The partnership came to an end shortly after this and Kelley left Dee. Kelley died in November 1595, while trying to escape from one of Emperor Rudolph's Bohemian citadels in which he had been imprisoned on a charge of sorcery. Dee mourned the passing of his friend and spiritual helpmate – 'one who might have wrought so many wonders had he a mind to discipline his exceeding impatient desires'.

The spirit conversations of Dee and Kelley make strenuous reading. They are dense with alchemical recipes and mysto-babble. Sometimes the language is puffed out with metaphoric ballast; other times a light and trivial exchange is pleasingly set down. There are dubious prophecies, such as when the Archangel Uriel presents Kelley with a vision of many ships on a sea and of a woman being beheaded by a black man. This was seen as a vision of the Spanish Armada and the death of Mary Queen of Scots whose hooded executioner would appear as a black man. Visions of this sort characterised a troubled period, with Leicester and Walsingham standing for the 'war party' at court, and Elizabeth trying – unsuccessfully – to circumnavigate potential strife with Holland and Spain. In the air was a tingle of millennial trepidation: a Puritan complained that 'Satan is roaring like a lion, the world is going mad, Anti-Christ is resorting to every extreme that he may with wolf-like ferocity devour the sheep of Christ.'

Another time, out of Dee's 'Oratory' came a spiritual creature, like a pretty girl, seven or nine years of age, with her hair rolled up before and hanging down behind very long, attired in a gown of 'changeable' green and red with a train. She seemed to dodge in and out of the heaps of Dee's books that appeared to move and give place to her. The following exchange took place:

Dee: Whose maiden are you?

Girl: Whose man are you?

Dee: I am the servant of God both by my bound duty, and also (I hope) by his adoption.

A Voice: You shall be beaten if you tell.

Girl: Am not I a fine maiden? Give me leave to play in your house. My Mother told me she would come and dwell there.

(*Dee comments*: She went up and down with most lively gestures of a young girl, playing by herself, and diverse times another spake to her from the corner of my study by a great perspective-glass – but none was seen beside herself.)

Girl (addressing another [spirit?] in the corner of the study): Shall I? I will.

Dee: Tell me who you are.

Girl: I pray you let me play with you a little, and I will tell you who I am.

Dee: In the name of Jesus then tell me.

Girl: I rejoice in the name of Jesus, and I am a poor little maiden, Madimi. I am the last but one of my Mother's children. I have little baby-children at home.

Dee: Where is your home?

Girl: I dare not tell you where I dwell – I shall be beaten.

Dee: You shall not be beaten for telling the truth to them that love the truth, to the eternal truth all creatures must be obedient.

Girl: I warrant you I will be obedient. My sisters say they must all come and dwell with you.

Dee: I desire that they who love God should dwell with me and I with them.

Girl: I love you now you talk of God.

Dee: Your eldest sister her name is Esémeli.

Girl: My sister is not so short as you make her.

(*Edward Kelley comments*: She smileth; one calls her saying, 'Come Away Maiden.')

The girl takes a book out of her pocket and opens it at picture of a man wearing a crown on his head. The man was Edward VI of England. She then turns to a picture of Henry VIII.

Girl: Here is a grim Lord. He maketh me afraid.

Dee: Why doth he make you afraid?

Girl: He is a stern fellow.

Other desultory exchanges take place and then, prosaically, Dee breaks off – 'We were earnestly called for to supper by my folks.'

Madimi turned out to be the most playful and wayward of Dee's angelic contacts. He came to regard her as his spiritual daughter – he even named one of his own daughters after her. Madimi would sport among the tomes in his study, consult her mother and sister in response to questions and erupt into little fits of tantrum and petulance. Over a period of seven years, during which she grew and blossomed into womanhood, she engaged in conversation with Kelley and Dee, her replies veering between maidenly meekness and theological bombast. Her most alarming visitation was when she appeared to Kelley in the crystal ball and shed her clothes one by one until completely naked and exhorted the scryer and magician to 'share all things in common . . . including our wives'. This led to the celebrated 'cross-matching' or wife-swapping experiment which so perplexed and offended John and Jane Dee and gave rise to the suspicion that Edward Kelley, who often criticized his own wife's shortcomings, was using the crystal as a vehicle of erotic manipulation.

Dee's flocculent dialogues and carnal caperings were held against him by commentators like Meric Casaubon (1659). His distinction as a scholar was eclipsed by a miasma of lurid legend, but recent studies have re-established him as a mathematician, geographer and scientist. For although denounced as a black magician, Dee believed that contacting angelic entities and obtaining knowledge from them was an ennobling process. Such beings were seen as deputies and representatives of the vast spiritual whole ruled over by Almighty God. He did not, like the Cathars, envisage a cosmos in which Good and Evil were forever at war, but a more orderly system in which numerous angels and demons pursued their divinely ordained roles from assigned sectors or 'Watchtowers'. In his lofty remoteness from the concerns of his fellows, one detects in Dee a Puritan tinge. He cared little for the diversions of the mob and, on 13 January 1583, noted in his diary how 'the stage at Paris Gardens fell down all at once, being full of people beholding the bear-baiting. Many being killed thereby . . . The godly expound it as a due plague of God for the wickedness there indulged and the Sabbath day so profanely spent.'

As for Dee's magic and relations with the angel-child Madimi, one can find an analogy in Pan's love for the nymph Echo, who had no body or substantial form. But this did not deter the goat-god who was provoked by her very elusiveness. Pan's romance with Echo was like chasing the memory of a sweet dream, a melting wraith. Some think that Pan was condemned to pursue his own reflection – a mind endlessly turning in upon itself.

Did John Dee find his wood-nymph or Echo in Madimi – a waif who tantalised him with thoughts of uncovering the deep mysteries of the cosmos? In a sense, he slew any fear he might have harboured, converting it to curiosity and crossing the threshold. He made 'spirits' work for him and give up their secrets. Initially it appeared a thrilling challenge, an esoteric route to riches and power, but as the years went by his transactions became 'routine'. Did Dee discourse with spiritual beings? Maybe – but a paradoxical and recessive law is at work here. When a magician confronts the 'unknown' by means of tools and conjurations, it tends initially to yield secrets and then 'step back', leaving him enclosed in a ceremonial space. He is using 'nature' as a sounding board and interactive arena for pathways and correspondences. Once the ritual ceases, the 'unknown' comes flooding back and attempts to swallow him. To avoid being swallowed by dread and panic, he must 'hide' in more ritual – in more discourse with demons and spirits – just as a caveman hides from a raging storm. In trying to decipher the mystery, he has in fact avoided it.

Therefore it is difficult to make a great deal of sense of Dee's writings, crammed as they are with amazing, inconsequential visitations and spirits of all sizes and appearances. But as Madimi observed, these 'beings' do not possess a knowledge deeper than that 'buried in the shadow of men's soules'. The dialogues seem destination-less, coiling around a metaphysical vacuum. Dee asks questions. The spirits reply in a way that demands elucidation: hence the web extends infinitely.

RESTORATION & REVOLUTION: NATURE & NOTHING

LORD ROCHESTER

> Birds, feed on Birds, on each other prey,
> But Savage Man alone, does Man, betray . . .
> For fear he armes, and is of Arms afraid,
> By fear, to fear, successively betray'd.
> Base fear, the source from whence his best passions came,
> His boasted Honor, and his dear bought Fame,
> That lust of Pow'r, to which he's such a Slave,
> And for the which alone he dares be brave.
> (*A Satyr against Mankind,* John Wilmot, Earl of Rochester, 1679)

After the death of Oliver Cromwell in 1658, there were signs that Britain was relapsing into anarchy. The Lord Protector's son Richard was weak; he had none of his father's iron resolve or decision-making capacity. Eventually a newly elected government was formed by General Monck who invited Charles II to return from exile and take over the throne, providing he first agreed there should be an amnesty for the anti-royalists. These terms were accepted and the King returned.

The Civil War and Interregnum had brought with them a disrupted social pattern. The old hierarchical order had collapsed and isolated cabals petitioned for basic rights and privileges to be extended to the common man. Further talk of divine right seemed ridiculous after it had been demonstrated that Parliament could arrest and behead a king. With the accession of Charles II came further social turmoil, as the King tried to win back for the monarchy a little of its lost power. In the midst of these opposing factions sprang up various religious groups, all seeking to define how God made his voice heard through ordinary men and women. Lord Clarendon, the king's chief adviser, acidly noted the growth of religious sects which 'discountenanced all forms of reverence and respect' and a tendency in children not to submit to their parents' ruling – 'but every one did that which was good in their own eyes'. Relations between masters and servants had deteriorated and, in place of generosity, there had grown 'a vile and sordid Love of Money'.

It was thought that the age was about to be punished for its moral failings when, in 1664, a blazing star passed across the northern skies, making 'a rushing, mighty noise, fierce and terrible, though at a distance and but just perceivable'. This portent unleashed a flood of tracts and prophecies heralding the imminent end of the world. Men claimed that London would be destroyed within forty days; self-appointed soothsayers and priests parroted millennial babble similar to that which had roused the peasants of the Middle Ages. Some claimed a flaming sword had been seen descending from a cloud with its point hanging over the city, while others had visions of hearses, coffins and piles of corpses. Generally it was whispered that the Almighty's anger had been brewing.

Prediction became reality a year later when a tradesman in East Smithfield discovered that his pregnant wife had caught the plague. No midwife would assist her, nor nurse tend her. On seeing her symptoms, both his servants fled the house. The man ran from door to door to find help, but people shuddered and drew back. Finally he made contact with a watchman who promised to send a nurse the following morning. So he returned home and tried to ease his wife's labour. He managed to deliver the baby – but it was stillborn. Heartstricken, the husband held his wife in his arms for a further half an hour until she passed away. He was still holding her in the morning when the watchman appeared with the nurse: 'So overwhelmed with grief was he, that he himself died a few hours after without any sign of the infection upon him, but merely sank under the weight of his grief.'

The plague spread; by September 1665 some thirty thousand Londoners were thought to have perished. The religious saw it as divine punishment for base practices and there were calls for penitence and reform. Solomon Eccles (or Eagles), a Quaker fanatic, ran naked through the streets of London, a dish of burning sulphur on his head, preaching repentance and prophesying catastrophe.

The second great disaster came a couple of years later when a baker called Farynor, who lived in Pudding Lane, woke up with a choking sensation. Realising that his oven was on fire he quickly evacuated the house, forgetting to rouse a maidservant who was asleep. She suffocated. The wind, changing direction, swept sparks into nearby Thames Street where, in the various cellars and warehouses, lay stockpiles of oil, spirits and tallow brought by merchant ships to the port of the London. Nearby were open wharves, stacked with hay, timber and coal awaiting transit. When the fire reached these, it very quickly began to rage out of control and a mass exodus ensued.

Samuel Pepys, whose wife had told him about the fire the next morning, strolled down to the waterside and saw crowds of people frantically trying to remove their goods from their property, flinging stuff into the river or loading it into lighters: 'Poor people staying in their houses as long as till the very fire touched them, and then running into boats or clambering from one pair of stairs by the waterside to another. And among other things, the poor pigeons I perceive were loath to leave their houses, but hovered about the windows and balconies till they were some of them burned, their wings, and fell down.'

Diarist John Evelyn, lover of tortoises and country gardens, surveyed the devastation, noting the sad ruin of St Paul's whose beautiful portico had been rent in pieces – 'flakes of vast stone split asunder' – although the inscription on the architrave remained intact. Splendid arched buildings had been razed to the ground, their ornamental fountains dried up and ruined, 'whilst the very waters remained boiling; the voragos of subterranean cellars, wells, and dungeons, formerly warehouses, still burning in stench and dark clouds of smoke, so that in five or six miles traversing about, I did not see one load of timber unconsumed, nor many stone but were calcined white as snow. The people who now walked about the ruins appeared like men in some dismal desert, or rather in some great city laid waste by a cruel enemy; to which was added the stench that came from some poor creatures bodies, beds and other combustible goods . . . Nor was I able to pass through any of the narrower streetes, but kept the widest; the ground and air, smoke and fiery vapour, continued so intense that my hair almost singed, and my feet insufferably surbated.'

Despite the backcloth of fire and pestilence and the dogmatic, clear-sighted moralising of John Bunyan, the age of Charles II is usually characterised by its scientific temper. After the eradication of vast areas of London, there was a cleansing of the senses – an awakening from the collective trauma and an attempt to usher in new ideas and principles. Christopher Wren's architecture, Isaac Newton's theory of gravity, William Harvey's discovery of the circulation of the blood and the founding of the Royal Society – all conspired to create the flavour of an English Renaissance. Certainly there had, following Cromwell's death, been a shift from the religious to the political. 'Good King Charles's Golden Days' may have been rife with religious dissent and persecution, but it was also a time when fashion and frivolity came to the fore. 'A strange effeminate age when men strive to imitate women in their apparel,' wrote Anthony Wood in 1663, 'viz. long periwigs, patches in their faces, painting, short white breeches like petticoats, muffs, and their clothes highly scented, bedecked with ribbons of all colours.'

The plays of the time feature various social types, from the mocking sophisticate to the blunt honest fellow of rural pedigree and the fan-brandishing society lady. Sharply outlined, often crudely contrasted, their plots are obsessed with money, sex and class. The predominant hypocrisy is advanced by matchmaking connivance and self-serving deceit. In Britain there were a few effective tragedies of the heroic mould. Basically the substance of drama avoided the elemental, the stupendous and divine, preferring an emphasis on amours, both calculated and ardent, played out against a background of leisure and affectation.

This preoccupation was caricatured in the image of the rake: the indolent, witty, often aristocratic knave who drank from morn till night, seduced anyone from ladies to page boys, duelled and japed, schemed and blasphemed until death halted his voluptuous and bacchanal exertions. In 1660 Clement Ellis commented that the noun gentleman 'is indeed already made to be of no better significance than . . . to denote a person of a licentious and unbridled life . . . a gentleman must be thought only a man, as may without control do what he lists, and sin with applause: one that esteems it base and ungentle, to fear a god, to own a law, or practice a religion; one who has studied to bring sin into fashion and with so much unhappy success, that he is now accounted a clown that is not proud to be thought a sinner; and he as ridiculous as an antique, who will not, without all scruple, proclaim himself an atheist.'

John Wilmot, second Earl of Rochester, proclaimed himself an atheist and felt no scruple over his disbelief. His brief, charmed life at the court of the Charles II was followed by downfall and disaster. After squandering his days amid a fury of women and wine, he died of venereal infection at an age when many of his peers were considering taking up a career.

Born on 1 April 1647 at Ditchley in Oxfordshire, John Wilmot was the son of a royalist general who had helped Charles escape after the battle of Worcester. The astrologer Gadbury added that he came into the world imbued with a noble and fertile muse. At the age of twelve he entered Wadham College where, it was said, he 'grew debauched'. Two years later, having gained an MA, he went on a tour of France and Italy, came back to England and established himself at the court of Charles II. His pranksterish, impulsive nature got the upper hand when, with the help of an armed guard, he abducted the heiress Elizabeth Malet, who had rejected him, for which offence he was placed in the Tower. He petitioned the King for his release and was successful. During the Dutch Wars, conducted with the intention of breaking Holland's grip on overseas trade, he was made a commander and distinguished himself, fighting bravely during the raid at Bergen.

Once released from naval duties, he married Elizabeth Malet (who had reconciled herself to his poverty), returned to court and cut a dashing figure as a wit and satirist. But his behaviour became increasingly wilful and out of hand. For a while, by employing guile and wit, he served as a gentleman of the royal bedchamber – a kind of rakish manservant to the king – at £1,000 a year. He called himself the 'prince of all the devils of the Town' and was frequently – some might say continuously – drunk. Other escapades include assaulting the poet Dryden, posing as a quack and selling patent medicines, and disguising himself as a footman to spy on the ladies at court. His determined immersion in physical sensation suggests that the more subtle pleasures eluded him. He once admitted that his behaviour could be attributed to an aversion to Puritanism and, more importantly, a desire to affront it.

Though vocationally dissipated, Rochester was an attractive personality, if not immune to visitations of terror or fancy. Between drinking and fornication lay a chasm of boredom. 'The world,' he wrote to Henry Savile, 'ever since I remember, has been still so insupportably the same, that 'twere vain to hope there were any alterations.' What terrors preyed on him did not seem to take the form of Bosch-like demons or physical grotesques. It was the void – a fear of meaningless and ultimate dissolution – that leaked between the cracks of his skull. He jumped from one sensation to the next as if afraid to savour too much silence or reflection. Yet when he chose, he could write with gravity and metaphysical wit.

Seeing little beyond material, sensual pleasures, he remained impervious to thoughts of heaven or an afterlife. His poetry, mainly slashing satire or bawdy masque, was distinguished by its combination of elegance and gutter profanity. It suggests a man who desires both to shock the prim-minded and to evince admiration from the lascivious sophisticates. It has a throwaway superiority and often appears to have been written a little too easily. If Rochester was frequently cruel and improvident, it stemmed more from a desire to appear witty or brilliant in the eyes of the court than to actually hurt or humiliate, though the harm caused may have often been equivalent.

Rochester had read the works of Thomas Hobbes (1588–1679) who, according to Gilbert Burnet, appealed less to his intellect than to his emotions. In his masterpiece *Leviathan*, Hobbes puts forward a materialist view of existence wherein mechanical explanations dominate and spirits and demons do not exist, 'for we erre, not knowing the scriptures . . . by introducing the Daemonology of the heathen poets, that is to say, their fabulous Doctrine concerning Demons, which are but Idols or Phantasms of the braine, without any real life of their own, distinct from human fancy; such as dead men's Ghosts and Fairies, and other matter of old Wives tales.' Thus the soul becomes a function or attribute of bodily existence and, after death, 'we become the lumber of the world'.

Fear of death was an essential element of Hobbes's system. He was himself born prematurely in 1588 when the Spanish Armada was approaching. 'Fear and I were born twins,' he said, citing his anxious nature. Hobbes traces human development as a struggle against death and terror, an escape from the state of nature 'which is worst of all, continual fear, and the danger of violent death; and the life of man, solitary, poor, nasty, brutish and short'. To dispell such apprehensions, human beings congregate, offer each other kinship and consolation, create nations, laws and material comforts. For Rochester such an outlook provided cynical satisfaction and probably fuelled his invocation to 'Nothing', a superb existential poem that has lost none of its lustre.

> Nothing, thou Elder Brother even to Shade,
> Thou had'st a being ere the world was made,
> And (well-fixed) art alone of ending not afraid.
>
> Ere Time and Place were, Time and Place were not,
> When Primitive Nothing something straight begot,
> Then all proceeded from the great united – what?
>
> Yet something did thy mighty power command,
> And from thy fruitful emptiness's hand
> Snatched men, beasts, birds, fire, water, air, and land.

The eternal paradox is stated. How can anything derive from Nothing? How can existence be spawned by non-existence? Even to call 'Nothing' by name is to instate it as a presence when it is actually an absence. Nothing in which all processes terminate engulfs wordly ambition. Yet non-being – though scarcely desirable – is preferable to Hell and Damnation. 'Nothing' has connotations, both metaphysical and disdainful, which Rochester stretches and counterpoints, skilfully playing negation against negation, the language sinously circling its own vacuum. Finally politics, philosophy, metaphysics, fashion and worldly wisdom are drained of meaning; a mantric repetition bleaches the world of significance. The great negative swallows all:

Nothing, who dwells with fools in grave disguise,
For whom thy reverend shapes and forms devise
Lawn-sleeves and furs and gowns, when they like thee look wise:

French Truth, Dutch Prowess, British Policy,
Hibernian Learning, Scotch Civility,
Spaniards' Dispatch, Danes' Wit, are mainly seen in thee;

The great man's gratitude to his best friend,
Kings' promises, whores' vows, towards thee bend,
Flow swiftly into thee, and in thee ever end.

A sardonic poise gilds the humility. The gravity and control are impressive. If Rochester had written more poems of comparable force, his stature would equal that of Andrew Marvell. Gilbert Burnet, who acted as royal chaplain to the Prince of Orange and was appointed Bishop of Salisbury in 1689, was the man to whom Rochester divulged details of his life and opinions. The cleric published *Some Passages of the Life and Death of John Earl of Rochester* in mainly dialogue form, allotting over 1,671 lines to himself compared with 302 to the ailing aristocrat. 'After I had waited on him once or twice,' Burnet wrote, 'he grew into that freedom with me, as to open to me all of his thoughts of both religion and morality, and to give me a full view of his past life, and seemed not uneasy at my frequent visits.'

Despite the fact that Rochester was half-dead and 'pissing matter', Burnet prodded and poked him for memories and reflections. It seems that he was hankering after a death-bed repentance and, for good measure, he extracted some grudging concessions concerning the usefulness of religion and the necessity of morality. But Rochester did not come within musing distance of his conception of Christian God.

> He said, he looked on it as a vast Power that wrought everything by the necessity of its nature: and thought that God had none of those affections of love and hatred, which breed perturbation in us, and by consequence he could not see there was either to be reward or punishment. He thought our conceptions of God were so low, that we had better not think much of him, and to love God seemed to him a presumptious thing and the heat of fanciful men. Therefore he believed there should be no other religious worship, but a general celebration of that Being, in some short hymn.

Rochester disapproved of clergymen who wrapped things up in mystery and ritual. Stories, parables and miracles were the wands they waved in order to wield power and authority. 'The believing mysteries', he told Burnet, 'made way for all the juggling of priests, for they getting the people under them in that point, set out to them what they pleased, and giving it a hard name, and calling it a mystery, the people were tamed and easily believed it.' In other words, priests appoint themselves as a custodians of truth and virtue, not because they revere such qualities, but in order they should be flattered and empowered. Like politicians, instead of banishing a present evil, they distract the unwary by promising a future good or Kingdom of Heaven which shall never come about. Religion is little more than manipulation through enforced superstition – a critique, incidentally, taken up hundreds of years later by Nietzsche and Michel Foucault.

ABSOLUTE FEAR: THE REVOLUTIONARY SPIRIT OF THE MARQUIS DE SADE

> The effect of liberty on individuals is that they may do what they please: we ought to see what it will please them to do, before we risk congratulations.
>
> *(Reflections on the Revolution in France*, Edmund Burke, 1790)

'How much the greatest event it is that ever happened in the world,' Charles James Fox exclaimed after the storming of the Bastille in 1789, 'and how much the best.' The taking of the fortress, containing only seven inmates, none of whom was a political prisoner, mattered little. But the liberating violence of the gesture was gratifying for the oppressed populace. At last the commoner was able to flaunt his grievance with the same disregard that the government had once shown against him. The Bastille was a symbol of authority that many had come to hate and the date of its destruction is still commemorated as a national holiday.

Originally the Revolution was viewed as a symbol of hope. It stood for the abandonment of protocol, the breaking-down of repression and the ushering in of a new openness. 'Happiness', said the Jacobin Louis de Saint-Just, 'is a new idea in Europe.' By establishing the principle of equality, it freed the peasant from ancient dues and obligations and payment of tithes to the Church. It brought with it the idea of self-determination: that an individual could take the reins of his destiny and be, in Henley's phrase, the captain of his soul. But after the positive opening shots, the election of a National Assembly, the Declaration of Human Rights, the outlining of a new constitution, abolition of feudalism and other corporate privileges, came a retrograde backlash that disillusioned so many liberal intellectuals in much the same way that Stalin's 'purges' did over a century later. It has been called 'revolutionary neurosis' but 'mob violence' or 'unfocused rage' might be as good a description.

Sometimes, after a drastic measure has been taken, a warped exultation passes through men, and they exchange proper reform – the long, hard job of restructuring an entire political system – for acts of violence against anyone identified as their enemies. In order to sustain the illusion of action, they succumb to a long-brewed hatred and resentment. Many, including the philosopher Hegel, saw this as a degeneration of the original idealism, the descent from high principles into 'Absolute Fear'.

Usually such violence occurs when political considerations annul intimate ones. A poor man in pre-Revolutionary France found himself so hard done by that ordinary domestic joys provided little solace. Through harshness and unremitting taxation, the regime had oppressed all that made his life worth living. So the Revolution arose from the same kind of protective-assertive fury that might be unleashed upon someone who wantonly attacked one's wife or children. The poor had nothing to lose but their misery.

An early victim was the Queen's friend Princesse de Lamballe, who was set upon by the mob when they entered the prison of La Force. She had returned to Paris to be at the Queen's side (some dubbed her Marie Antoinette's lesbian partner) during the troubled times of 1792. After being detained at the Temple Tower, where she had accompanied the royal family, she was dispatched to La Force. Armed with pikes, butchers' knives and sabres, the mob stormed into the official residences and penal institutions of the old regime, selecting and dispatching their victims. They stopped at neither cannibalism, disembowelment or sexual mutilation. The princess was brought before Maillard's tribunal, but she refused to swear her hatred of the King and Queen. The mob accordingly turned its rage on her. A sabre-stroke from behind severed her head. Her body was mounted on a pike and held up to the windows of the Queen's residence. For hours it was dragged through the streets until finally the executioner ripped open her chest and drew out her still-beating heart. Then he cut off her breasts and vulva which he drew over his lips, so that it fitted him like a moustache, causing laughter among his followers, as did the remark: 'The whore! No one shall ever thread his way into her again!'

At the command of Robespierre, a left-wing revolutionary who coined the slogan Liberty-Equality-Fraternity, Queen Marie Antoinette was beheaded. He told the people that the best way to maintain the momentum of the Revolution was to remove anyone who might impede its progress. The Glorious Revolution soon plummetted into the Bloody Revolution. In Paris alone, 2,600 suspects were tried, mainly nobles, but also scientists like the chemist Lavoisier, who discovered oxygen, and the poet Andre Chenier. An English observer, William Wordsworth, was shaken by the spectacle:

> Domestic carnage now filled the whole year
> With feast-days; old men from the chimney nook,
> The maiden from the bosom of her love,
> The mother from the cradle of her babe,
> The warrior from the field – all perished, all –
> Head after head, and never heads enough
> For those that bade them fall.   (*The Prelude*)

Finally Robespierre had his colleague, Danton, executed and appointed himself leader. His next task was to flush out the Jacobins. Marseilles was purged and Lyons, Bordeaux and Nantes. In the latter town the director of executions was a tireless sadist called Jean Baptiste Carrier. Under his command, five hundred children were taken to the meadows and shot or axed to death – some were so small that the blade failed to locate their neck and sliced their heads in two. Even the public executioner had a breakdown after executing four sisters. Carrier also invented a form of drowning called *noyades* in which a barge filled with prisoners was towed into the middle of river and then sunk. Should any of the prisoners escape to the shore, men were stationed on the banks with hatchets and clubs to complete the work.

The Marquis de Sade

One of the prisoners released from the Bastille stood out from the rest. Puffy-faced and corpulent, he was, ironically, detained in the Tower of Liberty which overlooked the poor district of St Antoine. During his stay, he had been enjoying special privileges which included visits regular visits from his wife and dainties like chocolate and white nougat, dried fruit, pots of jam, peaches and bottles of wine. This dissipated nobleman went by the name of Sade, and his 'tired eyes still held a certain brilliance and acuteness, which shone from him like a fading spark on dead coal'. Although Sade had been imprisoned for cruelty and sexual excesses, he claimed his writing embodied the proper revolutionary spirit. In the nineteenth century his very name had evinced fear and loathing, but now the pendulum has swung to the opposite arc. If he is treated respectfully – sometimes reverently – it is because he mapped out how far humans are prepared to go in pursuit of gratification.

Centuries before Sade was born, brutal pleasures had provided entertainment for the masses. Crowds had witnessed the torture of animals and humans and flocked to public executions like oxen to a drinking pool. It is disconcerting that 'gala day' – associated with celebration and festivity – derives from 'gallows day' when crowds would put on their best clothes to watch a head being chopped off or a neck throttled by a hangman. So it was not so much that Sade indulged in worse excesses than other libertines, but more the fact that he translated his perversions into challenging, often shocking texts. His novels and tracts were seen as promoting practices hitherto considered too shameful to mention. There is a hysterical enthusiasm in the way in which Sade delineates torture and perversion – in the evangelical manner he preaches a doctrine of ecstatic cruelty. He is, in a sense, the Martin Luther of debauchery. So, despite their confusion and obsessive repetition, Sade's writings arise from a kind of honesty. It is a curious fact of human psychology that someone may steal happily and with impunity for many years, but should anyone confront him – actually call him a thief – an outburst of rage and denial may result. Similarly Sade spelt out – admittedly in grotesquely exaggerated fashion – the hidden urges and lusts buried in the human personality and stirred up a similar rage. While people might recognise pleasurable sensations arising in them during inappropriate moments, they would resent being classed as perverts or masochists.

Sade's central doctrine was the doctrine of 'Nature', which he did not see as positive and benign, as Rousseau did, but as self-seeking and compassionless. 'Nature averse to crime,' he remarked in 1792, 'I tell you that nature lives and breathes by it, hungers at all her pores for bloodshed, yearns with all her heart for the furtherance of cruelty.' Sade's 'Nature' was the governing principle behind human behaviour which expressed itself by following whatever urge arose to its completion or exhaustion. The more protective and playful aspects of the all-encompassing canon were ignored. So far as Sade was concerned, Nature did not balk at rape, incest, buggery, murder, theft or wanton destruction, so why impose such false controls? Throw off these ridiculous constraints, he urged, and everyone will enjoy a much happier existence, especially women, who will have the same liberty to enjoy themselves as men: 'Oh enchanting sex, you will be free . . . like ourselves, as free to make a career on the battlefields of Venus as we are. No longer need you blush for your charming escapades, we will crown you with myrtle leaves and roses.'

As for sodomy, that is a vice which serves Nature's purpose, for 'she is far less adamant about procreation than we so foolishly believe'. Furthermore murder – yet another hymn to the ubiquitous deity – should not be punished, save by those who are angry enough to avenge themselves on the perpetrator: 'I forgive you,' said Louis XV to Charolais, who had killed a man for his own amusement, 'but I also forgive the man who will kill you.'

Curiously, when Sade was appointed a judge of the Revolutionary court, his liberal inclinations came to the fore. The man whose fictional fantasies constituted a nest of horrors was profoundly unsettled by sights he came to witness. 'Nothing', he wrote to Gaufridy following the Paris massacres, 'can equal the horrors which were committed.' Furthermore he lamented the wanton slaughter of priests, particularly the Archbishop of Arles, 'the most virtuous and the most respected of men'.

An overheated imagination may entertain itself with horrid scenes – but it does not invariably wish to actualise them. Sade liked to provoke the staidly conservative with narratives of shocking possibilities and stimulating desecrations but did not require them to be agonisingly reproduced.

THE ROMANTICS:
THE MINISTRY OF FEAR

DREAD

> Angst reveals man's fundamental ontological situation, his
> connection with non-being, so that all fear is not just dread of
> death, but of the nothing on which all being is based.
>
> *(Pan and the Nightmare*, James Hillman, 1974)

Sade's gospel of cruelty was an inversion of the once-fashionable
view holding the 'natural' to be fundamentally good. During the
mid-eighteenth century Jean-Jacques Rousseau (1712–78) had
ushered in a change of attitude towards the wild and the tame.
Civilisation, he declared, was rotten and corrupt. Once gathered
together in cities, men proceeded to dirty their souls in industry and
commerce. With ever-increasing greed, they leeched the earth,
fouled rivers, created mountains of refuse and spread urban blots
across the countryside. They were prepared to deceive and exploit, to
make fortunes out of catastrophes, to reap profit out of shipwreck,
famine and war.

Contrast the civilised debauchée with primitive man. After he has
eaten, the latter is well-inclined towards his fellow-men. If he does
have an argument with anyone, it's usually over something basic
like food. Well, he can settle that with a quick fist fight after which
the winner will go back to his meal and the loser seek his game
elsewhere. But with civilised man, it's different, for he can never be
satisfied whatever his gain. First he acquires essentials like food and

clothing and then his hunger graduates to luxuries like fine wines and expensive carriages. Next he wants to own entirely superfluous things like exotic ornaments, paintings and plants. Steadily his passions and appetites grow more absurd, more elaborate, and yet such is his power and standing that he is able to satisfy them. In order to fulfill his needs, 'our hero' makes slaves of more and more people, so that after amassing a fortune by pillage and exploitation, he is able to cut the throat of every single living being and make himself 'sole master of the Universe' – that is the 'secret pretension' of every civilised man.

Instead of a synonym for a cannibal or hairy untutored oaf, under the spell of Rousseau's prose 'savage' became a term of approbation. The 'noble savage' was held up as an exemplar because he had not been cruelly or decadently educated. His accomplishments emerged out of a two-way discourse between himself and the environment of which he was an expression. This environment had not been over-cultivated or prettified but left to itself. For savage, untamed landscapes had a unique ability to elevate the soul. The pure air of a mountain region moved men to noble thoughts. What was sublime and terrible in Nature – cataracts, gorges, gloomy precipices, volcanic eruptions – reminded man of his puniness in the mighty scheme of things. 'It would seem that in raising ourselves above the abodes of men,' Rousseau wrote of mountains, 'we leave behind us all base and terrestrial sentiments, and that, in proportion as we approach ethereal regions, the soul contracts something of their unalterable purity.'

Rousseau's analogy was apt, for it was an age of justification and explanation. Paintings were subjected to acres of analysis and, for the first time, the word terror came to be used in an aesthetic context. What had made stout men tremble and cower was now a word conveying a pleasant shiver down the spine of gentleman who beheld a sight like a foaming cataract on the Pyrenees or a high glacier in the Alps. Terror was as desirable thing to feel as love or religious joy.

In 1795 the Scottish geologist James Hutton published *The Theory of the Earth*, a ground-breaking textbook discounting the old 'catastrophist' idea that changes in rock strata denoted ancient cataclysms, eruptions, floods and earthquakes. Instead Hutton explained that earth-building was still going on, but infinitely slowly, for rocks move through deep time. A waterfall could take several million years to wear away the underlying rock and a mountain might grow just an inch in a thousand years. Hence the Georgian and Regency periods were not just times when men like Wordsworth and Coleridge praised landscape for the repose it brought to the human soul; they were also able to anatomise and classify its bedding planes and alignments.

The following year (1796) Edward Jenner developed a safe vaccine against smallpox and Meikle pioneered the threshing machine. Inventions like the steamboat, the cotton gin, lithography, the electric battery, the gas lamp, the glider and steam locomotive, were all pioneered and developed in the succeeding century. The increased pliability and abundance of available materials had released an enormous and diverse inventive potential.

Gothic Ripples

Whenever dramatic changes occur in society, men and women start to balk at novelty or complain of losing touch. Next they reach for their rose-coloured spectacles and look back to times when things had a satisfying if primitive candour. Hence the myths of the Middle Ages which are periodically revived: from Arthurian knights galloping out of fairy-tale castles to murky dragon-haunted wastelands ruled by dark lords and brooding barons; from monks cultivating herbs or shading illuminated manuscripts in quiet cloisters to the burning of witches; from wimpled ladies meekly sewing to a torturer sharpening his blades in a dungeon. Barbaric, civilised, sadistic, domestic, chivalric – all possibilities are contained here. Tableaux of this kind, plucked from an idealised past, were planted within the context of a novel or piece of poetry that attempted to rekindle an antique theme. In such writing the ruin was a potent symbol whose crumbling beauty was redolent of sadness and impending dissolution. As Mrs Ann Radcliffe observed in *Gaston de Blondeville* (1826), it pointed the finger of mortality at those who observed it:

Generations have beheld us and passed away, as you behold us, and shall pass away. They have thought of the generations before their time, as you now think of them, and as future ones shall think of you. The voices, that revelled beneath us, the pomp of power, the magnificence of wealth, the grace of beauty, the joy of hope, the interests of high passion and of low pursuits have passed from this scene for ever; yet we remain, the spectres of departed years . . .

Evocations of grandeur and decay – of bloody melodramas enacted in crag-perched castles and black ravines – aroused an excitement in the reader, tinged with fear and apprehension. In contrast, it also produced a feeling of safety. The heros, heroines and villains of the Gothic novel were propelled through a symbolic reality in which they underwent torture, terror and privation, to which only the reader – sharing the excitement yet evading the gruesome consequences – was privy. In a sense the reader was the true survivor: hence the notion of safety.

Perhaps it is apt to pause here and consider what fear meant to people like Byron, Keats or Mary Shelley, for it is a sensation of an entirely different order than that known by medieval man. In the latter, fear was pure fear – of a tangible nature perhaps – but for the Romantics, fear had a thrill or frisson attached to it. Surrounded by machines and industry, by contrivances that subdued man like a workhorse, they sought escape from such oppressive securities into upland regions where they could experience elemental emotions: terror, awe, sublime stupefaction and religious reverence. To the various flavours of dread – fear, despair and anguish – Kierkegaard devoted whole books in the 1840s: *Fear and Trembling*, *The Concept of Dread* and *The Sickness unto Death*, saying of one variety that it 'belongs to the child so essentially that he cannot do without it; even though it alarms him, it captivates him nevertheless by its feeling of swift apprehension. In all nations in which the childish character is preserved as the dreaming of the spirit this dread is found, and the deeper it is, the more profound is the nation.'

If the Danish theologian's explanation is a little fluid and copious, the gist of his argument may be translated. In discovering freedom, the individual confronts a void – a void of choice and possibility which he must tranform into a 'concretion' or aim. In trying to find his way, the sheer prolixity of phenomena overwhelms and alarms him, so he shrinks back in dread. Dread, then, is yet another manifestation of Pan, or the unknowable abyss that during the course of history yields many secrets and consolations, extending to humans choice, piquancy and variety, yet witholding its *raison d'être* or ultimate significance.

Similar to Kierkegaard's insight was that of George Borrow who, in *Lavengro* (1851), analyses this soul-stalking dread and suggests it endows life with a necessary tension. It urges the aware to complete their given tasks and not whittle away the years.

O that dark feeling of mysterious dread which comes over the mind, and which the lamp of reason . . . is unable to dispel. Art thou, as leeches say, the concomitant of disease? Nay, rather the principle of woe itself, the fountainhead of all sorrow co-existent with man, whose influence he feels when yet unborn . . . Fool . . . how dost thou know that this dark principle is not thy best friend? It may be, for what thou knowest, the mother of wisdom, and of great works: it is the dread of the horror of night that makes the pilgrim hasten on his way. Courage! build great works –'tis urging thee . . . What great work was ever the result of joy, the puny one? Who have been the wise ones, the mighty ones, the conquering ones of this earth? the joyous? I believe (it) not.

Either one stood perpetually on the threshold, trembling with uncertainty and foreboding, or one made a 'leap of faith' and landed securely in the lap of the Christian God – that was Kierkegaard's solution. But it was not Byron's or Shelley's: they sought inspiration in the dread and trembling, in the fear inmixed with awe, reverence and wonder. Wild scenery formed a background for walking and meditating. With his clubfoot, Byron was more handicapped in this area, but Coleridge, Wordsworth and Shelley were magnificent striders. In her journal (1816) Mary Shelley records a visit to the spectacular Mer de Glace, the confluence of three glaciers, below the slopes of Mont Blanc. At the time her husband, Percy, had been reading 'a sublime but gloomy theory' that the earth would revert to a mass of frost, and when she looked upon the glacier, with its dirty white surface traversed by blue-sided crevasses, she thought it 'the most desolate place in the world'.

Stark desolation helped to peel away layers of social pretension. Intercourse with pure mountain air rendered one's insights equally uncontaminated. If lightning, storm and thunder shook up the scene, that enhanced the drama for the solitary poet who stood on the bridge of being and faced Nature in her implacable indifference. 'There is in man,' wrote Friedrich Schlegel, 'a terrible unsatisfied desire to soar into infinity; a feverish longing to break through the narrow bounds of individuality.'

RIDING THE NIGHTMARE

> History, Stephen said, is a nightmare from which I am trying to awake.
>
> *(Ulysses,* James Joyce, 1922)

In an influential essay on the sublime and beautiful (1756), Edmund Burke argued that the goal of great art was the infinite and 'no passion so effectually robs the mind of all its powers of acting and reasoning as fear', which intensified the appreciation of natural phenomena. Art critic Sir Uvedale Price, a follower of Burke, wrote:

> it would be difficult to conceive any set of objects, to which, however grand in themselves, an addition of terror would not give a higher degree of sublimity . . . The sea is at all times a grand object; need I say how much that grandeur is increased by the violence of another element, and again, by thunder and lightning? Why are rocks and precipices more sublime, when the tide dashes

at the foot of them, forbidding all access or cutting off all retreat, than when we can with ease approach . . . The most savage rocks, precipices and cataracts, as they keep their stations, are only awful; but should an earthquake shake their foundations, and open a new gulf between the cataract – he, who removed from immediate danger, could dare at such a moment to gaze on such a spectacle, would surely have sensations of a much higher kind, than those which were impressed upon him when all was still and unmoved.

In other words, Sir Uvedale's pleasure at gazing on a sight like the Reichenbach Falls would be heightened if a mighty earthquake could be arranged to take place at the same time. Not only is he able to analyse sights that once filled travellers with superstitious dread, but to demand an additional seismic thrill. This attitude hints at a high degree of comfort and complacency. People had come a long way from the time when mountains were thought horrid and oppressive with cold, unhealthy airs. They were now able to regard landscapes as aesthetic artefacts, paintings that might be improved with an added dash of drama or sensation: hence the contrived wildness of the landscape garden.

An artist of the early Romantic period who absorbed such ideas and assiduously cultivated fear was the Swiss-born Henry Fuseli. He chose subjects like *Satan bridging Chaos*, the *Shepherd's Dream*, *Fairies from Shakespeare* and *Hamlet's Ghost*. Benjamin Haydon (1853) praised the latter as 'the finest conception of a ghost there ever was painted . . . There it quivered with martial stride, pointing to a place of meeting with Hamlet; and round its visored head was a halo of light that looked sulphurous, and made one feel as if one actually smelt hell, burning, cindery, and suffocating. The dim moon glittered behind; the sea roared in the distance, as if agitated by the presence of a supernatural spirit; and the ghost looked at Hamlet, with eyes that glared like the light in the eyes of lion, which is savagely growling over his bloody food.'

Fuseli, unlike his compositions, was not impressive to look at. What Haydon saw was 'a little white-headed lion-faced man in an old flannel dressing-gown tied around his waist with a piece of rope and upon his head the bottom of Mrs Fuseli's work-basket'. Today his most frequently reproduced work is *The Nightmare* (1782), which was painted after he had dreamed that he had made love to his unrequited sweetheart. It shows a young woman sleeping, her breast and legs dramatically thrust upwards, and the head of a phantom horse, with icy wisps of mane, rising above the bed. Perched on the woman's breast is a small hairy devil, impishly sinister. The horse's eyes bulge and its neck seems to strain to burst through the rent in the curtains and take possession of the world of shapes and solids. Rendered in apparitional whites and dusky browns, it is a shudderingly effective visual landmark.

In 1788 Fuseli brought out *Aphorisms on Art*, containing the following statements:

> The loathsome is abominable, and no engine of expression.
>   Sympathy and disgust are the lines that separate terror from horror; though we shudder, we scarcely pity what we abominate.
>   The axe, the wheel, sawdust, and the blood-stained sheet are not legitimate substitutes for terror.

Fuseli is suggesting that 'terror' is an altogether superior emotion to horror. The latter, in seeking to make the gorge rise, dwells overmuch on messy, visceral excesses while terror strives to express a desolation and grandeur, a refined, doom-laden sadness and sense of the inevitability of fate. It also has that element of dark fantasy which Fuseli's own paintings convey.

Like Fuseli, Coleridge, Shelley, Lamb and De Quincey were fascinated by dreams, nightmares and waking visions. They studied them, set them down in their notebooks and recreated them in poetry and prose. In ancient Greece, the lord of nightmares was Pan, who imbued the dreamer with a sense of fluctuation and instability. Night had the power of stripping away whatever patterns were woven in the day. And what of the association with the horse? The 'night-mare' refers to 'Mara' – the incubus that bears the dreamer to the otherworld of ghosts and shadows, the realm of Tom o'Bedlam and the Piper of Dreams. Horses were said to suffer from nightmares, at which times they would sweat, snort and shake their necks. Their manes, heavily knotted and impossible to comb, had to be burned out with blessed candles or excised by a cut shaped like a cross.

A classic account of the nightmare was furnished by John Bond (1763) who pointed out that it generally seizes people who are sleeping on their backs. Afflicted by fearful images, they groan and sigh, find respiration difficult and feel 'a violent oppression of the breast'. They struggle to break the bonds of the nightmare but are constrained by the body's inability. The sensation of paralysis – of something pinning down their limbs – heightens the accompanying terror, as if they are clenched in the 'jaws of death'. If they do succeed in breaking free, they are afflicted by palpitations, anxiety, langour and uneasiness, 'succeeded by the pleasing reflection of having escaped such imminent danger'.

By then the erotic content of nightmares had been translated, not in terms of the sleeper's repressed desires, but rather of quiescent innocence being disrupted by strong-minded young succubi. In *Pandaemonium* (1684) Richard Bovet gave an account of a poor young man lying speechless on his bed. He had been lying down for half an hour, trying to lapse into sleep but unable to do so owing to an appalling headache, when there came into his room two very beautiful young women who

endeavoured to come into the bed to him, being one on the one side, the other on the other side thereof, which he resisted with all the power he could, striking at them several times with his fists, but could feel nothing but empty shadows; yet they were so strong that they drew all the bedclothes off him, though he tried with all his force to hold them, and after they had stripped him of his shirt, and he had contested with them so long that he concluded within himself that he should die of their violencies, during all that time he had no power to speak or call for aid.

Sometimes the nightmare utilised the archetypal Pan-Devil spectre of which there is more than a hint in Fuseli's painting. Paul Radestock (1879) quoted a sleeper who saw at the foot of his bed a small, hideous creature with dark eyes and narrow, wrinkled brow. It had a goat's beard, upright pointed ears 'like Pan', a humped back and puffed-out chest. Taking hold of the edge of the bed, it shook it with tremendous force and said: 'You will not remain here much longer!' At this the terrified man awoke and hurried to the cloister where he threw himself down before the altar 'numbed by fear' and unable to move.

An eloquent sufferer from nightmares was the young Charles Lamb (1775–1834) whose classic essay on 'Witches and Other Night-Fears' appeared in the *London Magazine* – classic because it had a pertinence and depth absent from his more fanciful excursions. He begins by sympathising with the medieval peasants' fear of the supernatural, for they had no method by which they could separate natural phenomena from folklore:

That maidens pined away, wasting inwardly as their waxen images consumed before a fire – that corn was lodged, and cattle lamed – that whirlwinds uptore in diabolic revelry the oaks of the forests – or that spits and kettles only danced a fearful-innocent vagary about some rustic's kitchen when no wind was stirring – were all equally probable when no law of agency was understood. That the prince of the powers of darkness, passing by the flower and pomp of the earth, should lay preposterous siege to the weak fantasy of the indigent eld – has neither likelihood or unlikelihood a priori to us, who have no measure to guess at his policy, or standard to estimate what rate those anile soul's may fetch in the devil's market.

Lamb traces the source of his childish night-fears to a book by Stackhouse called *The History of the Bible*. The book contained many vivid pictures, including the witch raising up Samuel. But then, subtly, he does not hold the drawing responsible for his terrors, only for the 'shape and manner of their visitation' – in other words, the illustration provided the armature, the framework, on which the loose, runny fears could seize and assemble. In an extraordinarily prescient paragraph, deriving from Coleridge (who investigated his own nightmares exhaustively), he anticipates what Jung formulated over a century later: a universal unconsciousness hoarding preternatural archetypes: 'Gorgons and Hydras, and Chiméras dire – stories of Celéno and the Harpies – may reproduce themselves in the brain of superstition – but they were there before. They are transcripts, types – the archetypes in us, and eternal.'

In the final part, he confesses to being no longer tormented by night-fears, for he knows them for the 'mockeries' they are. His dreams, grown prosaic, are filled with staid architecture and buildings quite unlike the icy caves and pleasure domes of Kubla Khan. The very tameness of his soul's flights makes him conclude that prose is his natural element.

Stranger than Lamb's youthful imaginings were the nightmares of his young friend, essayist and opium addict, Thomas de Quincey, who evoked his dark alliance with the poppy seed and the alarming visions it induced. 'I seemed every night,' he wrote, 'to descend, not metaphorically but literally to descend, into chasms and sunless abysses.' Space was amplified 'to an extent of unutterable infinity'; a night seemed to take a century to pass and the minutest incidents of childhood were precisely recalled. Vast architecture loomed; mysterious seas welled and 'on the rocking waters of that ocean human faces began to appear: the sea appeared paved with innumerable faces, upturned to the heavens; faces imploring, wrathful, despairing, surged upwards by thousands, by myriads, by generations, by centuries – my agitation was infinite – my mind tossed – and surged with the ocean.' This vision should not be a fearful one, yet it is, for it reminds one of the pool of history, the drowning generations, faces that rise and dip out of sight, as if smoothed away by a gesture.

Dwelling on doom was a speciality of the opium-eater who described a nightmarishly fast journey by stagecoach from Manchester to Westmorland. An outside passenger, de Quincey was seated next to the driver, who had fallen asleep over his reins, when he saw ahead a young man and woman in 'a frail, reedy gig'. The heavy stagecoach was bearing down on them and de Quincey let out a warning cry. A few seconds before impact, the young man yanked his horse out of the stagecoach's path. The 'little cany carriage' received a harsh blow which 'resounded terrifically'. De Quincey looked back. The horse's forelegs were splayed on the crest of the road, the young man was trembling, and the lady throwing up her arms to heaven as 'from the manly tenderness of this flattering, murmuring, whispering love . . . suddenly as from the ground yawning at her feet, leaped upon her, with the flashing of cataracts, Death the crowned phantom with all the equipage of his terrors and the tiger roar of his voice'.

MURDER AS A FINE ART

If once a man indulges in murder, very soon he comes to think little of robbing; and from robbing he comes next to drinking and sabbath-breaking, and from that to incivility and procrastination.

('On Murder Considered as One of the Fine Arts', Thomas de Quincey in *Blackwoods Magazine*, 1827)

Not only were the Romantics prepared to analyse nightmares and the violence of nature, they were also able to confront violence in man. Shelley's play *The Cenci* (1819) deals with incest, murder and intrigue. Set in the year 1599, it tells how a debauched old man, Count Cenci, conceives an implacable hatred for his children along with an incestuous passion for one of his daughters, Beatrice, using cruelty and violence to satisfy it. To escape the unremitting contamination of her body and mind, Beatrice plots with her mother-in-law and brother to murder the tyrant. The crime is quickly discovered and the perpetrators brought to justice. Beatrice, who committed the murder, pleads with her judges, but they will not pardon her and she is executed. Her final speech is redolent with horror and pity:

Worse than the bitterness of death, is hope:
It is the only ill which can find place
Upon this giddy, sharp and narrow hour
Tottering beneath us. Plead with the swift frost
That it should spare the eldest flower of spring:
Plead with awakening earthquake, o'er whose couch
Even now a city stands, strong, fair and free;
Now stench and blackness yawns, like death. O plead
With famine, or wind-walking pestilence,
Blind lightning, or the deaf sea, not with man!
Cruel, cold, formal man; righteous in words,
In deeds a Cain. No, mother, we must die . . .

Evidence of a growing detachment towards things once regarded as beyond the pale can be found in the combination of jocular robustness and delicate cynicism in de Quincey's *On Murder Considered as One of the Fine Arts*. Briefly stated, the argument is that once a murderer has been condemned and the demands of morality satisfied, the connoisseur of homicide will naturally be drawn to compare the narratives of the different cases, the degrees of finesse or brutality involved and then to pass an aesthetic judgement. He cites Mr Howship, author of a book on indigestion, who shows no scruple in referring to a certain ulcer as 'a beautiful ulcer', so why not be prepared to acknowledge that merit may be perceived in certain criminal acts? De Quincey is here playing upon the divide between 'beautiful' as an aesthetic as opposed to moral epithet. Presumably a 'beautiful' murder signifies an act that was effective within the scope of its intentions rather than an alluring spectacle.

Aside from murder, de Quincey evokes the fear and fascination engendered by wanton, disorderly acts of destruction, like the terrible fire which occurred at Liverpool docks, when flakes of blazing cotton were carried by the wind some eighteen miles eastward and 'public sympathy did not at all interfere to suppress or even check the momentary bursts of rapturous admiration, as this arrowy sleet of many-coloured fire rode on the wings of the hurricane'.

Impish argument of this type is interspersed with deeper reflection. De Quincey identifies the morbid intoxication which murder may confer on both criminal and spectator. As civilians rather than combatants (the legitimacy of soldiers 'killing' for their country is usually accepted), we place the murderer in a special class, for he is able, as Coleridge observed, to generate 'the tremendous power which is laid open in any moment to a man who can reconcile himself to the abjuration of all conscious restraints, if, at the same time, thoroughly without fear'. Once supplied, such an intensity is not easily abandoned. In order to satisfy a growing appetite for excitement, the criminal may need to repeat his actions. The deed becomes a craving. He has entered a realm of heightened risk in which killing may be likened to 'a condiment for seasoning the insipid monotonies of everyday life'. From such observations arose the German word *lustmord*, indicating a murderer possessed by the thrill of his occupation in the same way that worshippers of Dionysus were intoxicated by the spirit of the vine. The 'joy' or heightened state of arousal dissolves moral distinctions. One grabs a repeater rifles, goes out into the street, shooting innocent bystanders willy-nilly, or stabs some poor stranger repeatedly. The philosopher Schopenhauer might say the blind, remorseless 'Will' is working through the individual who has no power to resist. Man is an empty vessel or puppet whose strings are jerked by an impassive, compassionless force. This force, manifest in lust, greed and vanity, draws him along and shatters him like a tidal wave. Only by renouncing this 'Will' may he gain redemption or insight into his essential helplessness.

As we have seen, fear provoked by a murder may give rise to both frisson and poetic inspiration. Ballads and verse narratives chronicling the deeds of murderers usually attain no great literary heights but Thomas Hood's *The Dream of Eugene Aram* is an exciting exception. There is a tainted elation in its thrilled depiction of the murderer-outcast who is branded with the mark of his calling. Aram walks apart from others, locked in a trance of torment and isolation:

> I know that murderers walk the earth
> Beneath the curse of Caine
> With crimson clouds before their eyes
> And flames about their brain;
> For murder has put upon their souls
> An everlasting stain.

Aram was a relatively well-educated criminal, a scholar and teacher. He was born in 1704 and publicly hanged at Tyburn Field outside the gates of York for murdering Daniel Clark, shoemaker in Knaresborough, fourteen years earlier, aided by William Flaxman, a flax-dresser. After relieving the 'stammering, pockmarked and weedy cobbler' of £220, they brained him with a pick and put the corpse, doubled up, beneath a rock in St Robert's Cave, Knaresborough. Because he had been seen in the company of Clark the previous evening, Aram decided it was timely for him to leave the district, going first to Nottingham and then to London where he lived a full and profligate existence, until a yearning for academic life tempted him to take up a post as teacher at the Grammar School, King's Lynn, Norfolk.

He was a stern and authoritarian teacher who performed his duties ably. But then, in June 1758, a Knaresborough visitor to the town recognised him. Aram denied his identity but two months later, under interrogation, he confessed to the crime and led the Justices to the remains. For about a year, he was confined to York jail where he wrote an elaborate defence, pointing out that the bones in the cave might be the relic of a saint or hermit – but this convinced no one. Found guilty, he attempted suicide by slashing his wrists the night before the execution and was dragged half-dead to the gibbet. His bones were left dangling in a nearby forest and there was no uproar when his skull was donated to the College of Physicians.

Seventy years later, the grim and tragic affair was transmuted and resurrected in Thomas Hood's black and swaggering ballad, stanzas from which, it has been noted by Colin Wilson and Pat Pitman, 'were often recited at Victorian musical evenings by that other callous criminal, Charley Peace'.

RESURRECTIONISTS

> Did I request thee, Maker, from my clay
> To mould me man, did I solicit thee
> From darkness to promote me?
>
> 　　　　　　　*(Paradise Lost,* John Milton, *1667)*

As we have seen, the bodies of murderers like Eugene Aram were often taken for dissection or 'anatomising', but the corpses of peaceable citizens were not always safe from medical enquiry. In the year 1811, a Scottish dwarf called David Ritchie died; his tomb bore an epitaph taken directly from Shakespeare:

> Good friend! For Jesus' sake forbear
> To dig the dust enclosed here;
> Blest be the man that spares these stones,
> And curst be he that moves my bones.

The quatrain was intended to be a deterrent, a curse aimed at those who appropriated mortal remains. Anatomists particularly prized the bodies of dwarves and giants whose cadavers furnished primary source material for lecture notes and medical textbooks. On account of its rarity, the corpse of a dwarf commanded a higher reserve price. Ritchie was understandably anxious that he should lie undisturbed, which he did for ten years, after which doctors from Glasgow opened up his grave and took out his bones for display.

It is curious to trace the route by which the human corpse – formerly an object of fear and superstition – became a highly prized, highly marketable commodity. No one could have accused the average man or woman in the eighteenth century of being fastidious. Crowds still flocked to public executions and consumed food from street vendors as they appraised the spectacle. Yet there was a widening consciousness of 'civilised' as opposed to 'uncouth' pursuits. If aspects of the age were characterised by madness and mayhem, they were counterbalanced by manners and mirrors. Etiquette books pointed out that habits like spitting or swearing in front of the titled was not the best strategy for social enhancement. An abundance of wigs, powder, petticoats, silk and perfume emphasised that the body was something to adorn and decorate rather than openly expose.

Accompanying this flowering of social awaresnsss was a withering of superstition. For instance, in medieval times it had been alleged that blood from a hanged man was a cure for leprosy; after that disease had abated, a host of lesser ailments, such as goitres and skin infections, became candidates for this potentially lethal application. But few civilised Augustans still believed a corpse was endowed with beneficent properties, and although premature death through disease, accident and illness was common, the allure of the grave – the tropical bloom of putrefaction – had started to acquire literary rather than practical implications.

Generally speaking, there was a decline in magic, superstition and needless fear, and a stronger emphasis on self-help, prompted by a greater availability of preventative and precautionary strategies. Important philosophers like John Locke had dismantled much superstitious and irrational association. In his *Essay Concerning Human Understanding* (1690), he had noted how 'Goblins and Sprites have really no more to do with darkness than light. Yet let but a foolish maid inculcate these often on the mind of a child, and to raise them there together, possibly he shall never be able to separate them as long as he lives; but darkness shall ever after bring with it those frightful ideas.' Locke's psychological acuteness opened a path for the deeper scepticism of David Hume whose essay on miracles stressed the uniformity of human experience: that night follows day, wood burns, people die, lead cannot float in air – such observations everyone could share and reach agreement upon. Miracles, by contrast, were 'a violation of the laws of nature'.

In this more critical atmosphere, a lifeless body assumed the status of an object. Death was a mechanical event like a branch shearing off a bough, a breath of wind snuffing out a candle. One can gauge how immured some were by the fact that a German child-rearing manual of 1787 makes the sensitive suggestion that, as it is necessary for children to learn about anatomy, care should be taken that they should not be exposed to anything that excites their senses. The genitals should be portrayed correctly but pictures are far too provocative. 'All these worries disappear,' the writer declares, 'if one makes use of a lifeless human body for this purpose. The sight of a corpse evokes solemnity and reflection, and this is the most appropriate mood for a child under such circumstances. By a natural association of ideas, his memory of the scene will produce a solemn frame of mind . . . There is often opportunity to see a corpse.'

Increasing knowledge of physiology was undoubtedly responsible for the feeling that the human body was a landscape to be mapped rather than a mystery to be venerated. As we have already noted, anatomical studies proper began in 1543 with *De Humani Corporis Fabrica* by Andreas Vesalius, an elegant and ground-breaking anatomical atlas with engravings by Jan Stevenszoon van Calcar. This was criticised in some circles for probing the secrets of God's creation – offending those who thought there should be proper limits to man's knowledge. This work prepared the way for the more authoritative and detailed *Icones Anatomica* (1743–56) by Albrecht von Haller in which anatomy and physiology were properly combined. The muscular fibres and their fundamental division were shown along with major veins and arteries.

These books represented the fruit of innumerable dissections and extirpations – practices which had traditionally caused offence. But so far as doctors were concerned, dissection was a necessary evil if medical science was to advance. In Calvinist Scotland and in parts of Britain, it was opposed on humane and religious grounds. Until the close of the seventeenth century, the only corpses available for dissection in Scotland were those of known felons or men who had died on the gallows. Edinburgh surgeons were restricted to one body a year for dissection, usually divided into ten parts and distributed among students.

Despite such a stipulation, no one was especially pacified, for the law was not an easy one to enforce. In 1694 the doctors of Edinburgh obtained permission to experiment upon the sad fatalities of poorhouses – 'those bodies that dye betwixt the tyme they are weaned and their being put to school or trades'. The poor were always at risk, but now the genteel were aware that corpses were marketable and that, were some sort of stand not taken, their own remains might be imperilled by the body-snatchers, especially if they happened to be a giant, a dwarf, a hydrocephalic or a hunchback. This upset the religious-minded – those who literally believed in the dead coming alive on Judgement Day. Were a body to be resurrected, that would be a startling enough, but how much more so if it arose headless and armless with a bloody cavern where its chest was! A dissected body, it was thought, might forfeit its right to eternal life. Thus in Scotland body-snatchers, or those who acquired bodies for selling on to medical science, were ironically called 'resurrectionists' or 'sack-em-men'.

Often heavily fortified by drink, these tomb robbers worked at night. First they dug down to the surface of the coffin. Being in a hurry, they cleared only the head area of the coffin of soil and then prised open the lid with a crowbar. Next the corpse was tugged out by means of hooks and ropes and the body stripped of any clothing. The latter was put back into the grave which was then filled in. Francis Clerihew, a law student of Aberdeen, recalled going along with some of his medical student friends on such a necromantic jaunt:

> Slowly we dragged the dead man up; and just as we got him to the surface out flashed the moon, full on his wan, discoloured face. His dull glassy eyes were wide open, and, as I thought, leered knowingly on me; his blue lurid lips were drawn back, and showed his white teeth; his arms hung dangling to the ground, and his head rolled about on his shoulders. In a trice, he was stripped of the graveclothes, tied neck and heels, and bundled into the sack. We pitched him over the wall, and two of my comrades set off with him to the gig, while Peter and myself remained to fill the grave.

Various catatonic or comatose states resembled death so closely that anatomists called a halt to their activities rather than dismember a living being. This happened to a London murderer in the year 1587 according to Stow's *Annals*. After being cut down from the gallows, the man's body was thrown upon a cart and taken through

Southwark and the City of London to the Surgeon's Hall near Cripplegate. The anatomist, opening his chest, found that his heart was still beating. The dissection was abandoned and the man lived for a further three days.

A similar event was recorded in eighteenth-century Germany but the reaction of the head surgeon was dispassionate. 'I am pretty certain, gentlemen,' he announced, 'from the warmth of the subject and the flexibility of his limbs, that by a proper degree of attention and care the vital heat would return, and life in consequence take place. But when it is considered what a rascal we should have again among us, and that, should we restore him to life, he would probably kill someone else, I say, gentlemen, all these things considered, it is my opinion that we had better proceed in the dissection.'

In such an atmosphere, it is hardly surprising that a Smithfield butcher who had stabbed his wife shouted after he was arrested: 'I have killed the best wife in the world, and I am certain of being hanged, but for God's sake don't let me be anatomised.'

Dissection was only one small area of investigation provoked by the human body. There were doctors and occultists who sought for 'the spark of life' or that which separated the animate from the inanimate. The religious might attribute it to the 'soul' or 'breath of God' kindling the flame of motion while experimenters had a more practical attitude. The latter attempted to kick-start muscular tissues into life or at least observe the effect of an electric charge on nervous systems. With the development of condensers and the Leyden jar, the science of electricity made dramatic and entertaining progress. Experimental physiology – sending electrical charges through nerves and muscles – became an accepted treatment. Some thought it could revitalise a flagging system and cure conditions like gout or stiffness of the joints. The anatomist most renowned for its medical application was Luigi Galvani who wrote a thesis, *In De Viribus Electricitatis in Motu Musculari* ('On Electrical Powers in the Movement of Muscles') in 1792, describing operations in which he drew across a iron balcony a length of copper wire on which hung the legs of dead frogs. When an electric current was sent along the wire, the frogs' legs twitched – from which, he concluded, electricity must be the life force or animating spirit.

By far the most important pioneer of electrical experiments in Britain was Faraday, but he had his regional enthusiasts, one of whom caused a furore. In the year 1836 a plain-speaking, West Country scientist published a description of an experiment in which he had created living insects. Andrew Crosse, the squire of Fyne Court, Broomfield, soaked a porous stone in a mixture of potassium silicate and hydrochloric acid and then ran an electric current through it. He was attempting to form silica crystals, but on the fourteenth day of the experiment 'a few whitish excrescences or nipples' were seen projecting from the middle of the electrified stone. Subsequently these enlarged, and struck out seven or eight filaments, finally transforming into perfect insects that crawled away.

Weeks went by, during the course of which Crosse manufactured hundreds of these insects, which detached themselves from the stone and walked about at leisure. The first person he told about his findings was the poet Robert Southey who was staggered. 'It's the very Devil, Andrew,' he exclaimed. Ironically, that light remark was to have alarming echoes, for 'creating life' was taking things too far in Regency Britain. Even before this incident, Crosse had gained a sinister reputation by simulating violent electric displays in the grounds of Fyne Court, using yards of iron wire, Leyden jars and large brass balls which would clang together. This led to him being reviled as 'a disturber of the peace of families' as well as a self-appointed rival to the Creator.

Being the object of so much 'virulence and abuse, so much calumny and misrepresentation' hurt Crosse deeply. He told a friend that he was no atheist but someone who held the 'Great Being' in reverence. But the stigma still held and local men, emboldened by cider, attempted to smash down his fences, fire his crops and kill his livestock. Others hurled stones at him when he went on his solitary Quantock walks. He was even accused of causing the potato blight. A young clergyman attempted to exorcise him; pacing up to Fyne Court, he held up a Bible and shouted, 'Reviler of our holy religion! Disturber of Christian peace! We came to ask Heaven's protection from you and your foulness!' The antagonism pushed Crosse deeper and deeper into a seclusion only made bearable by scientific companionship and the solace of a young and pretty second wife, Cornelia Crosse, the daughter of a neighbouring landowner; she became something a literary socialite and played hostess to poets like Wordsworth and Coleridge. When Crosse died in 1857, she gathered his papers and wrote a long memoir, complete with a selection of speculative fictions and verses extolling local features like the heather-clad Quantock Hills and the crystal formations in Holcombe Cave.

Crosse was thought to have been one of the stray sparks that helped to light the candle of *Frankenstein*, the celebrated 'horror' narrative by Mary Wollstonecraft Godwin, daughter of the political philosopher and subsequent wife of Percy Bysshe Shelley. After a 'blank and dreary childhood' spent around Dundee, she met the poet when she was fifteen and he twenty. They eloped and travelled through France and Switzerland, spending the summer of 1816 on the shores of Lake Geneva with Shelley's friend, the poet Lord Byron. When the weather grew stormy and oppressive, the writers spent much of their time indoors, devising for one another's amusement stories of a ghostly character. The poets produced rather half-hearted flesh-creepers, but Mary became truly inspired. She decided to write a story 'which would speak to the mysterious fears of our nature, and awaken thrilling horror – one to make the reader dread to look round, to curdle the blood and quicken the beating of the heart'.

'Have you thought of a story?' they asked her when she came down the following morning, and she had to to say 'No.' But then the talk turned to some electrical experiments in which vermicelli or Italian pasta had been put in Leyden jars and animated until 'by some extraordinary means it began to move with involuntary motion' – an idea which Mary immediately applied to the human body. What if a corpse could be animated in similar fashion? That night, unable to sleep, she experienced a waking dream in which she saw 'with shut eyes but acute mental vision . . . the hideous phantasm of a man stretched out, and then, on the workings of some powerful engine, show signs of life, and stir with an uneasy, half vital motion. His success would terrify the artist; he would rush from his odious handiwork, horror stricken. He would hope that, left to itself, the slight spark of life which he had communicated would fade . . . He sleeps but he is awakened; he opens his eyes; behold the horrid things stands at his bedside, opening his curtains and looking on him with yellow, watery, but speculative eyes.'

The next day Mary began writing *Frankenstein*. The novel so memorably begins – 'It was on a dreary night in November . . .'. Packed with sublimities, terrors and hostile icebound landscapes, the story has an authentic Promethean grandeur and its theme – taken from *Paradise Lost* – gnaws at the autocracy of the soul by sporting with the possibility that man is capable of 'making' himself, for he is basically an organic construct which can be replicated by the daring machineries of science: an unsettling, bravura exercise in romantic blasphemy.

Return of the Undead

Along with the thrilling apprehension of man usurping God's role and designing his own monsters, a backwash of traditional terrors rippled through the Romantic imagination. Tombs, graves and lofty turf-robed monuments raised their mouldering brows in stories and stanzas of the period and the stock supernatural presences of vampires, werewolves and ghosts continued to suck, slash and haunt.

In the summer of 1819 a periodical called *New Monthly Magazine* published a novella called *The Vampyre* (1819) by Dr John Polidori, a story of lust, murder and bloody resurrection, featuring a villain based on Lord Byron, whom Polidori had accompanied to Lake Geneva. Byron, to whose authorship the story was initially attributed, was outraged; he had found Polidori vain and ill-tempered, noting as they set sail from Dover that he 'was exactly the kind of person to whom, if he fell overboard, one would hold out a straw to know if the adage be true that drowning men grasp at straws'. The novella turned out to be immensely successful – but the author did not prosper much from it. Two years later, in August 1821, Polidori was struck dead 'by the visitation of God' according to the coroner.

In the year Polidori's novel was being feasted upon by the masses, the poet John Keats issued *Lamia*, a polished reworking of the legend recounted earlier in which Apollonius of Tyre unmasks a vampire at a wedding banquet. In Keats's version Hermes changes a serpent into a beautiful woman (Lamia) who seduces a young Corinthian philosopher until her spell is broken by the wise and wary Apollonius. Drydenesque couplets ripple along, brisk and fluid as the snaky heroine, who is changed from reptile to maiden with bilious vividness:

> The colours all inflam'd throughout her train,
> She writh'd about, convulsed with scarlet pain:
> A deep volcanian yellow took the place
> Of all her milder-mooned body's grace;
> And, as the lava ravishes the mead,
> Spoilt all her silver mail, and golden brede,
> Made gloom of all her frecklings, streaks and bars,
> Eclips'd her crescent, and lick'd up her stars . . .

Bound up with the lamia or female vampire is the femme fatale, a woman who draws erotic energy from the male. Arousing dread and desire in equal parts, she features as the bewitching lady in *La Belle Dame Sans Merci* (1819), the epitome of fatal, all-enslaving love:

> I saw pale kings and princes too,
> Pale warriors, death-pale were they all;
> They cried – La Belle Dame Sans Merci
> Hath thee in thrall!'

Keats grasped that sexual passion was essentially lawless, closer to anarchy and outrage than probity and control. It was simultaneously craved and feared – craved for the 'celestial flood of emotion & exaltation' it brought and feared because it melted the chain of male strength and pride. No law can make a woman love a man or a man love a woman. No statute can suppress a secret desire. No guidelines can control the dynamics of attraction. Sex has the power to humiliate and delude, to pamper the ego or crush it to a stain. No wonder the medieval church struggled so hard to control and subdue it.

Contrast Keats's irresistible ladies with the unappetising male bloodsucker Byron portrays in his Turkish romance *The Giaour* (or 'Infidel'):

> But first, on earth as vampire sent,
> The corpse shall from its tomb be rent:
> Then ghastly haunt thy native place,
> And suck the blood of all thy race;
> There from thy daughter, sister wife,
> At midnight drain the stream of life . . .
> Wet with thine own best blood shall drip
> Thy gnashing tooth and haggard lip;
> Then stalking to thy sullen grave
> Go – and with the ghoul and afreets* rave,
> Till these in horror shrink away
> From spectre more accursed than they!

Vampires never die. Revived by copious quantities of printers' ink, they constantly burst through the vellum bonds of their literary tombs.

In their employment of the undead, Keats, Byron and Dr Polidori were, relatively speaking, late arrivals. Popular interest had been fanned throughout the seventeenth century by a quantity of sensational journalism that made the normally shrewd Jean-Jacques Rousseau declare: 'If ever there was in the world a warranted and proven history, it is that of vampires: nothing is lacking, official reports, testimonials of persons of standing, of surgeons, clergymen, of judges; the judicial evidence is all-embracing.' This is typical scaremongering. To summarise the vampire stories of Eastern Europe would be a mindless, exacting task, for in these too-numerous, irrationally connected narratives that climax in inhumation, staking

---

* A demon or ghoul.

and burning, a high pinnacle of tedium is achieved – not even the browning pages of Hansard can compete with drollery of such quality.

In contrast with the vibrant credibility of the Romantics was the wearier tone of the Benedictine monk Dom Augustin Calmet (1672–1757), the author of *Dissertation on Apparitions, Spirits, Vampires and Revenants* (1749). There is a battered air about the opening of his explication in which he characterises each age by a fashion or whim. First he tells us it was once the done thing for Europeans to make pilgrimages to Jerusalem, but then the tide turned and priests and nobles started making journeys to Rome. That fashion passed, and then there appeared flagellants in many districts, who spent an inordinate amount of time scourging themselves. When whipping waned, country tumblers and dancers appeared on the scene. At every street corner one was met by the sight of bodies flinging themselves topsy-turvy. Eventually they petered out and were replaced by convulsionaries who entertained men by having religious fits in public. After the rash of fits expired, witchcraft became rife, but that too in time became forgotten and was followed by the philosophy of Monsieur Descartes, the physics of Mr Newton and the theories of Mr Law and his bank-notes. 'In our times,' he continues, 'another drama has been enacted for sixty years or more in Hungary, Moravia, Silesia and Poland; it is said that men who died months or years before walk and talk again, haunt men and beasts, overrun the villages, suck the blood of their relatives, and that there is but one way to rid the people of this dangerous affliction; the bodies must be dug up, impaled on spikes, decapitated, the heart cut out, or the corpse burnt.'

But no one actually perceived vampirism – rather they were seized and possessed by it. An example might be the case of Johannes Cuntze, a sixteenth-century alderman of Pensch in Silesia. On his way to dinner with the mayor, he stopped to examine the shoe of a mettlesome horse and received a kick on the head. This blow dislodged his reason. He started to complain that he was a great sinner and his body was burning. Furthermore he refused to see the priest, and rumours about him became rife, including that he'd had sold his soul to the Devil.

Colin de Plancy published his dialogues with the Devil in 1825. He described Old Nick as eight feet tall, well proportioned, with the traditional attributes of horns and tail but no hooves. His nose was large, owing to having been stretched by St Dunstan's red-hot tongs many hundreds of years before. The Devil told de Plancy that he acquired the features people attributed to him: 'Thus at the beginning I had no tail, until popular belief gave it me.' As for his horns, they were fixed to his forehead by ladies and nurses 'who wished to terrify their little charges'. All these projected attributes and blemishes ultimately brought about an identity crisis: 'I am disfigured so as not to recognise myself. They give me every name and every shape.' De Plancy himself was a child of

the Revolution who had been taught to live by reason alone. He appeared to have suppressed the religious impulse in himself and, according to Kurt Seligmann, 'wrote many books on the Devil' because he subconsciously sought 'God at heaven's back door'.

(*Previous page*) Dürer's mad, magnificent evocation of the Four Horsemen is undoubtedly a masterpiece. The drawing is strong, harsh and pitiless and the infernal vengeful figures seem impelled to trample and strike down whatever lies in their path. The first horseman, usually called Conquest, rides a white horse, aims a bow and wears a crown. The second, on a red horse and often shown wearing black armour, is identified with Mars or War. The third rides a black horse and holds a pair of scales: he represents Famine – an association emphasised in *Revelation* by a voice quoting the prices of wheat, barley and other staple foods which have increased eightfold. The fourth horseman, astride a pale horse, is Death, depicted as a skeleton, and also referred to as Plague or Pestilence. The hovering Angel of Death seems no more than a vacant cheerleader, and note the bishop in the bottom left corner who has been trampled by the skeletal horse of death and is about to be devoured by a devil-dragon. (British Museum)

Heinrich Aldegrever made this engraving of John of Leyden (right) after the fall of Munster, probably at the request of Bishop von Waldeck, who wished to capture something of the power and the glory of the messianical insurrectionist. John of Leyden is shown in the full splendour of his achieved ambition. He is King of Kings, richly apparelled and holding a sceptre. The scroll and orbs reflect his secular and spiritual authority; the two swords surmounted by the cross stand for his dominion over the Pope and emperor. The motto 'God is my power and strength' was a favourite of his. Hindsight – with its knowledge of his cruel fate – casts a pall of savage irony over this portrait.

The ideal portrait of Dr Faust hardly suggests the legendary, arrogant overreacher, but more the trickster figure, possessed of a strong degree of low cunning. The original figure behind Christopher Marlowe's and Goethe's masterworks was Dr Johann Faust, or Faustus (*c.* 1480–1540), a magician and astrologer who was born in Württemberg and about whom many incredible stories circulated. Scholars love to trace the Faust legend and his many historical manifestations. Starting out as an ambitious, self-seeking upstart, he has come to stand for the questing spirit of Renaissance man, who is willing to defy strictures and orthodoxies in order to arrive at the truth. By confronting and manipulating the forces of evil, he masters terror and superstition and becomes the director of his own destiny. The symbol has fared better than the man, for the original Faustus, alas, was torn to shreds by demons.

Trafficking with the dead has always been considered an unsavoury occupation and this illustration of John Dee and Edward Kelley, standing within a magic circle and summoning a spirit, depicts the type of things for which magicians were notorious: raising up the dead in order to obtain supernatural power or to wreak havoc or malevolence upon an enemy or rival. Why anyone should assume spirits have greater knowledge than living beings is not known. So far, most postmortal information, filtered through the mouths of mediums, has been characterised by its flocculent inanity. Of the two, only Kelley appears to have performed such rites, but any lengthy association with the world of spirits and angels is liable to give rise to such notions. The spirit summoned appears to be a female – could it be the spirit of John Dee's first wife, who died shortly after their marriage?

(*Opposite*) Urban Grandier was a priest accused by the Ursuline nuns at Loudun in western France of wielding diabolic power over their minds. It seems he was a sexually attractive man who took advantage of his position, but the evidence against him was fraudulent. During the trial the devils, who spoke through the mentally diseased nuns, were called as witnesses (why Christian judges should accept the testimony of a spiritual underclass known for their skill at lying is a mystery) and two documents were produced purporting to be Grandier's contract with Satan. Written backwards in 'mirror writing', one was signed by the priest, while the other bore the signature of six devils. Grandier, found guilty, was burned to death on 18 August 1634, but his curious history impressed many, including Aldous Huxley, who interpreted the episode (*The Devils of Loudon*, 1952) in terms of scapegoating, hallucination and sexual hysteria, as did Ken Russell, whose film on the same subject, starring Oliver Reed and Glenda Jackson, made a thrillingly lurid phantasmagoria. Possession is still a popular theme and the enigma of the multiple personality – of an individual possessed by several identities – has not yet been properly explained.

Resurrectionists dug up dead bodies and sold them to doctors or medical colleges. It was hard, unpleasant work and had to be done swiftly. In such illustrations the emphasis lies on horror and revulsion rather than the breaking of any sacred or supernatural pact between the living and dead. Bodies are saleable products which can be exhumed and marketed. They can also have their flesh stripped off and feature in anatomy textbooks such as in the famous illustration (right) by Jan Stevenszoon van Calcar for Vesalius' *De Humani Corporis Fabrica*. The body is hung on a rope which passes through the eye sockets and around the base of the skull. The diaphragm hangs from the wall on the right like a piscatorial trophy.

The Scottish duo Burke and Hare achieved notoriety for murdering healthy people and trading their fresh corpses to the distinguished anatomist Dr Knox. Burke was executed in January 1829 but the equally guilty Hare, who bore witness against his murky associate, was released. He was rumoured to have ended up as a blind beggar on the streets of London.

Body-snatching was not an entirely British phenomenon: the lower illustration shows the body of Mrs Cassell being exhumed by medical students from its grave in Indianapolis.

Thomas de Quincey described how the effect of opium was to make faces and shapes merge into one another like ripples on the sea and the ever-changing metaphors of his prose mimics a similar effect. Similarly, long before surrealism, the Milanese painter Giuseppe Arcimboldo (1527–93) was particularly adroit in this field. He spent twenty-six years in Prague as court painter to the Hapsburgs, amusing them with bizarre portraits composed of fruit, flowers, animals and objects. Some find his work witty; others disconcerting. This face (right) draws in landscape, architecture, rock, foliage and even a skein of smoke which, pouring from the chimney of a nasal-shaped residence, curves over to create an eyebrow. Such whims may take the form of nightmare terrors to those hallucinating or under the effect of opiates, and it is easy to forget that much of our visual perception is a result of our education. We interpret colours and shapes according to various cultural signifiers. Our most lucid diagrams employ a symbiology and perspective that can appear incoherent to other cultures.

The levitations of Daniel Dunglass Hume were witnessed by thousands, as he did not insist on working in darkness. Apparently he was able to float, stretch his body and make other people levitate in his company. Similarly the miracle of Christ walking on the water was said to involve weightlessness, as did the aerial antics of the 'flying monk' Joseph of Copertino (1603–63). In fact, the latter proved something of an embarrassment to the Catholic Church – he was constantly 'taking off', floating up to altars, perching on trees and even hovering six inches above his deathbed. His feats were witnessed by kings, dukes and the philosopher Leibnitz. Levitation is also attributed to St Teresa of Avila; she described how 'a great force beneath my feet lifted me up', causing her fear initially, but later the sensation gave way to buoyancy and a sense of rapture.

Was God an astronaut? Aliens have been visiting the earth for centuries and were known to prehistoric peoples, argued Erich von Däniken in his sensational bestseller *Chariots of the Gods* (1968). Several ancient scriptures refer to sky-defying vehicles and radiant beings, usually identified as deities. Ezekiel saw God among a swarm of winged creatures 'that had the likeness of man and who sparkled like the colour of burnished brass' – conceivably an allusion to metallic spacesuits. Von Däniken found in the biblical account of angels mating with the sons of man evidence of interplanetary cross-fertilisation. Further indication of alien contact can be found in Mexican designs like the Palenque Astronaut, showing a man lying on his back surrounded by a complexity of devices that could be interpreted as the elaborate circuitry of a spaceship. The figure is tightly enclosed like a modern astronaut and is operating handles or navigating instruments. However, others regard such interpretations as fanciful and see such pictograms as a precise set of symbols which are translatable within the cultural context out of which they arose. As each age gives way to the next, new correspondences are always being found between past and present, but they are often projections rather than genuine historical insights. (Mary Evans Picture Library)

As Cuntze lay dying, with his son beside his bed, a black cat leaped into the room and scratched his face. Soon afterwards he died. At his funeral, on 8 February 1592, a tempest arose and continued to blow as he was buried beside the altar of the local church. After his burial, his house was shaken by poltergeists. Doors swung open; there were numerous bangings; the whole building shook. The morning after these structural convulsions, footprints or hoof-marks were found outside in the snow. Cuntze's widow was so frightened she started sleeping with her maid, but the ghost of Cuntze appeared to her, demanding he should resume his conjugal status. And the parson of the parish dreamed that Cuntze was 'squeezing him' and awoke tired and exhausted.

All this unrest led to Cuntze's body being disinterred on 20 July, six months after his burial. His body was found to be undecayed and, when a vein in the leg was opened, the blood that flowed out was 'as fresh as the living'. The corpse was taken to a bonfire with great difficulty – it had become 'heavy as stone' – and burned to ashes. A diverting tale, yes, but also a superstitious 'cluster'. In deference to demonic intrusion, the norms of causation are dropped. A kick from a horse, a cat, a storm, a burial, an undecayed body – all are run together, implying connection, but these incidents – if indeed they took place – may be no more than a sequence of chance collisions.

Unruly Desires

Calmet attributed the vampire craze to ignorance, misidentification, hysteria and superstition. Later explanations blame desires suppressed or projected upon others rather than reconciled with our natures. Every infant draws milk from the breast, a fluid processed through the bloodstream. Later erotic refinements attributed to the vampire – all that puncturing and sucking – have their source in an infant taboo. In other words, feasting on mama's body has to stop; the child must grow up and direct his energies outward. However, unlike the Sphinx*, permanently displaying the insignia of terror on its wings, people tend to subdue rather than integrate their secret

---

* Death's Head Moth: see A Tragic Butterfly, pp. 146–8.

desires – hence their secret desires fight back and proceed to disintegrate them. The idea is perhaps over-familiar, blaming everything on repression, for essentially a vampire is doing little more than taking an unconventional repast. The prospect of becoming a vampire is less alarming than becoming a leper, an inmate of a high security prison or a schizophrenic. It is an exotic fear, scarcely to be taken seriously, yet potently attractive to those aficionados who deck themselves in plastic incisors, pale make-up and flowing capes. To account for its fascination is not difficult, in that the myth is concerned with preserving and maintaining the vital energies of the body: an aim shared by drugs companies which yearly invest many million pounds. If supplies of fresh blood enabled people to live forever, pints of it would be delivered in crates each morning by a perky, whistling bloodman decked out in scarlet coat and matching hat.

VICTORIANA:
THE REIGN OF GHOSTS

THE GREAT RUSH OF CREATION

> Above all else there was the problem of human personality and
> its possible survival of death. Was a human simply a member of
> the mammalian species that grew a big brain and used it to
> produce speech, thought, crafts, science and technology to
> ameliorate its physical condition, and religion to confront and
> exorcise its fear of death and loss of loved ones? Was a human
> being simply an incredibly complicated electro-chemico-physico
> mechanism linked by the fives senses to the physical world and
> its neighbours or was there something else?
>
> *(The Archives of the Mind,* Archie Roy, 1996*)*

The secularisation of fear, which began in the Renaissance, was
complete by the middle of the nineteenth century when the
dominant philosophy was materialistic and the spectres of industry
and commerce oppressed the population of Britain and Europe. The
belief that life was dominated by overarching deities and disembodied
spirits had all but evaporated and the Catholic apologist, John Henry
Newman, in the fifth chapter of his *Apologia* (1864), admitted that,
although convinced of God's existence, 'when I try to put the
grounds of my certainty into a logical shape I find a difficulty in
doing so . . . I look out of myself into the world of men, and there
I see a sight which fills me with unspeakable distress. The world
seems simply to give the lie to that great truth, of which my whole

being is so full, and the effect upon me is . . . as if it denied that I am in existence myself.'

Even John Stuart Mill, whose utilitarian philosophy promoted 'the greatest good of the greatest number', went through a kind of spiritual crisis when he decided that, even if all his principles were realised, it would afford him no great satisfaction: 'An irrepressible self-consciousness distinctly answered, "No!" At this my heart sank within me: the whole foundation on which my life was constructed fell down. All my happiness was to have been found in the continual pursuit of this end. The end had ceased to charm, and how could there ever again be any interest in the means? I seemed to have nothing left to believe in.'

And Charles Darwin, whose *Theory of Evolution* wielded unsettling social implications, there being nothing 'moral' about the best-adapted elbowing aside the weaker in the great rush of creation, deplored that he had lost his ability to enjoy painting and music, finding that his mind 'seems to have become a kind of machine for grinding out general laws out of large collections of facts, but why should this have caused the atrophy of that part of the brain alone, on which the highest tastes depend, I cannot conceive . . . The loss of these tastes is a loss of happiness, and may possibly be injurious to the intellect, and more probably to the moral character, by enfeebling the emotional part of our nature.' A secondary loss for Darwin was of religious faith – he had been disconcerted by the habits of a particularly ruthless wasp. 'I cannot persuade myself,' he wrote, 'that a beneficent and omnipotent God would have designed the Ichneumonidae with the express intention of their feeding within the living bodies of Caterpillars.'

A Tragic Butterfly

As a naturalist, Darwin regarded all living forms as inter-dependent, but it is significant that he singled out an insect as a villain. If the larger beasts sometimes attracted panegyrics, insects were often abhorred, with the exception perhaps of bees whose honey-producing qualities put them in a special class and ants whose modesty and industry were admired. The attitude had been rife even among intellectuals and naturalists. Henry More, the seventeenth-century Cambridge Platonist, remarked how loathsome spiders and caterpillars were, while Robert Boyle (1772) said that he could not look on a spider without feeling 'a notable commotion in my blood'. Even the normally well-disposed Oliver Goldsmith (1774) observed that many people, himself included, 'have an invincible aversion to caterpillars and worms of every species'.

And when they exhibit human-like characteristics, their capacity to frighten is intensified. In 1846, during the cholera epidemic in New York, Edgar Allen Poe retired to a house on the banks of the Hudson. Towards the end of the day, he was sitting by the window when, suddenly, a monstrous giant came down the hill before his eyes. The creature had a double pair of wings and a mouth in the shape of an immense spiralling proboscis protruding from a bush of black hairs, but even more alarming was 'the representation of a Death's Head, which covered nearly the whole surface of its breast, and which was as accurately traced in glowing white, upon the dark ground of the body'. The poet was trebly alarmed when this 'monster' opened it jaws and let out 'a sound so loud and so expressive of woe that it struck upon my nerves like a bell, and . . . I fell at once, fainting, to the floor.'

Poe vastly magnified the size of the Death's Head Moth or Sphinx. Far from swooping down the hill, it was stepping along a spider's web stretched across the window pane. Yet even whittled down to its true dimensions, the Sphinx has disquieting features. A book of natural history records that it 'can easily provoke a feeling of terror because of the mournful cry it emits and the funereal symbol decorating its chest'. The horror of the Sphinx's otherness was intensified by the addition of human features, like the fly with the human head in the eponymous horror film. August Strindberg believed the Sphinx was drawn to plague spots, battlegrounds, cemeteries, places of skeletons and decomposition and, by constantly haunting such morbid localities, the long-imbued association had left the signature of death on its anatomy as on a photographic plate, and its near-human cry was a mimicry of the desolation it knew so well.

When Poe stared at the Sphinx, he saw horror as direct appearance. There was no intangibility about an insect that bore the stamp of mortality like an ensign and whose habits and appearance had been meticulously observed. In natural history – science, biology and anthropology – the detail being accrued during the nineteenth century was phenomenal, but some found themselves overwhelmed. It was as if the fullness of the achievements of the period had placed them in a state of lassitude. In the same way that sharing the company of a hyperactive person may inspire exhaustion or self-questioning, the proliferation of machinery, the eager flood of medical and mechanical insights, the sheer plenitude of facts and fallacies, left many bewildered and doubting. Perceiving variety rather than unity, pattern rather than structure, mobility rather than fixity, they began to intellectually 'back away' from the impassioned materialism. How could trade and inventions provide answers to the deepest problems, the issues of life and death, the survival of the spirit? So, at the same time as factories made machines that duplicated yet more machines, and a diversity of objects and household appliances began to clutter the surface of the physical world, there waxed a breathless interest in the night-side of nature, in ghosts, doppleganger, wraiths, spirits, dreams and hauntings.

Seance

Alongside the growing preoccupation with other-worldly matters came an increased demand for those who claimed they could commune or draw information from spirits and hovering 'presences'. The long-laid ghouls who haunted the ancestral tombs of Bronze Age man returned not to terrorise, not to spread infection or madness, but to discourse politely with any listening ear. After the stir caused in 1848 by the antics of the Fox sisters at Hydesville, New York, in which the two daughters of the house claimed contact with a phantom rapper, the craze swept across America and over the Atlantic to Britain and Europe. Soon the gaslit seance room, with its select audience and ectoplasm-wreathed medium, was to become a much-fêted feature of British life in the second half of the century. Select audiences listened to eerie shrillings and explosive raps, seeing them as attempts to renew old ties:

A shadow flits before me,
Not thou, but like to thee:
Ah Christ, that it were possible
For one short hour to see
The souls we loved, that they might tell us
What and where they be.

(*Maud*, Alfred Lord Tennyson, 1855)

The most celebrated British medium was Daniel Dunglas Home (1833–86) whose reputation, despite a few sharp reappraisals, seems to have stayed intact. Accusations of fraud were frequently levelled at him – he was pilloried by Robert Browning in his poem *Mr Sludge the Medium* – but was never caught rigging the spectacular effects he invariably created. A delicate child, Daniel was born near Edinburgh, and at the age of nine he moved to Connecticut with his aunt. His psychic faculties manifested themselves early; his friend Edwin, who died young, appeared to him; they had made a childhood pact that, whoever died first, would reveal himself to the other. When the spirit forces became unruly, a Baptist minister attempted to exorcise him, but he could barely be heard for the violent rappings and bangs. Eventually his aunt, who thought the Devil had got into him, asked him to leave the house.

Home grew up to be an effeminate young man possessed of a fey charm that brought him numerous female admirers. As his unique abilities became known, he was drawn to leave America and take his skills to Britain and Europe. Soon he was advertised as 'The Modern Wonder', for not only was he able to levitate in lighted rooms, but to transfer the power to men in his audience who moved off the ground, too. At a typical Home seance, raps sounded, glimmering hands materialised, tables rose in the air, ghostly music drifted across the room and the dead spoke freely with the living. On occasions he thrust his face into flaming coals and took it out, showing no burns; elongated his trunk as he floated up to the ceiling; produced birdsong and animal noises; apported flowers across the room and into the laps of female admirers.

The medium's last years were spent with his second wife in Russia and on the French Riviera. The spirits did not appear with quite the same vigour as before but he would still hold an occasional seance. Meanwhile his body was wasting away with consumption – he died on the date and time he had predicted. The jury is still out on Home but many acknowledge it would be almost impossible to fake the effects he achieved. Others claim that supernatural agents were sinisterly manipulating him. 'Far be it from us,' wrote Eliphas Levi, 'to denounce Mr Home as a low-class sorcerer, that is to say, as a charlatan. The celebrated American medium is sweet and natural as a child. He is a poor and over-sensitive being, without cunning and without defence; he is the plaything of a terrible force of whose nature he is ignorant, and the first of his dupes is certainly himself.'

Life Review

Not only was there a great deal of trafficking in seance room and country house but attempts were made to put spectres into divisions and categories: crisis apparitions, animal ghosts, disembodied heads, wraiths, doppleganger and spirit voices. Apart from the nebulous area of spirit communication, material was collated relating to other mental phenomena: how the mind works under different conditions, whence hypnotism draws its strength, what sensations and illusions extreme situations are liable to trigger. There was a renewed interest in near-death experiences (NDEs), not so much in the context of hospitals and operating theatres, but in moments of duress and danger. Today mechanists attribute NDEs and similar effects (floating outside one's body, entering tunnels of light and meeting 'angelic' beings) to an oxygen-starved brain releasing chemical alarms and construing things in a faulty manner; dopamine, the pleasure chemical, is probably involved and time may appear to stand still. Over a hundred and fifty years ago, however, before the development of brain-imaging, credence was given to arcane data of this kind. A renowned collector of such oddities was the astronomer and psychic researcher Camille Flammarion, who drew attention to one of the most curious of psychological mechanisms: the phenomenon of 'life review' in which a person, during a fall or impending physical crisis, experiences a kind of weird elation accompanied by an instantaneous autobiography in which events are presented simultaneously.

The idea that dying – or crisis – acts as a stimulant to memory is far more than a filmic or literary conceit. Evidence suggests that incidents from one's life may replay themselves. Here is Flammarion recording the fall of a French cavalry officer:

> My friend Alphonse Bue was on horseback in Algeria, and following the edge of a very steep ravine. For some reason, his horse made a mis-step and fell with him into the ravine, from which he was picked up unconscious. During this fall, which could have hardly lasted two or three seconds, his entire life, from his childhood up to his career in the army, unrolled clearly and slowly in his mind, his games as a boy, his classes, his first communion, his vacations, his different studies, his examinations, his entry at Saint-Cyr in 1848, his life with the dragoons, in the war in Italy, with the lancers of the Imperial Guards, with the spahis, with the riflemen, at the Chateau of Fontainebleau, the balls of the Empress at the Tuileries, etc. All this slow panorama was unrolled before his eyes in less than four seconds, for he recovered consciousness immediately.

This gives the impression that the images proceed chronologically, but Father John Gerard, who had a skating accident as a boy, compared it to a picture in which 'everything was seen simultaneously and with equal clearness, yet without confusion, as an insect may be supposed to see through compound eyes'. Time appeared to halt, for although the duration was seconds, volumes were contained within it. Eugen Guido Lammer (1887), who survived being swept away by an avalanche on the Massif du Cervin in the Alps, recalled:

> During this deadly fall my senses remained alert. And I can assure you, my friends, that it's a fine way to die! One doesn't suffer!

A pinprick hurts more than a fall like this. And there's no anguish at the thought of dying either – or only to start with. From the moment I realised that anything I could do to save myself would be useless, it was for me a great liberation. This person who was being swept across the avalanche, thrown over the body of his companion, hurled into space by a tug of rope – this was a stranger more like a block of wood: my real self floated over the scene with the relaxed curiosity of a spectator at a circus. A wave of images and thoughts invaded my brain: memories of childhood, my birthplace, my mother. I could fill hundreds of pages with them! Yet during all this time I was coldly calculating the remaining distance before I would be thrown down dead at the bottom . . . All this without cries, without agitation, without sorrow: I was totally freed from the chains of Self. Years, centuries passed during that fall!

BLASPHEMERS AND DIABOLISTS

Indeed, we philosophers and 'free spirits', when we hear the news that 'the old god is dead', it is as if a new dawn shone on us; our heart overflows with gratitude, amazement, premonition, expectation. At long last the horizon appears free to us again, even if it should not be bright; at long last our ship may venture out again, venture out to face any danger; all the daring of the lover of knowledge is permitted again; the sea, our sea, lies open again; perhaps there has never been such an 'open sea'.

(*The Gay Science*, Frederick Nietzsche, 1882–7)

To the spiritually inclined, the 'life review' confirmed the presence of a Universal Mind. It showed people stepping out of a crisis and looking at incidents in their lives like fragments in a kaleidoscope. It had a 'religious' quality about it that appealed to spiritualists and psychic investigators who were often broadly 'Christian' in outlook, preferring not to contest the holy scriptures or offend people's sensibilities. But there was another current of Victorian scepticism that mocked and openly denied the existence of God. In the Regency period Shelley had been expelled from Cambridge for publishing *The Necessity of Atheism* (1810). John Stuart Mill had shocked the pious by declaring that, if God existed, he could not be altogether 'good' in view of the prevalence of cruelty, vice and suffering in the world. Frederick Nietzsche, more boldly, had proclaimed the death of God, a message suffused by a fierce pang of joy; for the interment of the Deity signified that now, at last, man would be able to act from pure self-regard, live a life uncluttered by superstition, guilt or fear. Religion, as Nietzsche saw it, had only been a long masochistic sermon, a tethering of the Dionsysian energies in favour of a tepid adherence to rote and ritual, a 'good life' without passion, without ferocity, without intellectual penetration.

If God had expired in some free-thinking households, in others he still paced back and forth flouting his opinions. His embodiment as a fear-inducing paterfamilias is well reflected in Edmund Gosse's *Father and Son*, the story of a father's attempt to shape every thought that passed through his son's mind and quash every jot of joy or self-indulgence. Not only was Gosse's father passionately religious, he was also a naturalist with a keen interest in coastal marine biology. The boy often observed his father 'while he soaked the flesh off the bones of fishes and small mammals'; the 'bare grinning skeleton of death' became to Edmund a familiar sight. When he was four, a lady showed him a large print of a human skeleton, saying, 'There! you don't know what that is, do you?' Upon which the small boy replied, 'Isn't it a man with the meat off?'

Christmas Day in 1857 proved bleakly hilarious. Edmund's father, seeing it as part of the abominable pagan rite of Yule-tide, allowed no decoration or mirth to soften the solemnity. In fact, so fervently did Philip Gosse hate Christmas that Edmund almost blushed if accidentally caught glancing at a holly berry. That day, his father declared, meals were to be served the same as normal and in no more copious quantities. But the servants, mutely rebellious, made a little plum pudding for themselves, and then, thinking it unfair to exclude the poor boy, wheedled Edmund into the kitchen and let him eat a small quantity of the pudding.

Shortly after, suffering a guilt-induced stomach-ache, he confessed his sin to his father: 'Oh Papa, Papa, I have eaten of the flesh of idols!' He was sobbing so convulsively that his father had difficulty in understanding but when the meaning was clear, he cried, 'Where is the accursed thing?' Taking Edmund by the hand, he dragged him before the startled servants, seized the remnants of the pudding, 'and with the plate in one hand and me tight in the other, ran till we reached the dust-heap, when he flung the idolatrous confectionery on to the middle of the ashes, and then raked it deep down into the mass'.

Idolatry fascinated Edmund who cross-examined his father on the nature of sin. He was told that God would be quick to express His anger if anyone in a Christian country bowed down to wood and stone. Shortly afterwards, when both his parents were out, Edmund hoisted a small chair on to a table, knelt before it and recited his daily prayers, substituting for the deity the words 'O Chair' – and then waited for God to exhibit his anger and chastise him. 'I was very much alarmed,' he wrote, 'but still more excited; I breathed the high, sharp air of defiance. But nothing happened; there was not a cloud in the sky, not an unusual sound in the street. Presently I was sure nothing would happen. I had committed idolatry, flagrantly and deliberately, and God did not care.'

Exciting developments in natural history caused Edmund's father deep vexation. Darwin's theory refuted the truth of Genesis: God did not make the world in seven days. Life appeared to have evolved over millions of years, and the proof lay in the fossil record. This could not be. Philip Gosse made it his mission to reclaim the Almighty and put Him back in the centre. Was it not possible to join the divergent visions of religion and science? He pondered over the matter until he found an extraordinary solution. God had created the world instantly, with fossils already embedded in the rock 'in order to tempt the geologists into infidelity'. The idea had more ingenuity than conviction, yet he worked long and hard on it, eventually producing *Omphalos* (1857) which, upon publication, was ignored or sneered at by the progressively minded. Even his friend Charles Kingsley wrote back and told him that he could not 'give up the painful and slow conclusion of five and twenty years study of geology, and believe that God has written on the rocks one enormous and superfluous lie'.

While the dogmatism of Philip Gosse was alarming, some found its opposite equally reprehensible: the weary acceptance of everything coupled with a refusal to educe any particular moral or meaning. G.K. Chesterton preferred monotheism to polytheism. 'If people won't believe in God,' he announced, 'they'll believe in anything.' Chesterton was a staunch upholder of spiritual worldliness and the divinity of ordinary objects. He showed astonishment at being alive and valued a truly light-hearted attitude: 'In perfect force, there is a kind of frivolity, an airiness that can maintain itself in the air . . . Angels can fly because they take themselves lightly.'

But he did have his darker, more melodramatic moods. In one of his essays he recalled a conversation with one of his fellow students at the Slade School in 1893, a young gentleman who would have not balked at being descended from a rat, a slug, an ape. He was a gadabout who delighted in exploring the various modes of dissipation (some think Chesterton had young Aleister Crowley in mind) and the immature Gilbert Keith was drawn to him. They liked to discuss God, morality, the Universe and other imponderables. The student had 'a horrible fairness of intellect that made me despair of his soul. A common, harmless atheist would have denied that religion produced humility or humility a simple joy; but he admitted both. He only said: But shall I not find in evil a life of its own?'

Chesterton responded by pointing to a bonfire burning in the darkness below the steps. 'In a fighting democracy that upheld Christian standards,' he told his companion, 'you'd be burnt as a devil-worshipper.' To which the student replied in his tired, fair way: 'Perhaps, only what you call evil I call good.'

He went down the great steps alone, and I felt as if I wanted the steps swept and cleaned. I followed later, and as I went to find my hat in the low, dark passage where it hung, I suddenly heard his voice again, but the words were inaudible. I stopped, startled: then I heard the voice of one of his vilest associates saying, 'Nobody can possibly know.'

The student's reply reverberated through Chesterton's conscience: 'I tell you I have done everything else. If I do that, I shan't know the difference between right and wrong.'

The essay is remarkable for the impact it achieves without specifying the nature of the young man's felonies and excesses. Omission of detail leaves a more potent afterglow of damnation than a catalogue of explicit vices. Evil, when specified, often emerges as petty and vicious, such as cruelty to animals or children, while a few dark hints coupled with Chesterton's moral outrage create a genuine foreboding.

Gallic Diabolism

As can be gathered from Chesterton's rather stagey moral indignation, in the cultivation of cynicism and blasphemous defiance the French outdo the English, and the 'horrible fairness' of Chesterton's young villain pales beside the excesses of Isidore Ducasse, author of *Maldoror*, a work of snarling egocentricity which later influenced the surrealists who prized its contorted artifice and nihilistic despair. Maldoror has something in common with Melmoth, the Faust-figure of Maturin's novel *Melmoth the Wanderer*, another archetypal outcast, damned yet almost heroic in his pride and arrogance. Melmoth sold his soul to the Devil in exchange for supernatural power; subsequently he spent his time searching the world for someone prepared to take on his unenviable destiny. But whereas Melmoth is distant, inscrutable and remote from the concerns of ordinary men, Maldoror is bursting with bile and rancour, but his target is not middle-class gentility but God Himself, whom he utterly despises, portraying the Divinity as a murderer, a cannibal, a visitor of brothels who wishes to conceal his indiscretion ('Tell them a bold lie, tell them that I have never left Heaven') and a drivelling irresponsible drunkard, quite unsuited to hold the reins of the universe. His stature reaches its lowest ebb with the sentence: 'While the cold wind whistled through the firs, the Creator opened his doors and showed a pederast in.'

Black Wine

If, among the intelligentsia and the scientifically minded, God fared badly during the Victorian Age, the Devil cut a dashing figure among the literati. In fact, association with him became a fashionable affectation during the 1890s. In France a sophisticated brand of Satanism had surfaced, induced by men like Baudelaire and Huysman, and the ripples of this current crossed the Channel to England. Writers ceased to express romantic revolt against God and turned their attentions towards the dark side. Shaking one's fist at the visage of the stars gave way to drowsy lusts and languid blasphemies. Max Beerbohm wittily parodied such posturing in the short story *Enoch Soames*, where he portrays a Catholic diabolist from Preston, author of a slim volume called *Fungoids*. In such a fashion-conscious age, even the Devil could not elicit sympathy if not possessed of youth and a profile:

> Round and round the shuttered Square
> I strolled with the Devil's arm in mine.
> No sound but the scrape of his hoofs was there
> And the ring of his laughter and mine.
> We had drunk black wine.
>
> I screamed 'I will race you Master!'
> 'What matter', he shriek'd 'tonight
> Which of us runs the faster?
> There is nothing to fear tonight
> In the foul moon's light!'
>
> Then I look'd him in the eyes,
> And I laugh'd full shrill at the lie he told
> And the gnawing fear he would fain disguise.
> It was true, what I'd time and again been told:
> He was old – old.

Such lightness of touch is absent from the writings of Baudelaire who took his diabolism more seriously. But he was not so much a devil-worshipper as a poet with an original viewpoint. His enjoyable *Litanies of Satan* identifies the Devil as the champion of the outcast. Satan is Lord of the Gutter Twilight wherein dwell the petty criminal, prostitute, pimp, drug addict:

> O Prince of exiles, who have suffered wrong,
> Yet, vanquished, rise from every fall more strong,
> Satan have pity on my long despair!
>
> To lepers and lost beggars full of lice,
> You teach, through love, the taste of Paradise.
> Satan have pity on my long despair!
>
> You who give suppleness to drunkards' bones
> When trampled down by horses on the stones.
> Satan have pity on my long despair!

Baudelaire's interest in Satanism was sufficiently academic to embrace the concept of the Black Mass. To perform this obscene parody, purists maintain, one should be an ordained priest of the Catholic Church. The 'mass' is not a self-validating act of worship but an inversion, an obscene parody of the Christian Eucharist, whereby Satan is substituted for God. Originally the practice formed the climax of the Witches' Sabbath when copulation with Satan took place.

It was not the poet Baudelaire but the novelist Joris-Karl Huysmans (1848–1907) whose diabolism aroused loud debate and censure. His novel *A Rebours* (1884) – a piquant blend of occultism, recondite sensation and literary reflection – stirred a mild scandal across the Channel by accelerating the moral decline of Dorian Gray. By the time *Là-Bas* (1891) appeared, Huysmans' interest in the dark side of magic had become obsessive. The hero of this novel, a writer called Durtal, is preparing a biography of Marshal Gilles de Rais, who massacred and abused over a hundred children. He receives a letter from an unknown woman whom he later discovers is Hyacinthe Chantelouve, wife of a Catholic historian. She is acquainted with a priest called Canon Docre who performs the Black Mass. Durtal persuades her to take him along. They enter a damp chapel with dingy, cracked walls. The face of Christ is painted so that it laughs derisively from the walls and the choirboys are elderly homosexuals with painted faces. Canon Docre declaims a blasphemous parody of the mass – 'Thou hast forgotten the poverty thou didst preach, thou hast seen the weak crushed . . .'. The women in the congregation begin to have convulsions. The choirboy performs an act of oral sex upon the Canon who afterwards distributes his seed among the congregation; he also soils the altar.

The Black Mass can be seen as an inversion of Catholic ceremony. Its lineage is obscure but it would seem to stem from a vitriolic contempt, a desire to defile the faith that produced the exuberant ferocities of Torquemada. Its shock impact depends very much upon the orthodoxies of the period, and in these enlightened or merely rudderless times, black masses have been advertised in various nightclubs in Britain and America.

The Mark of the Beast

An alleged celebrant of black masses and 'one of the most depraved, vicious and revolting humbugs who ever escaped from a nightmare or lunatic asylum' was born during the final quarter of the Victorian age. While some may contest Preston Sturges' estimate, it is true that Edward Alexander Crowley or Aleister Crowley (1875–1947) generated a collective shudder or frisson that translated well into sensational journalism. On attaining his mid-forties, he achieved the distinction of being called 'The Wickedest Man in the World' and 'A Monster of Depravity' – titles that simultaneously titillated and petrified.

Born at Leamington Spa, a son of strict Plymouth Brethren, he attended Cambridge University where he acquired a reputation as a poet and dabbler in the occult. Leaving university, he joined the Order of the Golden Dawn, explored China and India, organised mountaineering expeditions, wove spells and caused scandals. An outré figure in Edwardian London, he was acquainted with W.B. Yeats – thought his work 'lacked virility' – Arnold Bennett and

Somerset Maugham; the latter made him the centre-piece of his sensational bestseller *The Magician*.

A man of strong appetites, Crowley smoked hashish, sniffed cocaine, imbibed bodily secretions for ritual purposes and indulged in every variety of sexual rite. As England's leading 'black' magician, he worshipped at strange shrines; as a climber he scaled the high peaks of the world; as a traveller and scholar, he scoured remote corners of the globe, absorbing exotic foods and religious practices. Having frittered away a fortune, in old age he designed a special tarot pack. He was cremated at Brighton in 1947. His greatest achievement – in his own view and those of his scattered followers – was founding a new solar-phallic religion based upon self-determination or 'Do What Thou Wilt' and 'Every Man and Every Woman is a Star', the first invoking destiny and purpose, the second emphasising the unique, separate status of each living soul.

Despite such apparently laudable strictures, Crowley's status as a Utopian or Platonian thinker was never high. The complex disarray of his personality – his broad range of interests, his savage epicureanism, his startling, often shocking life – attracted the attention of the scandal sheets. He died much as he had lived, amid the flames of gossip and ignominy. However, with the advent of the 1960s and a renewed interest in ecstatic, drug-induced states, his rebellious, anarchic nature found new sympathisers and bookshops reported that Crowley titles were often taken without payment – a case of customers doing what they wilt!

His posthumous celebrity is easy to account for. He was a clown of the Abyss, walking a tightrope between the opposing cliffs of civilisation and mayhem. While shocking conventional proprieties, he displayed enough humour, erudition and culture to interest those members of the educated and erudite who were themselves possessed of an anarchic or subversive streak.

As a writer of prose, he is seldom consistently satisfying or accessible, but there is a concise pressure behind works like the *Confessions* where, instead of flaunting his leaves in the sun, the magician sets down the record plainly and forcibly. Literary exhaustion has taken hold, impelling him to trim his metaphorical excesses – at last the voice is brisk, urgent, authoritarian. The result is one of the strangest, most eloquent autobiographies of the period – a jarring, paradoxical work, crammed with gossip, abuse and vitriolic asides, yet also standing as the record of a man obsessed with personal evolution or 'magical' advancement.

The core of Crowley's character combined creativity with collapsibility. The Beast 666 did not mind things falling apart – loss, pain and suffering were all part of the web of existence. He acquired riches and spent them just as promptly. He betrayed friends or, shocked and shattered, they deserted him. Through frayed nerves or alcohol abuse, his wives died or went insane. At least two of his offspring were sacrificed to ill-fortune. But he appeared not to mind if the centre of his life slipped and possessions and loved ones were torn from his grasp. A hardline Dionysian, he swooped from riches to ruination and welcomed the rebirth that the latter (hopefully) brought. As Jean Baudrillard observed, 'The sadistic irony of catastrophe is that it secretly awaits for things, even ruins, to regain their beauty and meaning only to destroy them again. It is intent on destroying the illusion of eternity, but also plays with that illusion since it fixates in an alternative reality.'

And it is this attitude of dancing defiance (so easily degenerating into a mannered callousness, a stubborn coldness, a destructive indifference) that is responsible for the appeal, fear and repulsion his character provokes. Set on exploring the 'every self', Crowley did not value one mental state above another; always he stressed inter-relation, holding that 'ecstatic affirmation and sceptical negation are neither of them valid in themselves but are alternate terms in an infinite series, a progression which is in itself a sublime and delightful path to pursue. Disappointment arises from the fact that every joy is transient. If we accept it as such and delight to destroy our own ideas in the faith that the very act of destruction will encourage us to rebuild a nobler and loftier temple from the debris of the old, each phase of our progress will be increasingly pleasant.'

Noble words. His own career, however, hardly stands as a calm record of spiritual ascendancy, more a frantic assault, a determined ransacking of every variety of experience, from the brutal to the subtle, from the sensual to the ascetic. Investigating his past lives, Crowley saw himself as a reincarnation of Edward Kelley, whose delinquency, arrogance and instability he found more attractive than the pedantry and learning of John Dee. Magically speaking, one of his more original acts was to revive the Enochian 'calls' or the 'secret language of the angels' that had been dictated backwards to Dee and Kelley – apparently, if the words had been transcribed the normal way, their magical charge might have been prematurely released.

In 1909, along with his magical assistant, Victor Neuberg, he went off to the Moroccan desert and drew a pentacle and circle on the sand. Using the Nineteenth Call to enable access to the various 'Aethyrs' or spiritual planes, he called up various devils, angels and monstrous appearances.

In the most exciting of these, the Tenth Aethyr, he confronted Choronzon, the demon of the Abyss, who appeared in various disguises – as a snake, a beautiful courtesan, an old man – in order to deceive and overwhelm the magician. The record of this invocation, *The Vision and the Voice* (1911), has a florid glamour. It is a kind of spiritual wrestling match, a Marlovian pantomime, packed with denunciatory rhetoric as Choronzon flatters and philosophises, castigates and compliments, while Crowley and Neuburg attempt to maintain control. Theatrically speaking, the dialogue of this bizarre masque is rather good, the splendidly enraged demon vomiting out strong lines: 'I am the Master of Form, and from me all forms proceed. I am I. I have shut myself up from the spendthrifts, my gold is safe in my treasure-chamber, and I have made every living thing my concubine, and none shall touch them, save only I. And yet I am scorched, even while I shiver in the wind. He hateth me and tormenteth me. He would have stolen me from myself, but I shut myself up and mock at him, even while he plagueth me. From me come leprosy and pox and plague and cancer and cholera and falling sickness.'

Admirable, too, is the way in which Choronzon rebuked Crowley: 'O thou who hast written two-and-thirty books of wisdom, and art more stupid than an owl, by thy own talk is thy vigilance wearied, and by my talk art thou befooled and tricked, O thou who sayest thou shalt endure.'

At one point the demon, in the form of a naked savage, leaps from the triangle into the circle of protection and sets upon Neuburg. 'He flung him to the earth,' recorded Crowley, 'and tried to tear out his throat with froth-covered fangs.' The alarming intrusion was quelled by Neuburg invoking the names of God and striking the demon with his magic dagger. Disgruntled, Choronzon left the circle, made one more unsuccessful attempt at seduction, then grimly conceded his ruses had not infiltrated the Kingdom of the Holy Ghost: 'I writhe in blackness and horror of hate, and prevail not.' Finally the demon gave up and vanished, after which Crowley wrote the word 'Babalon' in the sand with his ring, lit a huge fire to purify the place and obliterated the pentacle.

'HAST EVER BEEN DOWN A MINE?'

> Lately in the wreck of a Californian ship, one of the passengers fastened a belt around him with two hundred pounds of gold in it, with which he was found afterwards at the bottom. Now, as he was sinking – had he the gold? or had the gold him?
>
> *(Unto this Last,* John Ruskin, 1860)

While magicians like Aleister Crowley were mere dilettantes, exploring the Edens and badlands of consciousness, other Victorians were forced from childhood to inhabit a physical reality of oppression: the manufacturing environments of fear in which nineteenth-century workers found themselves. The mills, factories and workshops of Victoria's reign were hellish, insanitary enclosures, unconstrained by laws pertaining to hygiene or safety, through which men and women were processed like Marx's commodities. To many poets and visionaries these toilers in darkness lived and breathed a topography of despair, like those adrift in James Thomson's *City of Dreadful Night* (1874). Thomson's city was a metropolis or 'necropolis' of the mind, through which grieving, hopeless citizens, their faces set in tragic masks, brood on their miseries as they walk past funereal façades and over the river of suicides.

Though less nightmarishly unreal, conditions in mines were appalling, with children and young people hauling ponderous tubs of coal all day and returning home so tired that, instead of taking themselves to bed, they threw themselves on a stone in front of the fire and passed out. There was little discrimination between the sexes. 'The men work in a state of perfect nakedness,' the Shaftesbury Commission (1842) reported, 'and are in this state assisted by females of all ages, from girls of six years old to women of twenty one, these females being themselves quite naked down to the waist . . .'. One sub-commissioner complained at seeing young females, clad in trousers, crawling on all fours, with belts around their waists and chains passing between their legs; the large holes in their trousers revealed a sight so 'disgustingly indecent or revolting' that no brothel could beat it.

One young miner was the Cornish poet John Harris (1820–85) who, at the age of thirteen, accompanied his father into the depths of Dolcoath Mine, over 2,000 feet deep and linked by some 75 miles of interconnecting passages. The journey was ricketty and perilous. Ladder after ladder, ledge after ledge had to be climbed down until the 'working' was reached. There the rock was blasted and the loosened pieces loaded into a barrow from which it was wheeled to the plot or collecting place and drawn up to the surface.

No safety precautions existed at Dolcoath. Amid the dripping heat and sulphur fumes, buckets would crash down from severed chains and fragments of rock shatter on the stagings. Ore-laden barrows creaked back and forth, their way lighted by candles which flickered like glow-worms. The din of hundreds of picks impacting on rocks made a vibrating mesh of echoes. Occasionally a violent accident would take place and these human disasters, coupled with the torrid, explosion-lit atmosphere, inspired the poet to make a comparison between Dolcoath and Hell. The likeness was apt – a pitch-black hole full of dark, sweating shapes, smoke, explosions and clanging machinery. Harris both hated and dreaded it, yet it so deeply impressed his youthful imagination that he was able to forge a response:

Hast ever been down a mine? Has ever been
Down its fable grottoes, wall'd with gems,
And canopied with torrid mineral-belts,
That blaze within the fiery orifice?
Hast ever, by the glimmer of a lamp,
Or the fast-waning taper, gone down, down,
Towards the earth's dread centre, where wise men
Have told us the earthquake is conceived,
And great Vesuvius hath his lava-house,
Which burns and burns for ever, shooting forth
As from a fountain of eternal fire?
Hast ever heard, within this prison-house,
The startling hoof of Fear? the eternal flow
Of some dread meaning to thy soul?

Is this 'hoof of fear' the hoof of Pan – inducing 'panic' and
foreboding? In Dolcoath, John Harris confronted the sublime and the
terrible. What was the 'dread meaning' that flowed to his soul? Was
it similar to the 'huge and mighty forms' that induced awe and
perplexity in the young Wordsworth? The atmosphere of Dolcoath
was infused with danger. Harris did not know what would happen
next, whether there would be a rockfall, explosion or machine
failure. It was this overshadowing uncertainty – this brooding on the
unknowable – that set the kite of his inspiration soaring. He resolved
to trap the terror in language. When he succeeded, his talent gained
recognition and a couple of philanthropic gentlemen found him a
job as a door-to-door preacher or 'Bible-reader' at Falmouth.
Undoubtedly this improved his health and extended his lifespan –
but he never wrote anything better than his mining poems. His later
collections are basically acts of mimicry which – though they trip
and chime piously – hardly touch the real world. They lack the
visually appalled power and ragged mastery of his early writings.

Although he endured poverty and hardship, John Harris left a
personal estate valued at £1,098 or around £57,000 in today's
money. While never achieving the poetic success he craved, he
managed to attain the status of a lower middle-class gentleman who

owned some shares, investments and pensions. That he had dreamed of attaining massive wealth is apparent in his poem *The Mine*, in which the estate of a rich man – a former miner who discovered a rich mineral seam – is evoked in paradisial terms:

> Grey deer are leaping round them, snowy swans
> Steer over silent lakes, and cooing doves
> Drop from tall trees to drink at glassy falls,
> Whilst in his noble dwelling Wealth sits down
> Dangling his shining keys . . .

If Harris had acquired the wealth he desired, would he have been happier than the diligent preacher-poet? Too much money may produce an equivalent deficiency in human sympathy. With wealth often comes an inability to understand the problems of others simply because the basic needs are readily accessible. Above a moderate sufficiency can only be heaped a luxurious dross: hence wealth brings its own unique fears. What is it about the smooth plastering of an ordered life that makes cracks appear? After a certain interval, a shiver may penetrate the high walls and well-watered gardens of a rich man's estate: the apprehension that one dark day, through bad luck or fiscal misfortune, these possessions could be taken away.

To that appalling possibility Samuel Butler gave ironic consideration in *The Way of All Flesh*. 'A man', he wrote, 'can stand being told that he must submit to a severe surgical operation, or that he has some disease which will shortly kill him, or that he will be a cripple or blind for the rest of his life; dreadful as such tidings must be, we do not find that they unnerve the greater number of mankind; most men go coolly enough even to be hanged, but the strongest quail before financial ruin, and the better men they are, the more complete, as a general rule, is their prostration. Suicide is a common enough consequence of money losses; it is rarely sought as a means of escape from bodily suffering.'

Fearing the loss of one's wealth posits how ownership stretches the boundaries of the personality. A property with a damaged roof a hundred miles distant can engender the same worry as a ceiling leaking in one's living room. No longer an isolated unit, the rich man has become a distended skin stretched over people and artefacts. The gabled mock-Tudor mansion is part of the self along with the presentable spouse, the Chippendale sideboard, the pond with fish in it, the garden with pergolas and statuary. So, if ill-fortune confiscates these, suicide may seem preferable to living divested of such hard-earned symbols.

LITERATURE OF THE CRYPT

A thing that has not been understood invariably reappears; like an unlaid ghost, it cannot rest until the mystery has been solved and the spell broken.
(*Analysis of Phobia in a Five-Year-Old Boy*, Sigmund Freud, 1909)

The brutal industrial reality inhabited by men like John Harris is noticeably absent from the Victorian ghost story with its tendency towards traditional decors and level-headed middle-class protagonists. In fact, in reading classic ghost stories of the nineteenth century one is struck by how moderate and disquisitional they seem compared with the exposed intestines and popping eyeballs of the spectres of the post-video age. Accounts of possession and poltergeist phenomena are found in the journalism of Defoe and earlier chroniclers, but ghosts find their deepest affinities in the Romantic flowering of the Georgian and Regency periods. They were a natural adjunct to the decaying shell-encrusted grottoes and creepered folly towers – the self-conscious Gothic or 'Gothick' of Strawberry Hill and Fonthill.

If one reveres certain periods of antiquity, one reveres the 'Spirit of the Age' and to believe in ghosts was almost a prerequisite of a Romantic attitude, a way of affirming that a certain heroic attitude, associated with a distant 'Age of Faith', lived on and breathed relevance into the present. Romanticism stood for the renaissance of the spirit and sought to unlock the numinous trapped in man. It aspired to eternity but was frustrated by the fact of bodily corruption. It sought out the mystical, the divine spark trapped in matter, yet also hid in nostalgia and fancy – evoking a remote and wonderful Middle Ages of the mind. Before an awe-inspiring, unpredictable universe, Romanticism wrestled with the sublime emotions of love, pity and fear, and relished the details of its own defeat. Eventually the Romantic Spirit was absorbed or transmogrified by the literature of horror, nihilism and black magic. The eternal yearning and tortured eroticism of Keats, Byron and Shelley came back in the form of vengeful, melancholy and embittered spectres.

The Victorians inherited the macabre mantle of the Romantics but added a little grisliness of their own. Aside from distinguished contributions from Dickens and Wilkie Collins, the bulk of work came from minor writers of the period who, by modern standards, seem admirably restrained. Furthermore economic and political expansion, the impact of places like India and China on the literary sensibility, helped to create a genre of 'Empire Gothic', an example of which is *The Mark of Beast* by Rudyard Kipling.

A drunken Englishman called Fleete pollutes a temple effigy in an Indian province by stubbing out a cigarette on the statue's forehead. Immediately he is touched by 'The Silver Man', a faceless leper with a body of 'frosted silver', and an informal priest of the temple; 'making a noise exactly like the mewing of an otter, [he] caught Fleete round the body and dropped his head on Fleete's breast before we could wrench him away'.

The priests of the temple had been angered by Fleete's behaviour but the Silver Man's reprisal appears to pacify them. After enduring the touch of the leper, a large blister appears on Fleete's breast, resembling spots on a leopard, and his horse becomes terrified of him. He is overtaken by a craving for lamb chops and is found crawling around in the flower-beds wanting to eat outside like an animal. Fleete's friends decide that they have to offer him assistance. East of Suez, they conclude, Providence ceases and Asian devils have their way. This reality must be confronted on its own terms. If Fleete has been cursed, the logical thing is to force the Silver Man to uncurse him. They find the leper, strap him to a bedstead and perform some appalling tortures on his body with heated gun barrels. This works; Fleete is cured and the priests of the temple deny that a white man ever touched their idol.

Less technically sophisticated than Kipling and far less anchored in the modern world, the stories of Sheridan Le Fanu (1814–73) create an atmosphere by means of tentative suggestion as well as coarse gruesomeness. He was a pioneer in the depiction of neurosis, and many of the delusions and dreads of his characters are explicable in terms of his own tortured personality, with its volatile blend of French and Irish ancestry. If the French side strains for stylistic elegance, the Irish pours forth in darkly garrulous imaginings.

An admirer of Swedenborg, who had written of the wonders and torments of heaven and hell, Le Fanu believed that certain abnormal physical and mental conditions open the channels of communication with spirits and demons. It is all a question of altering one's perceptions – whether from the effects of stress or physical abuse. After the death of his wife, Le Fanu withdrew from the world, becoming a recluse, only going out at night or to visit some bookshop where he would pick up a volume on demonology or spirit lore. He worked mostly at night in bed beside glimmering candles, then would awake at about 2 a.m. Then, after fortifying himself with a few cups of strong tea, 'he would write through a couple of hours in that eerie period of the night when human vitality is at its lowest ebb, and the Powers of Darkness rampant and terrifying'.

Le Fanu became increasingly disturbed towards the end. He had a regular nightmare concerning a decayed, forbidding old mansion 'which threatened to crush the paralysed dreamer' – an image perhaps of the collapsing fabric of his bodily and mental health. When the end came his doctor remarked, 'I feared this, that house fell at last.'

V.S. Pritchett admired Le Fanu's story *Green Tea* which is cast in barely noticeable epistolary form. It concerns Doctor Hesselius, a kind of clinical metaphysician, who meets the Reverend Jennings – a deeply troubled clergyman. Initially Jennings is afraid to confide but eventually he opens up, relating how he embarked on a study of paganism, fortified by tobacco, coffee and tea. At first he used ordinary black tea but later became addicted to the green variety, which he found intensified his power of thought. After a day's library hunting, he returned home on an omnibus and saw a little black monkey grinning at him. This spectre dogged his footsteps and became more active and aggressive, sometimes appearing in the pulpit, springing on to the page in the Bible that he happened to be reading to his congregation. No one but the Reverend Jennings saw the creature, and he thought that he was unwittingly sliding into the machinery of Hell. Anxious to help, Dr Hesselius tells the clergyman to contact him when he next sees the monkey, so that he can carry out an investigation. The following day Dr Hesselius receives an urgent call. He rushes over to the house but finds the unfortunate man has cut his throat with a razor. It transpires that the clergyman's odd delusion was provoked by consuming large quantities of green tea which excites the brain, forming 'a surface' on which spirits may wreak mischief.

In other words, a physical agent – green tea – draws the veil separating the world of matter from that of spirit. A mental trapdoor flips open admitting a little black malevolent monkey, the archetypal Pan or trickster figure, who taunts the unfortunate clergyman to the point of suicide. Critics have interpreted the hairy nimble primate as a symbol of repressed sexuality – although the clergyman's true passion seems to have been for his books. *Green Tea* was not a particularly horrifying story, but it was an original one, for Le Fanu was anticipating Conan Doyle in the use of scientific analysis to account for psychic events.

A Face of Crumpled Linen

One admirer of Le Fanu was M.R. James, whose ghost stories are effectively written tales of unease with strongly drawn backgrounds. His frequent allusions to and quotations from spurious documents anticipates Jorge Luis Borges, who was also fond of appraising the literary merits of the non-existent. James formed clear ideas about how stories of the supernatural should proceed. 'The ghost', he wrote, 'should be malevolent or odious: amiable or helpful apparitions are all very well in fairy tales or in local legends, but I have no use for them.' He distrusted the occult tale, for that put the whole issue on a quasi-scientific plane, and thought that 'a slight haze of distance' was beneficial to the ghost story. His technique is straightforward although highly polished. A fairly long leisurely opening with one unsettling hint, then a few more pages of relaxed narrative with more hints, followed by an intense horrific revelation which is usually left unexplained. As one moves towards the climax, the use of summary becomes more pronounced; inessentials are cut and the pace quickens. It does not seem so when reading, but it actually is a rather abrupt method, like talking to someone at length on a mildly interesting subject until a faint glaze falls over his eye, then savagely administering a few hard kicks on the shins.

One of his most anthologised tales, *Oh! Whistle And I'll Come To You, My Lad*, begins with a professor of ontography taking a holiday on the Norfolk coast. A colleague had asked him to look over a Templars' preceptory and, during a game of golf, he comes across the site, probes the ground with a knife and digs out a cylindrical metal tube. Taking the whistle back to the inn, he cleans it and discovers a Latin inscription carved upon it – 'Whistle, and I'll come to you.' He blows through it and is startled at the note, which had 'a quality of infinite distance . . . He saw quite clearly for a moment a vision of a wide, dark expanse at night, with a fresh wind blowing, and in the midst a lonely figure.' Later, when he tries to get to sleep, he sees this figure again upon the beach, a bobbing black object, a man running, jumping, apparently clad in pale draperies. Then, becoming aware of a movement in the empty bed on the opposite side of the room, the same apparition reveals itself; apparently blind, seeming to feel about in a groping, random fashion, it had 'an intensely horrible face of crumpled linen'.

This vision has been sarcastically attributed to an inhibited academic's guilt complex over masturbation. No explanation is offered for the manifestation, which was convincingly filmed for the BBC by Jonathan Miller. The whistle which literally calls back the past is an excellent ploy and the setting is well evoked – yet despite these surface merits, *Oh! Whistle* is flawed by its papery characters and lack of emotional depth. The evil wraith alone is not enough to lift a story which presents so few insights or ideas.

A critic once noted how Breughel the Elder introduced a vague and distant figure into the backgrounds of his paintings, as a kind of mystery component; Monty James sketches a similar device into his foregrounds, except its identity is never seriously in doubt: it is the pursuing spectre of death and bodily corruption. His scholars lift the lid on long-interned skeletons who play havoc with their sensibilities. But beyond unhinging the minds of know-all academics, his apparitions have litte rhyme or reason. If there is something lacking, it is an attempt to mesh atmosphere and psychology, as J.M. Barrie did when he made a strong maternal instinct the *raison d'être* for the lost spirit in Mary Rose. Monty James's tales often show a pleasing obliquity and erudition, but the insights seem to be absent or ordinary. The solidity and security of James's life and background may be partly to blame. Son of a Suffolk rector, Provost of King's College, Cambridge, and of Eton, the diligent don's literary productions tend to be ingenious and well constructed but ultimately sombre and barren – like a not-too-interesting Victorian parish church.

Enter the Count

Both Le Fanu and M.R. James attempted a vampire tale but neither managed to produce anything as unsettling as *Viy* (pronounced Vay) by the shy, self-torturing Nikolai Gogol (1809–52), a Russian author of hypochondriac tendencies. Into what would otherwise have been a workmanlike fusion of folklore and social observation, Gogol injects madcap absurdism and religious fervour.

A philosophy student, Thomas Brutus, along with a couple of friends, leaves a theological seminary and sets off on foot to spend a holiday with his parents. At nightfall the three students stop at a village and ask an old woman to put them up. She agrees and places one in her hut, another in a shed and the third in a sheep pen. Thomas Brutus lies down to sleep and sees the old woman advancing towards him with her arms outstretched. His body is locked by some evil enchantment and he cannot push her away. Straddling his back, she beats and bruises him, then rides him up into the sky, using her broomstick as a crop. To protect himself, he recites a prayer, forcing the witch to descend. Once grounded, he turns on her, hoping to thrash the monster to death, but finds himself chastising 'a lovely girl with magnificent tresses hanging loose and lashes long as arrows'. She is moaning and raising her bare white arms in fear. Filled with terror, he flees from the spot. Later the rector instructs him to keep a deathwatch over the body of a woman in the church. With nothing but a lighted candle, Thomas Brutus keeps vigil beside the open coffin. When he finds the body is that of the beautiful witch, he is overcome with fear. He draws a chalk circle around his feet to ward off evil, but the corpse, animated by a ferocious desire, rises up and advances towards him, then returns to her coffin, which itself takes off and flies around the church with a high, whistling sound. The windows shatter; the doors are wrenched off; the icons crash to the floor. Thomas Brutus recites an exorcism but the demons respond by summoning Viy, the chief of the earth spirits, a hideous gnome covered in clay with feet shaped like tree roots and eyelids that droop to the ground. Brutus knows that he must avoid looking at him if he wishes to survive. But curiosity overcomes him and he takes one glance and is literally scared to death. The cock crows for the second time and the spirits attempt to fly away but many remain, caught in the doors and windows of the church. When the priest calls in the morning, he finds the dead man and is appalled at the profanation of the holy sanctuary.

The horror of *Viy* lies in its blending of physicality and morbid fantasy. It is by turns harsh, sensitive, slightly crazy and possessed of a topsy-turvy logic. Before supernatural elements overwhelm the narrative, the rowdy, hard-drinking students are vividly presented along with the Bratsky monastery and the Cossack community. Neither is the sexual aspect of vampirism shirked: the witch's attractiveness is brought to the fore – a bewitching seductress who literally 'unmans' Thomas Brutus.

Perhaps it is merely a superficial knowledge of Gogol's life which makes one detect fierce repression here. The climactic end is akin to a violent unclenching, the psyche bursting apart like an exploding puffball, letting fly dark spores of terror and loathing. Sexual timidity hides at the core but other traumas are apparent. The attractive witch denotes the female libido; the flying coffin mental instability; the evil gnome the powers of darkness and decay; the chalk circle the fragile limits of human influence.

While *Viy* is relatively little known, *Dracula* by Bram Stoker is ubiquitous and renascent. Judged purely as an example of narrative skill, the vampire novel rates high, for it is told through the media of four journals, three sets of correspondence, newspaper reports, a ship's log and – innovatory at the time – a phonograph record. The method was inherited from Charles Maturin's *Melmoth the Wanderer*, a tale of a doomed but salvation-seeking magician, the literary equivalent of Gustave Doré's etchings of the Wandering Jew.

Dracula is the king of vampires and sucks blood from his victims in order to sustain life for an indefinite length. Perhaps it is his batlike connotations which make the gorge rise – after all, his blood-drinking habits are scarcely different from the flesh-eating habits of the larger proportion of humans, many of whom enjoy black (blood) pudding! Undeniably the novel has the disagreeable atmosphere of an unventilated crypt. Shadowed in grey-blue light, devoid of humour, steeped in neurosis, palpitations and the fetid breath of broken tombs, *Dracula* is powerfully rather than elegantly written. Its impactive gloom is not diluted by the faintest trace of nuance, irony, character analysis or philosophical reflection. Cold soil, gushing blood, garlic, crucifixes, iron stakes and wolves are its primary symbols. In one shudderingly unpleasant scene a tearful mother rebukes the Count for making away with her newborn child for cannibalistic purposes. Also the sexual overtones are far more pronounced than in previous horror stories. It is recorded that Stoker himself, reacting against his wife's frigidity, enjoyed regular liaisons with prostitutes from whom he contracted syphilis. Perhaps the dilations of terror and loathing in the vampire novel express his physical distress.

Professor Leonard Wolf wrote that from the novel 'there rises images so dreamlike and yet so imperative that we experience them as ancient allegories. Everywhere one looks, there flicker the shadows of primordial struggles . . . sex in all its unimaginable innocence, or sex reeking with the full perfume of the swamp. And these urgencies are seen or sensed through a hot wash of blood which . . . fascinates us nearly to the point of shame.' This is well-put, although the fascination of that wasteful expenditure of blood is questionable, unless one shares the Count's enthusiasms.

The eroticism, however, is another matter. Passages of lick-lipping sensuality hint that the Count's activity has a pleasurable pay-off, while his trio of female vampires are agile, voluptuous and dentally immaculate. According to Glen St John Barclay, they perform an act of oral sex upon the thrilled, trembling Jonathan Harker: 'Lower and lower went her head . . . Then she paused, and I could hear the churning sound of her tongue as it lapped the sharp white teeth and lips.'

With the advent of post-Freudian innuendo, the vampire's thirst lost its functional innocence. He was demoted to an ordinary sex-fiend like Frank Harris or Casanova. For the true horror of the Count has always been a reptilian singlemindedness that places itself outside human sympathy. Like a shark or famished tiger, Count Dracula needs regular refreshment and has little time for niceties or distinctions. To ensure survival, he will eliminate anybody – a trait he shares with Al Capone, Hitler, Stalin and others, the main difference being that they are less supernaturally gifted and present more convincing impersonations of human beings.

7

TWENTIETH CENTURY: THIN ICE OF CIVILISATION

THE BIG CRUNCH

> Only part of us is sane: only part of us loves pleasure and the
> longer day of happiness, wants to live to our nineties and die in
> peace, in a house that we built . . . The other half of us is nearly
> mad. It prefers the disagreeable to the agreeable, loves pain and
> its darker night despair, and wants to die in a catastrophe that
> will set life back to its beginnings and leave nothing of our house
> save its blackened foundations. Our bright natures fight in us
> with this yeasty darkness, and neither part is commonly
> victorious, for we are divided against ourselves and will not let
> either part be destroyed.
>
> (*Black Lamb and Grey Falcon*, Rebecca West, 1942)

In 1900 the German scientist Max Planck announced the Quantum
Theory, stating that light rays, X-rays and other rays were not
emitted at an arbitrary rate from a body. Instead atoms absorbed and
emitted radiation in tiny, discrete packets known as quanta. This was
the beginning of a long series of investigations that brought about
the steady subversion of reality. The ghostly microworld of the
electron, in which there are points of departure and arrival but no
connecting routes, proved a source of fascination and perplexity.
Physicists exploring these systems concluded that human life
appeared asymmetric, travelling in one direction only, from present
to future. Disconcertingly, some scientist were to posit a 'block

universe' whose initial Big Bang expands then contracts again into a Big Crunch. This induces a state of affairs like the Day of Judgement and would have made a suitably lurid backcloth for one of Thomas Muntzer's or John of Leyden's apocalyptic sermons. For history will start to wind backwards as radiation converges on stars; apples compose themselves on compost heaps and spring back into trees; humans step out of graves, pink flesh forming on their rotting skeletons, and grow into adolescents and toddlers.

What intrigued scientists disconcerted others. Although the microworld composes us, few people feel they actually live in it, preferring to perceive wives or friends as solid forms rather than as collusions of waves or particles. Many of us cannot even imagine the sun as a flaming ball of gas or the moon as a chunk of rock. Amid the hecticity of existence, we perceive the celestial bodies as phenomena that calm and reassure. Every morning the sun rises to warm our day; the moon comes out at night to soothe our dreams. In a turbulent and ever-changing world, these Newtonian certainties provide a crumb of comfort.

Dancing Sun

However, anyone present at the strange event that took place at the Cova da Iria, a natural amphitheatre at Fatima, Portugal, during the summer of 1917 might have to review any fixed ideas concerning the orderliness of solar behaviour. For what was seen – or thought to have been seen – had all the eeriness and unpredictability of the subatomic realm, all the qualities of the medieval millennial cults discussed earlier, for it channelled celestial sensation and divine transmission.

Two years previously, four children had been tending sheep in the vicinity when they saw a white figure hovering in the air. It had no feet or hands and was 'like someone wrapped in a sheet'. The same four children saw this apparition twice again during the course of that summer. Later the ghostly form was identified as the Blessed Virgin who promised to appear to the children and communicate a vital message to mankind at the time and date specified. News of these visions spread. The children's parents and the community became vociferously involved. After heated debate, the children were questioned by the religious authorities and kept in confinement for telling lies. But popular outcry procured their release, and on 13 October 1917 they went to their regular place to perform their devotions. By now the affair had become a matter of national standing – an estimated crowd of 70,000 had gathered in hope of seeing a miracle.

The weather was dull, dark and rainy and the children, accompanied by their parents, had to push through a mass of umbrellas to reach the holm-oak where the Lady was scheduled to appear. They knelt and prayed and passed into a trance. The Virgin appeared to them (unseen by others) and told them that, 'Men must correct their faults and ask pardon for their sins, in order that they no longer offend our Lord, who is already much offended.' Then she wished the children goodbye and left.

So far, this account has been subjective, limited to the children's interior perceptions. But at this point, something different began to happen. It has been described as a solar miracle, a heavenly sign, a dire warning. No commentator can be certain of what it was, but to summarise the various eye-witness reports, the sun described a series of circles in the sky or 'danced'. One witness – a scientist from Colombra University – reported:

> The sun's disc did not remain immobile. This was not the sparkling of a heavenly body for it spun round on itself in a mad whirl. Then, suddenly, one heard a clamour, a cry of anguish breaking from all the people. The sun, whirling wildly, seemed to loosen itself from the firmament and advance threateningly upon the earth as if to crush us with its huge and fiery weight. The sensation during those moments was terrible.

Was it terrible? Was the sun dancing or was it purely a mental construct? When the brain 'assembles' reality out of millions of tiny electrical impulses, there is always a strong subjective component that is dictated by the emotional configuration of the percipient. Hence some classify the events at Fatima as mass hallucination, others as religious revelation. At all events, the crowd's heightened state of awareness may have 'fabulised' the commonplace, for some present claimed they saw nothing unusual.

Angel of Mons

Those Catholics who witnessed the 'miracle' at Fatima had less need for hovering angels or intervention through a supernatural agency than did the British troops on the Western Front in the First World War. The squaddies' patron was St George – traditionally his spectral presence had appeared at testing moments on the battlefield. At Antioch in 1098, a heavenly army was reported to have rescued a band of crusaders from engulfing hordes of Saracens; the host included the saints George, Demetrius and Mercury, who, with a fluttering of banners and crunching of hooves, charged down the hillside and revived the Christians' flagging morale.

Nearly a thousand years later, the *London Evening News* featured a story by Arthur Machen entitled *The Bowmen* which has become part of the 'mythos' of the First World War. It tells how the English troops, under harrowing conditions and in the face of heavy odds, were assisted by the bowmen of Agincourt who miraculously appeared and dispatched with their arrows ten thousand German soldiers. *The Bowmen* appeared in September 1914 as a response to the retreat of the British Expeditionary Force from Mons. To the intensely nationalistic fantasy, Machen later added an introduction wherein he surmised that his story had inspired the crop of reports of the 'angel' seen at Mons. He was surprised when another author, Howard Begbie, produced the book *On the Side of the Angels*, which criticised Machen for his 'amazing effrontery', pointing out that an extraordinary range of visions – angels, knights, saints, bowmen and ghostly riders – had been seen before Machen devised his tale; he had merely picked up an actual event out of the air. The 'angel' version of the story first appeared in a church newspaper in May 1915. According to the testimony of an army officer, his company was retreating and the German cavalry were about to cut them down; they turned to face the enemy, 'expecting nothing but instant death when to their wonder they saw, between them and the enemy, a whole troop of angels'. The heavenly hosts halted the advance of the Germans and allowed the British time to reach their fort.

'If an angel appeared to Abraham under an oak,' commented Norman Douglas in *Late Harvest*, 'there is obviously no reason why an angel should not appear unto Lance-Corporal Richard Snooks, of the 69th Punjab Pushers, somewhere in France. But it surely does not resound to the credit of our troops – in fact, it is a distinctly ignominious confession to make – that the battle of Mons might have been lost but for the intervention of . . . a handful of angels, armed with bows and arrows . . . to supplement the efforts of the English soldiers utilising all the most modern appliances of artillery.'

Twenty years after the incident at Mons, another example of mob hysteria took place when Orson Welles adapted for radio H.G. Wells's *The War of the Worlds*. The drama was first broadcast on Hallowe'en in 1938, at a time when the world was in a state of political unease. Hitler had invaded Austria and the Japanese were marching on China. This may account for the sensational impact the play achieved. It was cunningly presented as a series of bulletins and interviews – these became increasingly hysterical as the depredations of the Martians spread and intensified throughout the USA. Hundreds of thousands of listeners, who had not heard the introductory disclaimer, were thrown into an appalling panic. Residents of New Jersey fled their homes and made for the hills; there were reports of suicides; telephone lines and highways were blocked for hours; and people ran screaming through the streets. Naturally Orson Welles quickly established a 'reputation' as a producer.

Blitzkrieg

The War of the Worlds was transformed into actuality less than a year later. Germany had invaded Poland and Britain declared war on Germany. After the opening moves, in which motorised Panzer divisions mowed down Polish cavalry, destroyed railway communication and demolished the Polish air force, surrender came swiftly and the German offensive heightened with attacks on Holland, Belgium and France. When Nazi bombers began patrolling the sky, pounding British cities, an awareness came into being of the distant enemy, the faceless man huddled in a cockpit who wreaks appalling damage yet never meets his victims face to face. 'As I write,' George Orwell opened one of his essays, 'highly civilised human beings are flying overhead, trying to kill me.'

The raids were intended to terrify and break the spirit, as surely as the Allied reprisals that devastated the Ruhr, Cologne, Hamburg, Berlin and Dresden. By undermining civilian morale and replacing historic squares and avenues with cratered moonscapes, they spread a web of tension and unease over the land.

The aircraft made doodles in the sky, leaving weird loops and aerial tracks, abstract, fascinating, yet remote from the destruction they signalled. At night the buildings of London were transformed into lunar palaces of ivory and bone. During the blitz the atmosphere was electrifying, almost surreal in its blend of appalling destructiveness and pyrotechnic vitality. William Sansom recalled the darkness shrivelling back

in the yellow flash of gunfire, in the whitish-green hiss of incendiaries, in the copper-red reflection of the fires, in the yellow flare of the burning gas main, in the red explosion of the bomb . . . These were the lights – but there were also dark streets, where suddenly a house of blackness collapsed with a roar, shifting down heavily like some bricked elephant lumbering to its knees, thickening the darkness with poisonous clouds of dust, shrouding the moment after its fall with a fearful empty silence, broken only by small sounds, the whispering of broken water pipes, slight shiftings of debris, moans and little cries of the injured . . .

Hordes of terrified, fleeing cats shrieked and leapt among the smouldering debris, trying to seek shelter underneath the rubble, trying to recover a lair that had been irretrievably lost. Walls would crash down like stage scenery, exposing the innards and plumbing arrangements, a structural anatomy lesson. People's privates lives and intimate belongings were thrown open like a peepshow:

They say that women, in a bombing-raid,
Retire to sleep in brand-new underwear
Lest they be tumbled out of door, displayed
In shabby garment to the public stare.

You've often seen a house, sliced like a cheese,
Displaying its poor secrets – peeling walls
And warping cupboards. Of such tragedies
It is the petty scale that most appals.

(Norman Cameron)

But it was the Allies rather than the Germans who were responsible for the greatest explosion of all. Ironically the event was received in the vibrant way that liberals had once greeted the storming of the Bastille. 'This is the greatest thing in history,' announced President Truman after the first atomic bomb had been dropped on the Japanese city of Hiroshima. The bomb, made from uranium-235, was called 'Little Boy' and was conveyed by a B-29 Superfortress bomber called *Enola Gay*. Dropped from 31,000 feet, 'Little Boy' killed some 80,000 people in the initial fireball and blast-wave. On 9 August a second bomb – a plutonium A-bomb called 'Fat Man' – fell on Nagasaki, killing around the same number. Within five years, half a million people had died of radiation burns and the accompanying sickness. Emperor Hirohito announced Japan's surrender the day after the second bomb. Truman told an audience at Columbia University that deploying the atom bomb had been no 'great problem' because it had achieved peace in the long run.

For the residents of Hiroshima and Nagasaki the ferocity and instantaneousness of the blasts had appalling consequences. In the duration of a flash their cities had been reduced to ashes, bricks, powder. Those surviving had little sense of identity or orientation. The context of their being had been violated. Locked in a zombie twilight, like lost souls in Dante's *Inferno*, they copied the rhythm of movement but could not configure the reality that had betrayed them. 'When asked whence they had come,' reported M. Hachiya in *Hiroshima Diary* (1955), 'they pointed to the city and said "that way"; and when asked where they were going, they pointed away from the city and said "this way". They were so broken and confused they moved and behaved like automatons. Their reaction had astonished outsiders who . . . could not grasp the fact that they were witnessing the exodus of a people who walked in the realm of dream . . . A spiritless people had forsaken a destroyed city.'

If the effects were catastrophic and sickening, to the detached onlooker the actual spectacle of the blast was thrilling to look upon. 'The lighting effects beggared description,' reported Brigadier-General Thomas Farrell, on the first atomic bomb test at Alamogordo on 16 July 1945. 'The whole country was lighted by a searing light with the intensity many times that of the midday sun. It was golden, purple, violet, grey and blue. It lighted every peak, crevasse and mountain range with a clarity and beauty that cannot be described but must be seen to be imagined. It was the beauty the great poets dream about . . .'.

Wotan

Beyond Hiroshima and Nagasaki, beyond the awesome toll of the death camps, public executions and massacres, the millions who died from enforced starvation and epidemics, loom two pre-eminent dictators, Hitler and Stalin, beside whose exploits the depredations of Genghis Khan and Ivan the Terrible seem relatively mild. In a memorable passage, C.G. Jung talked about the archetypes shaping human behaviour. He compared them to an old water-course in which deep gullies have been cut. They are the pre-ordained routes of nations, shaped by passions that control and direct the collective. Sometimes they dry up or are left abandoned, but when the energies of the nation-state are aroused or thwarted, the pressure builds and finally locates these ancient channels. Having found its ancient predisposition, the flood rolls forward, swelling in force and fury, tearing down dams and breakwaters. Like a branch, a leaf, a speck of foam, the individual is unresistingly swept along.

The analogy was used in Jung's essay *Wotan* (1936) in which he tried to dignify the Nazis in terms of fire, festival and comradeship, but Adolf Hitler was more cynically aware of the turbid forces he was arousing. 'All great movements',,' he noted in *Mein Kampf*, 'are popular movements, volcanic eruptions of human passions and emotional sentiments, stirred either by the cruel Goddess of Distress or by the firebrand of the word hurled among the masses.'

One imagines that men like Hitler and Stalin generate nightmares in others rather than reel and sweat before self-induced phantasms. But this is not so – for power, to a great extent, is illusory and time can bring about dramatic reversals. One moment Mussolini is the bellowing Duce; a year later, mutilated and hung up by his heels alongside his mistress, he is a drab sack of flesh and bone. Any dictator possessed of cunning and ruthlessness knows his power is a form of leasehold. In a world of shadows and shifting allegiances, there need only arise another as ruthless and devious as he. So being a tyrant does not preclude a nervous disposition. If anything, one has to be additionally aware, for the greater the toll of victims, the greater the harvest of vengeance and reprisal. Hence a dictator often finds himself extending the circle of killing, for the only way to preserve himself is either to eliminate all living resistance or to generate so much terror that nobody dare oppose him.

Even so, in the still of the night, clad in pyjamas and a suit of skin, the dictator may feel unprotected. Can there be such a thing as a proper ally or friend when so many fear him? Even the friends he has are friends only because they dare not be enemies. And yet a dictator must sleep after a day of torrential oratory and official receptions. The euphoric force of Hitler's speechmaking would not have been possible without a concomitant exhaustion – when all that frothing invective cooled to room temperature and silence gathered around a small baggy-suited man with a neat moustache and weak, soulful eyes.

Hermann Rauschning, quoting a close contact, wrote of the times Hitler would awake in the night, screaming and in convulsions: 'He calls for help, and appears to be half-paralysed. He is seized with panic that makes him tremble until the bed shakes. He utters confused and unintelligible sounds, gasping, as if on the point of suffocation.' During one such fit, he was seen standing in his room, swaying and crying out, 'It's he, it's he, he's come for me!' Perspiring and white-lipped, he let out a string of meaningless sounds, gibbered scraps of sentences and relapsed into silence. He was given a drink and suddenly screamed: 'There! There! Over in the corner! He is there!'

In old age, Stalin, too, was prey to phobias and dreads. Ever-suspicious and fearful of betrayal, his mood darkened after his seventieth birthday. Chain-smoking, doodling wolves on scraps of paper, oppressed by paranoias and delusions, he would travel on his private train protected by a vast entourage – guards were posted every 100 yards along the track. An insomniac, he demanded his cronies kept him company throughout the night. Nikita Khrushchev confessed how he came to dread these regular summonses. Not only were they required to watch Westerns with Stalin and appear to be suitably entertained, they had to consume immense dinners and drink throughout the small hours – in fact, Beria ordered that he be served coloured water until Stalin discovered his ploy.

As a milder form of sadism, the dictator might exert comic humiliations on his guests. 'Once Stalin made me dance the Gopak, squat down on my haunches and kick out my heels,' Kruschchev recalled. When Stalin orders one to dance, one dances – or later trips a measure before a firing squad! Finally, after a three-day orgy of drinking, smoking and eating, he died of a massive stroke. During the course of that long expiry, Beria poured scorn and contempt on his old master, but whenever there was a stirring of the eye or limb, or a minute sign of recovery, Beria would shrivel and become the craven, humble servant again. Stalin took three-and-a-half days to expire and a period of national mourning was declared.

That was Stalin in decline. His mind had blurred – not even the cynical pleasure derived from the execution of others roused him from depression. Just as Caliban did not care to see his face in a mirror, Stalin, who had once thought of becoming an Orthodox priest, did not care to see *Hamlet* performed in Russia. It was not a banned play – but putting it on might incur a dangerous disapproval. With its nest of fetid conspiracies and poisoned rapiers, the court of Elsinore might strike eerily concordant chimes among those living in his regime. *Hamlet* fascinated the Russians because it posed the question: 'Knowing all this, what is to be done?' It deals at inordinate length with procrastination and doubts – quandaries dear to the Russian soul. The great Russian director Meyerhold longed to stage *Hamlet* but Stalin closed down his theatre in 1938. Two years later the 'raven' called, and Meyerhold's beautiful wife Zinaida was stabbed through the body seventeen times and then knifed in the eyes, while he was kicked, maimed and forced to drink his own urine. Afterwards the head of the NKVD, Lavrenti Beria, moved his sixteen-year-old mistress into the empty Meyerhold flat.

Stalin himself had a talent for dark comedy. In exploiting fear to the utmost, he sometimes touched a nerve of insane ebullience. He would look over his 'lists' of people who caused a vague disquiet in his imagination, check a name, savour it, stand poised with his nib above the paper, remarking to his malevolent dwarf-henchman, Yezhov, who was later to be dispatched by his master – 'No, we won't touch the wife of Mayakovsky.' He hovered his nib over the poet Boris Pasternak, paused and pronounced benignly, 'Let this cloud-dweller be.' Reassuringly he told the historian Yuri Steklov that he was safe, patting him on the back, only a few hours before the 'raven' came for him in the night.

In his biography of Alexander Solzhenitsyn, D.M. Thomas tells us how once Stalin called the head of the music bureaucracy, saying how he 'greatly enjoyed' the broadcast of Yudina, the celebrated pianist, playing the Mozart Concerto no. 23 – might he have a recording? Unfortunately no copy had been made. Shaking, the producer summoned the pianist, orchestra and conductor, herded them into a recording studio and, knees knocking, ordered them to play the piece. The first conductor collapsed out of sheer terror; his replacement turned out to be equally petrified, and a third conductor had to be called to complete the performance. Only Yudina herself remained equable and unperturbed. The recording was completed and a single copy rushed off to the dictator.

Shortly after, Yudina received a gift from Stalin of twenty thousand roubles. She replied with a brief note: 'I thank you Josif Vissarionovich, for your aid. I will pray for you day and night and ask the Lord to forgive you your great sins before the people and the country. The Lord is merciful and He'll forgive you. I gave the money to the church that I attend.'

Stalin had killed men for cracking jokes at inopportune moments, for tiny suspicious actions, for showing the minutest stirrings of individuality, and here was this outspoken female donating his gift to a church and offering prayers for his soul. Thomas commented: 'Surprisingly, nothing bad happened to Yudina. Stalin may have thought she acted so crazily she must be a holy fool, and therefore to be left well alone. He was also capable of admiring courage. Let her go on playing for him, praying for him.'

THE TOUCH OF PAN

Again a footfall sounded far away upon an unruined world . . . and He was gone – back into the wind and water whence He came. The thousand faces lifted; all stood up; the hush of worship still among them. There was a quiet as of the dawn. The piping floated over wood and field, fading into silence. All looked at one another . . . And then once more the laughter and the play broke loose.

(*The Touch of Pan*, Algernon Blackwood, 1917)

In the miasma of confusion and bloodshed that characterised the first half of the twentieth century, one might assume men found little time for rural deities of past ages. But such an assumption would be groundless. At the turn of the century, a magazine called *Pan* flourished in Germany, devoting itself to Nietzschean ramblings, knights in armour and the salubriousness of Teutonic rusticity. The pipings of the goat-god reached England and were heard amid the undergrowth of Edwardian writing. With dry amusement, Max Beerbohm observed that 'current literature did not suffer from any lack of fauns . . . We had not yet tired of them and their hoofs and slanting eyes and their way of coming suddenly out of woods to wean quiet English villages from respectability.'

Definitely Pan was not dead, as Plutarch's anecdote suggested*, but was still with us, gnawing at the edge of the microchip, lurking

---

*   See opening chapter.

in the corners of those virtual realities in which we try to escape. Despite the depletion of his forest habitat, innumerable subsequent Pan-encounters took place when men and women, standing alone in some unfrequented, formerly sacred spot, felt an excessive, inexplicable panic. Mountaineers on high precipices would come over cowed and depressed, seized by an engulfing cloud of misery. The force was so potent that it led some close to the brink of suicide.

John Buchan, novelist and Governor General of Canada, recalled an incident in the Bavarian Alps. He was walking through a pinewood with a local forester when the panic swept over both of them. Without speaking, they broke into a headlong run until they collapsed exhausted on the highway below. Another man recalled a night fishing incident that took place on a beach in Deal, Kent, in the 1960s. As he cast his line and waited for the bass to come, 'the warm night suddenly grew cold. An icy wind tainted with an indescribable foulness was blowing towards me from the face of the cliff directly behind me. I had a terrifying sensation of being attacked by some supernatural force. My whole mind was dissolving into a whirling black chaos and my physical strength seemed to be draining away. I felt myself to be the direct focus of an emanation which was unendurably evil and unbelievably powerful. Somehow, like one groping in a nightmare, I managed to dismantle my rod and stumble to where the motorcycle was propped at the foot of the cliffs.'

In May 1966 Pan appeared in material form to Ogilvie Crombie, an Elizabethan scholar and member of the Findhorn Community, devoted to the promotion of all things natural. Walking down the Mound in Edinburgh's Old Town, he had the sensation of walking naked 'through a medium denser than air but not as dense as water'. This was followed by 'warmth and tingling like a mixture of pins and needles in an electric shock' and then he saw, walking beside him, a brown-eyed shaggy-legged faun who played on his pipes and told him: 'All human beings are afraid of me.'

Wild Man of the Pamirs

Not only was Pan still active amid the encroaching luxuries of civilised existence but other atavistic throwbacks made brief, enigmatic comebacks. Most surprisingly, the Wild Man – the uncouth club-wielding brute of the medieval imagination – was encountered in the remoter regions of Asia. In 1925 Major-General Mikail Stephanovich Topilsky was pursuing the forces of the White Army through the Pamir Mountains of southern Russia. His troops drew his attention to footprints in the snow which led to a cave by a cliff-face too steep for a man to climb. Nearby was a deposit of human-like faeces containing the remains of dried berries. Hearing a rustling disturbance in the cave, the soldiers opened fire with machine-guns on what they thought was a band of rebels in hiding. But out of the cave staggered a wild hairy man with dark eyes. Uttering inarticulate gasps of pain, he fell dead at the soldiers' feet. A doctor examined him and declared him not to be human. At first glance, he seemed to resemble an ape, but close inspection revealed that he was not anatomically different from man, possessing the same genitalia, but his body was covered with thick hair, his hands were slightly wider, and his feet much wider and shorter. He had a flat nose and Mongol-type face with slanting forehead, large, even-shaped teeth and massive lower jaws. The soldiers were shaken and moved by the sight of the strange hominid, lying there with bared teeth and desolate eyes, and felt compelled to give him a burial. They placed him under a cairn of stones and left him there amid the frozen wastes, perhaps the last true Wild Man – descendant of our Neanderthal ancestors – ever seen alive.

The Pamirs were one of the few remaining place where a prehistoric leftover – if such the 'wild man' was – might survive. As the population expands, the surface area of the globe stays constant. More and more people occupy less and less space. People have to opt for filing-block skyscrapers or a dome at the bottom of the ocean. Formerly an epithet radiating a charge of fear, 'wild' now obtained a pleasurable dimension, a frisson denoting open forest or lakeland where one could relax and interact with the benign and varied forms of nature. If wild beasts were present – bears, wolves and mountains lions – so much the better. It spiced the appeal of the district – after all, they were the aboriginal inhabitants with proper rights to graze and wander. Yes, animals had rights, too: to live and thrive unhunted, unmolested, unskinned.

If culling proved necessary, it was to be by instant and humane methods. Wilderness – in theory at least – was a precious area, no longer to be overcome and tamed pioneer-fashion, but to be fenced around, preserved and labelled National Park or Nature Reserve. These were areas in which industrial man could aerate his soul just as Jean-Jacques Rousseau had delighted in the diamond snows and air-baths of the high Alps. Land was no longer a commodity. Gone were the days when a peasant might have a whole field of his own to work, and instead the notion of body-space became a legislative issue. This steady 'filling up' and possession of the world's space entailed the passing of more and more laws. More people implied less freedom. Such factors, allied to the pressure of holding down a job and maintaining a family, sent men and women looking for new ways of relaxing or letting go of their inhibitions. There were bars, dance halls and discotheques, but there were few modern ceremonies that allowed young people to lose restraint or go dangerously mad. Those looking for equivalents find an outlet in substance abuse: 'I got stoned' or 'smashed out of my skull' or 'blew my mind'.

In such a frustrated context, Pan made his presence known through the common if unwelcome phenomenon of the 'panic attack'. Usually attributed to stress, overwork and sundry mental problems, sufferers found it 'difficult to cope'. Everything seemed to 'get them down'. A crowded street, a busy waiting room, a wooded lane – all produced fits of terror and shaking. Why? What was leaking into their systems and causing this? Arguably it was the same 'all' at work as thousands of years ago, inducing fear and alarm, yet qualitatively different from the primordial terror. The latter was induced by the prowling unknown – by the hostile wilderness beyond the campfire – while the modern panic attack seemed to be caused by an excess of knowledge and obligation. To sufferers, it seemed as if the bedrock facts of their daily lives – all the laws, mortgages, emotional upsets, filial obligations – were dissolving and congealing into a single mass – formless, threatening and pitiless. In other words, Pan was penetrating the centrally heated skins of the twentieth century and demonstrating that knowing too much can be as frightening and chaotic as knowing too little.

Borley Rectory

The 'Pan' experience impinges on one. It is not a thing one pursues. The very act of concentration or 'intentionality' tends to cancel it out. But once an experience has been categorised, there is a natural gravitation towards analysing its contents. From such an impulse arises the educative process that transforms yesterday's terrors into tomorrow's pleasures. Where formerly one fled shrieking from a ghost, by the 1920s it had become something to pursue as ardently as a beautiful woman. While the literati were sporting among the inky glades and parchment meadows, intent on trapping the elusive goat-god, the eminent psychic researcher Harry Price was cataloguing the phantoms reputed to reside in Britain's most haunted house: Borley Rectory.

Price has been criticised for preferring the limelight of newspaper publicity to the small, patient glow of empirical research, but it was through Borley Rectory that he gained his reputation as Britain's premier ghost-hunter. Since the rectory was built in 1863, various ghostly visitations had disturbed the incumbents: apparitions, poltergeist activity, spontaneous 'spirit' writing and planchette communication. Eerie stories emerged of kidnap and intrigue, of an affair between a monk and a nun ending with a rape and a murder. The families who lived in the rectory had troubled histories, too, which seemed to intertwine with the bizarre phenomena. Price itemised the latter as 'raps, taps and knockings; displacement of objects, clicks and cracks; sounds as of a door closing; knocks, bumps, thuds, jumping or stamping; dragging noise; wailing sounds; rustling or scrabbling noises; metallic sounds; crashing, as of crockery falling; wall-pencillings; appearance of objects; luminous phenomenon; odours, pleasant and unpleasant; sensation of coldness; tactual phenomena; sensation of a presence; and a fulfilled prediction.'

The climax came on 27 March 1938 with a planchette message from an entity called Sunex Amures who announced he was going to burn down the rectory that night – an event delayed eleven months until 27 February 1939. Such dramatic incidents make *The Most Haunted House in Britain* (1940) a minor occult classic. The level-headed, ostensible practicality of Price endows him with a Buchanesque authority. Here indeed we have a doughty explorer of the spiritual borderlands who employs scientific apparatus to trap the unwary ghost. 'In case the reader may wish to know,' he writes, 'what a psychic investigator takes with him when engaged on an important case, I will enumerate some of the items: a pair of soft felt overshoes for creeping, unheard, about the house in order that neither human beings nor paranormal "entities" shall be disturbed when producing "phenomena"; steel measuring tape for measuring chambers of hidey-holes; steel screw-eyes, lead post-office seals, sealing tool, strong cord or tape, and adhesive surgical tape, for sealing doors, windows or cupboards; a set of tools, with wire nails, nails, etc; hank of electric flex, small electric bells and switches (for secret electrical contacts)'. The list proceeds remorselessly, like a mad handyman's bottomless toolbox. Additionally there is a 'flask of brandy' for reviving investigators who fall faint from fear or injury. Borley's spirits had the unpleasant habit of tossing things around pell-mell – violently enough at times for Price to have added a miner's safety helmet to his list of gadgetry.

But was it the spirits? According to Charles Sutton (1950), Price used to walk behind investigators at Borley, casually shattering windows and attributing the delinquency to poltergeists. During a guided tour, he insisted the suspicious Mr Sutton walk ahead, but when the latter heard the sound of breaking glass, instead of pursuing the noise, he turned on Price and asked him to empty out his pockets: 'He refused to do so, so I plunged my hands into both his coat pockets and found that they contained a number of pebbles and stones of various sizes.'

The Borley story stands as a clever, complex narrative, and the rectory as an unpleasant, creepy place. But aside from Price's window-smashing expertise, most of the phenomena appear unrelated or linked only by messages from the planchette, raising the suspicion that Price might have employed the latter as a literary device to bind otherwise disconnected events.

After Borley, Price's most famous antic took place at the centenary of the death of Goethe in 1932. The year before he had announced that he would prove the fallacy of transcendental magic by performing a demon-invoking ritual – or act of 'black magic' – on top of the Brocken in Germany. Several Germans involved in the Goethe celebrations thought Price's experiment to be in the Faustian tradition – accordingly he was invited to fill a slot in the programme. Price agreed. After gathering the requisite accessories – bats' blood, scraping of church bells, soot and honey – he waited for Walpurgis Night to break on the highest peak in the Harz Mountains. There he found the organisers of the festival had drawn for him a magic circle, accurately designed in mosaic, near the Granite Altar. Unfortunately the moon could not be seen for mist – but nothing could be done about that.

Attending Price were the genial rationalist and radio personality Professor Joad; a spotless white-robed maiden; and a goat whom, it was hoped, the spell would transform into a youth of surpassing beauty. In addition, there were forty-two photographers, seventy-three pressmen and a hefty movie camera. Price recited the medieval incantation clearly but the goat remained a goat – as he had indeed predicted it would – but this unfortunate adventure resulted in him being dubbed the Goat Man; aptly enough, for Pan also is the Cosmic Joker, who visits mockery on the portentous and serious-minded.

KNIFEMAN IN UTOPIA: RUMINATIONS ON MADNESS

> On the pavement
> of my trampled soul
> the soles of madmen
> stamp the prints of crude, rude words.
>
> *(I,* Vladimir Mayakovsky, 1912*)*

At the Théâtre Récamier in Paris in February 1959 an unusual drama was staged with considerable success. Its author was the celebrated dramatist of the absurd, Eugene Ionesco, and its title was *Tuer Sans Gages* (or 'Killer without Reward') – indicating a gratuitous, motiveless killer. The principal character was Bérenger, a

Chaplinesque figure, well-meaning, liberal, benevolent, dragging a slight aura of pathos in his wake. As the play opens, he is being shown around an ambitious new housing scheme by its creator, the municipal architect. This is an especially attractive sector of the town with gardens, ponds and fountains. Moreover, the architect explains, the climate in this part of the city is regulated so that, however much it rains elsewhere, the moment you cross the boundary of the *cité radieuse*, you enter a world of perpetual spring.

Hearing all this, Bérenger is immensely enthusiastic. He praises the far-sighted housing scheme and the architect's skill and humanity. There is only one thing that puzzles him. Why are the streets of this beautiful quarter completely deserted? He is perturbed when the architect tells him that the inhabitants have either left or locked themselves into their houses because they fear a mysterious killer who stalks the streets, luring his victims to death by showing them a photograph of a colonel. Bérenger is shocked and depressed but the architect's attitude is blasé, hardened, matter of fact. After all, he argues, what is so bad about one solitary madman? Is not the world stuffed full of misery – 'Children murdered, starved old men, widows in distress, orphans, people in agony, judicial errors, houses that collapse on their inhabitants . . . mountains that come down in landslides . . . massacres, floods, dogs run over by cars – that's how the journalists earn their daily bread.'

The second act continues to explore the conflicts and confusions that underlie this so-called ideal community. We hear various cross-sections of society speaking, including a teacher giving a nonsensical history lesson and an efficiency expert calculating the money to be saved by stopping employees going to the lavatory five times a day and making them concentrate their natural functions into one session lasting four-and-a-half hours per month. Clearly the gracious architecture is merely façade; for the same social evils exist, stirring fear and unrest. At the end of the play, while walking the streets alone, Bérenger is confronted by the killer, a giggling dwarf in shabby clothes who carries a knife. Trying to persuade the killer, a degenerate idiot, to discard his pointless vocation, Bérenger embarks upon a huge speech, covering ten pages, in which he outlines all the reasons against senselessly taking the life of another: Christian, humanist, social responsibility, the vanity and pointlessness of all human activity. But none of Bérenger's words make any impression on the killer who chuckles and proceeds to advance with his knife.

It is interesting that Ionesco borrowed Corbusier's concept of the 'radiant' city as the setting for an absurdist drama showing a place that is basically a sham, a model community that is irredeemably fouled, a 'planned' paradise in which everyone lives in fear of an idiotic, compassionless murderer. The message of the play seems to be that revolution is not accomplished through architecture or anything else. Man is a flawed and fallen creature, and whatever external perfection you impose on his surroundings, the same old worm will awaken in the bud.

Only God and a Stone are Sane

In an age of social eruption and mass genocide, the killer-madman overshadowing Ionesco's drama stands as a representative image. He is an archetype who dominates much of the twentieth century, for judged by humanitarian standards so many of the acts of those in control might be deemed evil or, more charitably, schizophrenic. Definitions of madness have often been hazardous and relative. Prominent liberals were designated as mentally aberrant in the Soviet Union; passionate Communists were treated to long psychiatric sessions in the United States; and the Jewish writer Isaac Bashevis Singer opined, 'Only God and a stone are sane.'

The noun schizophrenia, meaning 'split personality' or loss of coordination between the manifold functions of the brain, was coined just before the First World War – a time of fragmentation, disassociation and alienation. In art, in music, in literature, the emphasis fell on splitting, fracturing, falling apart, the centre failing to hold. 'Buy, buy the damnation of your soul,' urged the surrealist leader Louis Aragon (1924). 'You will destroy yourself at last, here is the machine for capsizing your mind. I announce to the world . . . a new vice has just been born, one madness more has been given to man: surrealism, son of frenzy and darkness, step right up, here is where the kingdoms of the instantaneous begin.'

It was the Scottish psychologist R.D. Laing who set about elevating the whole process of going crazy by styling schizophrenia as unconscious rebellion – an attempt at sanity in a seriously disordered world: 'If the formation itself is off course, then the man who is really "on course" must leave the formation.' Madness was a form of involuntary opting out. Such ideas, bolstered by Michel Foucault's similarly radical *Madness and Civilisation* (1961), exerted influence for about a decade but did little to solve the problem of those whose minds buckled beneath the pressures of existence.

Later Laing's idealism came to be scorned. The idea that the mad should be entrusted to take charge of their destinies was naïve and irresponsible. And so were the facile attacks on hospitals as places of punishment and regulation. They gave the impression that mad people were not the problem, only the institutions that cramped their natural expression. Films like *One Flew Over the Cuckoo's Nest* – showing patients as victims of a repressive capitalist system – spread the misinformation further. E.F. Torrey wrote,

> You can psychoanalyse patients, change the social conditions and release them all into the community but these actions alone will produce little or no improvement in their condition. Indian Chief [a character in Ken Kesey's novel] will not be spearing salmon in the Columbia River but rather will be a mentally ill, homeless person in Portland sitting with frostbitten toes and hallucinating under a bridge.

Nevertheless Foucault and Laing were right to point out that, just as we store our sullied memories in the attic of the unconscious, a similar process is enacted in our treatment of the insane. They are kept in places where they will not be seen, save by relatives or those of a sympathetic disposition. The bad things we are, or may become, are best relegated to institutions that hide the flawed products, genetic rejects, of the social processing mechanism. In his angry book *The State of Shame* (1948), Albert Deutsch presented a picture of American psychiatric hospitals that rivalled the death camps of the Nazi holocaust. He wrote of 'hundreds of naked mental patients herded into a huge, barn-like, filth-infested wards, in all degrees of deterioration, untended and untreated, stripped of every vestige of human decency, many in stages of semi-starvation'.

As much as in Elizabethan times, the mad continue to create a deep dread – a desire to withdraw from their presence. They demand a feat of imaginative sympathy few are willing to muster. People realise they have little choice save to be nakedly and helplessly themselves. This frankness is disconcerting. Those who do not wish to take up their burden – who do not wish to acknowledge that destiny played them a twisted card – prefer them to be concealed and forgotten. What can a progressive society do with those who do not know what progress is?

Dystopian Fictions

After the humanistic vision of Wells and Shaw, based upon the anodyne of scientific and material progress, was rendered a mockery by the medieval barbarities of the death-camps, madness was seen as an escape from harsh reality. It became increasingly difficult for intellectuals to express faith in mankind's innate goodness. Theories of creative evolution gave way to the traditional thesis of the latent-beast-lurking-in-man. Dystopian fictions like Orwell's *1984* and Golding's *Lord of the Flies* (1954) prevailed over works like Huxley's *Island* (1962) which postulated a way forward. The literature of horror lost its moral pivot (never particularly secure) and themes of possession like Thomas Mann's *Doktor Faustus* (1947) and Malcolm Lowry's *Under the Volcano* (1947) proliferated. Civilisation did not rest on hard foundations but on marshy ground which at any moment might give way and engulf it:

> A mad animal
> Man's a mad animal
> I'm a thousand years old and in my time
> I've helped commit a million murders
> The earth is spread
> The earth is spread thick
> With squashed human guts.

> (Marat Sade, 1964)

Deaths on a vast scale defy the conceptual reach of most human beings. How can one imagine the deaths of sixty million Russians under Stalin? How can one take in the horrors of Auschwitz or Dachau? The brain numbs under the impact of the unreality. Empathy does not invariably ensue as, instead of bodies, they become huge abstractions stretching over the horizon of the inner eye.

In *Four Minutes to Midnight* (1981), Nicholas Humphreys noted the mental mechanism which responds to the personal, the intimate, but stalls at vast, giddying fatalities. 'In a week when 3,000 people are killed in an earthquake in Iran, a lone boy falls down a well-shaft in Italy – and the whole world grieves. Six million Jews are put to death in Hitler's Germany, and it is Ann Frank trembling in her garret which remains stamped on our memory.'

Un-American Activities

As we have seen, xenophobia is a manifestation of fear and the threatened animal is usually the fiercest. Patients in lunatic asylums are more dangerous frightened than angry. This applies to the politics of fear as generated between nations. To fear one's neighbour is to awaken to the fact that the terrible thoughts going through your head are also going through his. If you think of eliminating him, why then he has probably thought of eliminating you. So whatever guns he acquires, you had better acquire, for though you are sane, he is mad, though of course he thinks you mad, and himself sane, but then he would because he is mad. There is no way out of this dilemma save walking naked and shaking hands.

But how can a politician, say, walk naked if he has to operate within a larger mechanism of subterfuges? If one wants to stay high-minded, one should not enter politics at all. Openness and lack of suspicion will not necessarily advance a politician's career as speedily as blatant prejudice, singling out scapegoats or setting fire to men of straw. 'The most gifted demagogue ever bred on these shores,' Richard Rovere wrote of the Wisconsin senator Joe McCarthy who, to secure popularity and re-election, opted for the issue of 'Communists in government' as being the most topically arousing. His timing was excellent: it was not long after the Alger Hiss spy scandal, when 'Reds under the Bed' and anti-Russian phobia was at its height.

On 9 February 1950 McCarthy asked an audience of women Republicans in West Virginia: 'How can we account for our present situation unless we believe that men high in the government are concerting to deliver us to disaster. This must be the product of conspiracy, on a scale so immense and of an infamy so black as to dwarf any previous such venture in the history of man.' He held up a sheet of papers and flourished them. 'I have here in my hand a list of 205 names that were made known to the Secretary of State as being members of the Communist Party and who nevertheless are still working and shaping policy in the State Department.'

It was McCarthy who formed the Un-American Activities committee, a generously broad designation allowing the inclusion of a multitude of unrelated diversions and fads. As Arthur Miller observed, 'Un-American had numerous meanings depending on the level of sophistication to which it was addressed. Broadly, of course, it meant pro-Russian or pro-Communist but could also mean opponent of big business or of big unionism or a proponent of birth control or atheism. It was a catch-all for every kind of opinion.'

Years later, Miller wrote *The Crucible*, drawing a parallel between McCarthy's Communist witch-hunt and the persecutions at Salem in 1692. At its opening in Broadway, he recalled how 'a sheet of ice formed over the first-night audience when it sensed the theme. In the lobby afterwards, acquaintances would pass as if I weren't standing there at all. It was dismissed by the critics until McCarthy and the Terror were safely passed. One was a hunt for witches, the other for Communists, but they involved the same function of the human mind. Once you develop a siege mentality, anything is believable. The enemy is wily and therefore the more unlikely a person looks, the more likely he is to be the secret enemy.'

Fortunately McCarthy's influence could not last. Lacking integral idealism, he had made a political crusade out of a personal phobia, and such a posture proved inadequate in the long term.

Theoretically the 'red' enemies could be anywhere but were more usually found in places where McCarthy's limited inspiration veered: Congress, Broadway and Hollywood. His reputation collapsed when it became obvious that none of his scapegoats were rabid Communists; without the presence of the hidden enemy, McCarthy deflated and shrivelled. He had beaten his drum so brutally that the skin had collapsed, revealing the hollow interior.

Why were men like McCarthy allowed to realise their ambitions in a democratic regime? Why were they not stopped at an early stage? Aside from apathy and indifference, many deliberately held their judgements in suspension. Freud put his finger on the eternal struggle between the need to know and the fear of knowing. He identified the manner in which people suppress insights in order to conform or please others. They are, in fact, afraid of facing the implications of what they see – frightened that in doing so they expose themselves to attack. Suppressing fundamental insights enables them to drift comfortably with the social current. They end up doing what they do not want to do, being with people they do not want to be with, supporting causes that do not matter to them. Such strategies not only bar self-awareness, they also deter growth and change. Psychic timidity allows the subject to hide in a shell almost indefinitely – aware that any fundamentally honest act may force him to hatch out. Birth is always a painful process and it may be rendered more so if delayed to middle age.

There is yet another – far more dangerous – psychosis to which people like McCarthy are prone. This is when a man appears utterly detached from the havoc and despair he is generating. He is able to torture, imprison and kill with impunity. He does not go through life absorbed in his body – his ego has become 'disembodied' from the feeling part. He has opted to 'hide' in the painless realm of the abstraction. Instead of treating his adversary as a vulnerable fellow-being, he forces himself to see a label bearing the legend Communist, Jew or heretic. Hence, without a twinge of conscience, he can send thousands to death in the service of a theology or principle. Such men – Hitler, Stalin, Himmler and Beria – may prove deft at dispensing their policies. This is because ordinary emotions drain none of their energies from the task in hand. They have achieved something like the autonomy of machines.

The Fallen Hero

If Joe McCarthy was the archetypal bogeyman, swollen with rancour and acrimony, incapable of presenting a coherent policy, Jack Kennedy was seen as the reverse. Despite rumours of his boisterous sexuality and his father's affiliation with Chicago mobsters, his charm and buoyancy quelled the murmurings of reactionaries and rednecks. After his election to the presidency in 1960, it was not long before he became transmogrified into a mythic figure. Like Baldur or Adonis, he was touted as a symbol of hope and political redemption, and indeed his speeches were an inspiring combination of optimism and restraint born out of the granite face of the Cold War. 'Mankind must put an end to war,' he told the United Nations General Assembly, 'or war will put an end to mankind.'

After a short period in office, in which enlightened civil reforms were introduced and the threat of nuclear war only narrowly evaded, America was stunned by the news of Kennedy's assassination. It took place in 1963 during an electioneering visit to Dallas, Texas. Had a lone Communist sniper, Lee Harvey Oswald, done the deed? Or was it part of a conspiracy involving Chicago mobsters, rogue elements in the FBI allied to Kennedy's political opponents? None of the public was cognisant with the infernal wheels behind wheels that eerily turn behind the suited façades of government bodies. At the time, the shooting of Kennedy seemed like an assault on reason, a violation of purpose in existence. If such a thing can happen to the president of the most powerful nation in the world, who can deemed to be safe or special? The tragedy was Greek in its essential bloodiness and harsh swiftness.

The funeral was a monumentally solemn affair, superbly orchestrated – a ritual bandaging of the massive wound of the nation. Only something slow, purposeful and inordinately weighted by tradition could tell the population: life is this, dignity, purpose and ordered ceremony and not the stark nihilism of that rifle-shot. Seven grey horses with black-painted hooves drew the gun-carriage with its flag-draped coffin. The mythographer Joseph Campbell remarked: 'I saw death before me, the seven ghostly steeds of the grey lord Death, here come to conduct the fallen hero on his last celestial journey, passing symbolically upward through the seven celestial spheres to the seat of eternity, whence he had once descended . . .'.

HOPE SPRINGS INFERNAL: THE DEVIL IN THE TWENTIETH CENTURY

> Satan being thus confined to a vagabond, wandering, unsettled condition, is without any certain abode; for though he has, in consequence of his angelic nature, a kind of empire in the liquid waste or air, yet, this is certainly part of his punishment, that he is continually hovering over this inhabited globe of earth; swelling with the rage of envy, at the felicity of his rival, man; and studying all the means possible to injure and ruin him.
>
> *(The History of the Devil, Daniel Defoe, 1726)*

Jack Kennedy was a Catholic president. Whatever double-dealings might go on behind the scenes, the American public preferred a façade of presidential piety. Self-proclaimed atheists seldom occupied posts of high responsibility in the USA any more than vehement Christians did in the USSR. If the president does not believe in God, the reasoning went, he may well lack a sense of personal morality. In the past, religious rhetoric was used to back up political campaigns; there had also been a tendency to 'demonise' political opponents exemplified in Senator McCarthy who instilled the same kind of terror as a medieval witchfinder. His Satan was Communism just as his purported God was Democracy.

In similar vein Billy Graham lashed out at Communism on behalf of the Deity: 'A great sinister anti-Christian movement masterminded by Satan has declared war upon the Christian God!' For the middle of the twentieth century, this was a nostalgically medieval reaction. Hadn't Frederick Nietzsche, over a hundred years earlier in *The Gay*

Science, announced the 'death of God' as though it were an exciting, liberating event?

A bold declaration, yes – but few were actually delighted.

While there had been problems with the old universe of good-versus-evil, living in a godless universe proved a chilling proposition. No Heaven, no Hell, no Purgatory, no Limbo, no promise of eternal life, only that same faceless, all-engulfing Nothing which chilled the veins of Lord Rochester, made Soren Kierkegaard tremble and Jean-Paul Sartre reel with nausea. Man was just an incident in the cycle of evolution – one of the many life-flames destined to flicker and dwindle into a sniff of smoke. As for the illusion of consciousness – the self-directing 'I' or ego – that was a frisson effect of the neurotransmitters of the brain.

If God's standing was hardly secure, the Devil's was even more uncertain. At the waning of the Middle Ages, the Prince of Evil had divided into two figures. For peasants, he was a stumbling bumpkin whose low cunning was perpetually foiled by priests and moral superiors, while the intellectually urbane preferred to see him as a witty, decadent sophisticate:

> I called the Devil and he came,
> His face with wonder I must scan;
> He is not ugly; he is not lame,
> He is a delightful charming man;
> A man in prime of life, in fact,
> Courteous, engaging and full of tact.
> A diplomat, too, of wide research
> Who cleverly talks about State and Church
> A little pale, but that is en régle
> For now he is studying Sanskrit and Hegel.
>
> (Heinrich Heine)

In a Chicago production entitled *Hell Up to Date* (1892) a newspaper reporter interviews 'Sate' and is taken on a tour of the inferno. 'Hell is now run on the broad American plan' – a large-scale commercial venture. Captain Charon has abandoned his little tub of a rowboat for huge Mississippi-style steamers on the Styx, 'the only navigable river in hell'. The inventor of the barbed wire fence is made to sit on his spiky creation and tramps are washed, policemen clubbed until they see stars, quack doctors forced to take their own remedies, monopolists baked like popcorn and clergymen condemned to listen to their own sermons on phonographs.

So Satan, the arch-demon, was temporarily resurrected as a joker, an entrepreneur, someone who has lived a bit, seen the world and yielded to a few temptations. Such instant recognisability rendered him useful for advertising placards and brochures where he might appear in the role of lascivious tempter or gastronomic roué, egging one on to purchase a high-calorie chocolate cake or an elaborately coiffured tower of ice-cream capped by a nest of strawberries.

Not only did 'Sate' become the subject of parody, he was diminished to a mere psychism or projection. In a study of 1923, Freud identified the Devil as an archetypal version of the moody, frowning father-figure. In the beginning there was one God who, owing to irreconcilable elements in His nature, became split in two. His dark side established itself as a separate principle, Satan, and this process, identifiable in the myths of many cultures, also took place at a personal level. A father may both be kind and benevolent (God the Father) and cold, distant and punitive (the Devil) and the contrasting aspects account for our spiritual tensions: 'The unresolved conflict between, on the one hand, a longing for the father, and, on the other, a fear of him and a son's defiance of him, has furnished us with an explanation of important characteristics of religion and decisive vicissitudes in it.'

By contrast C.G. Jung was more positive. 'How can I be substantial if I fail to cast a shadow?' he asked. 'I must have a dark side also if I am to be whole; and inasmuch as I become conscious of my shadow, I also remember that I am a human being like any other.' The Devil was merely the shadow of God, or the human unconscious, where all the repressed desires are bound up like Satan in chains. These desires may find negative expression – in war, violence, rape or incest – but they are not in themselves bad, only akin to an excess of rich dark compost which should be spread over the rest of the soil in order to nurture growth and development. During dream-experiences, Jung believed he had confronted many devils, some harking back to his Alemmanic roots, such as the night before his mother's death when he had found himself standing in a dense, gloomy forest, strewn with gigantic boulders. Suddenly he heard a piercing whistle followed by crashings in the underbrush and the appearance of a gigantic wolfhound with a bloody, gaping maw. Jung identified it as an emissary of the Wild Huntsman, for it was January, the time of the Fohn storms, when Wotan led the troupe of dispossessed souls, like those encountered by Walchelin almost a thousand years earlier in Normandy. But Jung, who later witnessed the Wild Hunt and the host of the dead over Bollingen, was not prepared to countenance his God-fearing mother as a trophy for the Devil and concluded that Wotan deputised for 'the greater territory of the self' that lay outside Christian morality.

Satanic Abuse

However, there were those, including Billy Graham, who rejected the idea of the Devil being nothing more than Wotan restyled or the dark side of daddy. They sought to restore his full infernal status by pin-pointing evil as an active agent. Taking refuge in the atavistic securities of the Old Testament, they viewed global catastrophe in terms of the Antichrist fulfilling the chaos that is his destiny. In the assassinations, holocausts and 'abortion murders' of the century, they detected the signature of an evil genius. In particular, during the 1990s, Christian fundamentalists pounced upon contemporary 'evidence' that the Devil was rooting among the unloved, the angry and godless, inciting them to corrupt and abuse children. Thousands of instances were reported in America, England, Australia and Europe, many containing identical allegations.

The first British satanic child abuse case (1991) that went to trial involved two sisters, then aged ten and fourteen, who claimed they had been raped and sexually assaulted during rituals that took place at a gypsy memorial stone in Epping Forest. The accused, who comprised the girls' parents, godparents and a family friend, had drugged the children with an 'orangey aphrodisiac drink' and danced before them in cloaks and masks. The girls were later sexually assaulted by a 58-year-old gypsy called George Gibbard and his lover, Rosemary Ridewood, an active Christian who was also the girls' godmother, and a godfather, Ronald Smith. The latter placed babies on the altar, killed them and made the girls dismember the corpses and eat the flesh. The bodies were buried in the forest or taken home and stowed in plastic bags under the stairs. During the rituals, Ronald Smith, who claimed gypsy descent, spoke in tongues and invoked Lucifer and Lucillus; they were, he told the girls, 'angels' of the Devil. Furthermore, the older girl claimed, she had been taken at night to the gypsy stone, which had been decorated with horns and a black cross, and there raped, buggered and forced to perform oral sex.

Cracks in the prosecution case appeared on the third day when, under cross-examination, the younger girl admitted she had made up the long list of names and addresses that she gave to the social worker. She added that she could avoid being punished by her grandmother by furnishing the elderly lady with details of ritual assaults and indecencies. No bodies or signs of molestation were produced. The judge summed up the girls' evidence as 'uncertain, inconsistent and improbable' and ordered a 'not guilty' verdict.

Anthropologist Professor Joan la Fontaine was commissioned to write a report (1998) on satanic child abuse. In her view, high unemployment, social deprivation, class-war, recession, plus a plague of movies and videos dealing with devil-worship and alien visitants, created an atmosphere in which scapegoating and notions of conspiracies of black magicians could flourish. Children talking about Batman masks might easily mislead gullible social workers whose antennae were ever-alert for the Devil and all his works. In the United States similar pressures were at work, reinforced by the tensions of the Cold War and the economics of the Lone Ranger in the White House during the 1980s.

A great many of the cases hinged on the notion of repressed or hidden memory, some of which were recovered by hypnotherapists whose high-minded intentions were hampered by over-literal imaginations. The problem stemmed from the widely held assumption that the deep unconscious is a reservoir of the soul: a hidden 'self' is reflected there, a mirror of pure undiluted truth.

Unfortunately, as any priest or psychologist knows, the soul – or the deep unconscious – is a well of fantasy, dream and myth-making, and the wrong type of interrogation may uncover material of a bizarre, extraordinary kind. An instance is the case of Nadean Cool, a nurse's aide from Wisconsin who, during a decade of regression-based 'treatment', came to 'remember' herself entrapped in a baby-eating satanic cult, being raped, having sex with animals and coerced into watching the murder of her eight-year-old friend. She also discovered that she had 120 different personalities – including a duck. When she emerged from 'therapy', she managed to acquire some two million dollars by way of compensation and the term 'false memory syndrome' started to be bandied about.

It was fortunate that Nadean's therapist was not a witch-hunter or she might have ended up amid a heap of burning brushwood. For with an increased interest in reincarnation and the salvaging of previous identities, a growing number of people claimed they had suffered incineration for heresy or witchcraft. In March 1962 a well-known psychiatrist and doctor of medicine, Arthur Guirdham, received a letter from another doctor who referred to him the case of Mrs Smith – a lady who suffered from nightmares and shrieked so loudly that she and her husband feared the street would be awakened. Guirdham accepted the case and, as doctor and patient became increasingly close, it was revealed that in a past life Mrs Smith had belonged to the persecuted sect of the Cathars, most of whom, as was related earlier, were persecuted or burned by the Inquisition or their soldiery. Her knowledge of thirteenth-century France appeared to exceed that of modern scholars and there is a gruelling account of how she was herded into the flames and executed. In a letter to Guirdham she recalled:

We all walked barefoot through the streets towards a square where they had prepared a pile of sticks all ready to set alight. There were several monks around singing hymns and praying. I didn't feel grateful. I thought they had a cheek to pray for me. I must be rather a wicked person. I don't think wicked thing when I'm awake, but I dream awful things. I hated those monks being there to see me die. A girl at school once said she dreamt of Christ's crucifixion. I would rather be crucified than burnt. The pain was maddening. You should pray to God when you're dying, if you can pray when you're in agony. In my dream I didn't pray to God. I thought of Roger and how dearly I loved him. The pain of those wicked flames was not half so bad as the pain I felt when I knew he was dead. I felt suddenly glad to be dying. I didn't know when you were burnt to death you'd bleed. I thought the blood would all dry up in the terrible heat. But I was bleeding heavily. The blood was dripping and hissing in the flames. I wished I had enough blood to put the flames out. The worst part was my eyes. I hate the thought of going blind . . . The flames were so cruel after all. They began to feel cold. Icy cold. It occurred to me that I wasn't burning to death but freezing to death. I was numb with cold and suddenly I started to laugh. I had fooled those people who thought they could burn me. I am a witch. I had magicked the fire and turned it into ice.

The Bloxham Tapes

If Guirdham's reconstruction of Mrs Smith's life as a Cathar in thirteenth-century France was not totally convincing – save for those willing to follow a bitty and tortuous historical trail – many television viewers at the end of the 1970s were spellbound by a series of programmes in which Arnold Bloxham, a Swansea hypnotist, regressed a number of subjects. Bloxham had first developed the technique as a therapy to allay a patient's fear of death. He decided to show him that the soul did not dissolve into cosmic space but perpetuated its role in another identity. The experiment relaxed the man and made him accept the hereafter as an opportunity. Bloxham was encouraged and, as he became increasingly proficient, his fame spread and more patients asked for his services. Eventually he became the subject of a short television series, introduced by Magnus Magnusson.

During one of the filmed sessions, Graham Huxtable, a soft-spoken Welshman, changed from a figure of urbanity to a gruff-voiced, illiterate gunner's mate with a powerful cough and a growling drawl. Asked who was on the throne, he replied 'German George', and told them how he had been press-ganged while working the fields with 'Old Moll', his horse. He used the naval slang of the period and told of his adventures aboard a ship called Aggie (*Agamemnon?*) whose captain went by the name of Pearce. The climax cane when the Aggie engaged a French vessel, and during the ensuing gunfire the gunner's leg was blown off. The oaths and groans made painful listening. A naval historian who heard the tape said he was impressed by its 'authenticity' but research could not trace the Aggie or Captain Pearce in the far-from-comprehensive naval officer lists of the period.

In the Hindu system reincarnation is bound to the karmic notion that 'in each today you choose your tomorrow'. But Frederick Nietzsche preferred 'eternal recurrence' or the idea of lives being lived over and over again as a perpetual affirmation of their intrinsic value. 'What does this mad myth signify?' scoffed the novelist Milan Kundera. 'If the French Revolution were to recur eternally, French historians would be less proud of Robespierre. But because they deal with something that will not return, the bloody years of the Revolution have turned into mere words, theories and discussions, have become lighter than feathers . . . For how can we condemn something that is ephemeral in transit? In the sunset of dissolution, everything is illuminated by the aura of nostalgia, even the guillotine.'

Hell is Other People

A chain of existences raises problems for those who view each life as single and finite, and nature as an immense backdrop against which human destiny is enacted. If everything is an unending sequence, how can there be a day of judgement when scores are settled? The idea cancels the solid narrative satisfactions of the good being rewarded and the wicked immersed in flame. Hell – the traditional abode of Satan – has no place in such a scheme. But that torrid resort had already been subject to an impertinent transmutation when Jean-Paul Sartre declared 'Hell is other people'. In his play

Huis Clos, Sartre showed three characters in a Second Empire drawing room (a pacifist, a woman who had murdered her baby and a lesbian) tormenting each other by their outlooks and mutual – but frustrated – desires. Their antipathy and failure to sympathise have doomed them to perpetual misery and misunderstanding.

At a more elemental level, Sartre's premise is that fear and anger start in the nursery where the seeds of self germinate. After an early undifferentiated stage, wherein the world appears a blur of abstract shapes, the toddler will one day be challenged by Another whose estimate of him does not match his own. The presence of Another brings with it threats and apprehensions. The child's image is maligned or 'confiscated' by a presence that defines him in its own special way. He may be challenged or blocked by this Another when all he knows is the 'I' inherited at birth and over which he has no choice. To quell or heal such assaults, he may try to breach the gap that separates the Other. If his gestures provoke a conciliatory response, the outcome may be friendship and unity; if rejected, anger or hurt.

In the case of the latter, the resultant damage may disperse or, alternatively, fester for years, finding reinforcement when it merges with the psyches of the similarly damaged of whom there are, inevitably, millions – for friction and dislocation are the stuff of humanity. The anger will project itself upon an object, perhaps be articulated as a faction or army, for there is no end to the incompletion of the self. And even when the Another, or enemy, is effaced, afterwards there is always a moment of reflective dissatisfaction, almost a loss of self, during which the question forms: What do I do now? And it is never long before a substitute Another arises and takes the place of the vanquished. In this way the ancient stigmata is renewed.

So Hell is no longer a physical reality, a scorching emporium of devils and sinners, but a state of mind, a stance of guilt and resentment. Those hankering after a more topographical approach might consult *Overlord* (1995), a poem by the mystic and historian of spiritual culture Nicholas Hagger. Purporting to show karmic forces at work during the Second World War, this neo-Homeric epic shows Churchill and Hitler as analogous to Michael and Lucifer.

Dantesque passages of grim satire enumerate the chambers of Hell and their denizens who are sympathetic to the Führer. The first Hell is packed with authors and rationalists and the second with sex maniacs like Messalina, Casanova and Frank Harris. The third contains gluttons and drug addicts like De Quincey, Lucullus and Henry VIII, and the fourth avaricious misers. The fifth is peopled with warmongers and military tyrants such as William the Conqueror and Philip II, and the sixth with sadists and criminal lunatics. The seventh holds the ideologues Hagger disapproves of, such as Karl Marx, and finally there is Satan's own diabolic penthouse where he reclines with his bosom cronies:

> Beyond the seven hells
> Is pitch darkness of chaos, where light is
> Absent, where Satan dwells in the centre
> Of a thorn, guarded by prickles, hanging
> Like a bat (as his form Odin hung on
> The World Tree), near a cesspit where all waste
> Matter decays before, recycled, it
> Flows back into existence; surrounded
> By Arch-demons, forms his emanation
> Spawned in fornications, incarnations
> Both aliases of himself and children
> Such as Baal, Sammael, Beliar, Abaddon,
> His Hindu-like manifestations as
> Idol, seducer, fornicator and
> Destroyer; and by all his disciples:
> Simon Magus, Roderic Borgia (Pope
> Alexander the Sixth), Adam Weishaupt,
> Eliphas Levi, Aleister Crowley,
> Rasputin; in a thicket of Darkness
> Whence like the Axe through underground caverns,
> Decomposed, broken down into new forms,
> Its force and consciousness again released,
> Matters flows out into the universe,
> Polluted with deception and falsehood.

To anyone partial to leafing through infernal travel brochures, this type of poem is a revelation and Hagger's tickertape fluency is truly copious.

The Dream of John Haigh

Considered purely as entertainment – of more commercial value than the Devil or Hell – was the ubiquitous, ever-thirsty vampire. Beginning in the Edwardian era, numerous films were made – some classics – celebrating the antics of the undead. Bela Lugosi starred in a number, including *Return of the Vampire*, where he portrayed a vampire named Armand Tesla. Drake Douglas recalled a typical sequence in the movie: Tesla's chief adversary sits playing the family organ, while Lugosi (in evening clothes of course) threatens her. With a sweeping gesture, she removes the music book from the rack and reveals a lighted cross; Lugosi disappears in a clap of thunder. Finally Tesla – who has slain his werewolf assassin – is dragged into the sunlight and the flesh runs from his skull like melting wax, a delightfully gruesome end.'

It sounds funny enough – but what does all it amount to? Horror films, fright wigs, skeletons and gory essays in virtual reality supply a social function. They provide small, fictitious worries and tensions upon which men and women can divert their concentration and so gain temporary release from the large worries – war, disease, famine, oppression, death of loved ones – that truly wreak havoc with their lives. In effect, a commercial horror film is a placebo, a cathartic cartoon.

But that does not distract from the fact that a grimmer truth lurks behind these celluloid projections – hundreds of enthusiastic blood-drinkers and necrophiliacs have gained a place in the criminal annals. A notable English representative was John Haigh, the vampire of London, who was born in 1910 to parents who were Plymouth Brethren. This puritanical sect forbade drinking and gambling and also considered radio, films, comics and newspapers to be sources of corruption. At sixteen Haigh became a choirboy in the Church of England and later an assistant organist. Haigh's mother also believed in dreams and portents and influenced her son who confessed he had this repeated dream:

I saw a forest of crucifixes, which gradually turned into trees. At first I seemed to see dew or rain running from the branches. But when I came nearer I knew it was blood. All of a sudden the whole forest began to twist about and the trees streamed with blood. Blood ran from the trunks. Blood ran from the branches, all red and shiny. I felt weak and seemed to faint. I saw a man going round the trees gathering blood. When the cup he was holding in his hand was full he came up to me and said 'drink'. But I was paralysed. The dream vanished. But I still felt faint and stretched out with all my strength towards that cup.

Oddly enough, not being a pitiless man, Haigh could not understand why God allowed Christ to hang so long on the cross. By contrast, he killed his nine victims and drank their blood with relative efficiency. He also drank his own urine every day up to the period of his trial, following the text in the Bible, 'Drink out of thine own cistern and running waters out of thine own well.'

Haigh claimed his persistent dream underlined his desire to kill and drink blood. The thought of a deed – hideous yet gruesomely seductive – instils itself in the mind, first as a dream, and then, as it is denied expression, accrues strength through nocturnal replay until the criminal, more in the grip of subconscious lusts and yearnings than the average man, enacts the fantasy in flesh.

Why Take Death Lying Down?

But not all tales of the undead returning are gloomy and blood-spattered. Hope – and a little black humour – may be found in some accounts of revenants, as in case of Kalenben Balabhai, who died on 2 January 1989. Kalenben was a hundred years old and her end was expected. Solemnly her relatives carried the body to the cremation ground of her village, Gujarat in India, and placed it on the funeral pyre. As they prepared to ignite it, her family were shocked when the 'corpse' sat up and demanded to be taken home. When she discovered that her flat had already been let to a couple, Amuan and Selim Kahaan, by her son Luxan, she flew into a rage and actually threw some of the Kahaans' furniture out the window before the police arrived to establish some order.

Usually resurrected bodies are joyfully welcomed back into the bosom of their families. But this is not invariably so. According to a Reuters report on 20 July 1991, a Romanian widow fainted when her husband, Neagu, aged seventy-one, demanded to be let in to his house. About a week before, Neagu had choked on a fishbone and died of a heart attack. Three days after he was buried, the gravediggers at the cemetery heard a knocking and found him lying in the coffin among wilted flowers. When Neagu attempted to take up his old existence, his wife and children, fearing that he might be a ghost and exert a baneful influence, refused to have anything to do with him. In fact, it took Neagu a full three weeks to persuade the police, town hall officials, doctors and priests to officially erase his death from the records.

More gruesome and ethically inscrutable was the case of the eighteen-year-old Romanian girl declared clinically dead in January 1992. She was taken to a mortuary in Bucharest where she lay perfectly lifeless until the attendant proceeded to rape her. Then she regained consciousness – much to her assailant's horror. The police later arrested the rapist, but the parents refused to press charges 'because their daughter owed her life to him'.

Angels and Small Greys

If vampires and devils made a comeback, so did their opponents, angels, derived from the Greek word *angelos* or messenger. While rage against satanic abuse was frothing, these magnificent forms, sometimes winged, sometimes disguised as ordinary folk, appeared to a variety of people in Europe and America. They rescued skiers who were about to plunge over precipices, helped people on sickbeds, revived the weary and down-hearted, reared up in forests and meadows, golden and glowing. As Joseph Felser (1996) observed,

> Wherever one turns these days, an angel pops up: yet another book on angels on the shelves of the local Barnes & Noble; yet

another television program in which someone claims to have been saved from doom by the timely intervention of the angelic hosts; yet another angelic gee-gaw in some or another catalogue devoted to 'spiritual pursuits'. There are angelwatch networks, angel tee-shirts, angel mugs, and so on, ad nauseam. But what does it all mean?

Felser develops his argument by quoting John Lilly who put himself in contact with two 'guardians' or beings whose 'magnificent deep powerful love overwhelms me . . . If they come any closer . . . I would lose myself as a cognitive entity, merging with them. They further say I am separated into two, because that is my way of perceiving them, but that in reality they are one.' This triplicate identity suggested to Felser the Blessed Trinity: Father and Son bound by the Holy Spirit, implying that the mystery of divinity is contained in each separate individual.

Less captivating than angels – less terrifying than medieval devils – are the creatures from outer space who abduct earth people and spirit them to their craft where they strip them down and perform lubricious investigations on their bodies. There was a spate of such kidnappings in the 1980s and 1990s and it formed the subject of Whitley Strieber's bestseller *Communion*. The basic scenario involved the appearance before female subjects of glimmering lights, followed by abduction by small grey creatures who laid them on a kind of pallet and carried out internal examination, followed by the scraping of tissue and the insertion of eggs or ova by the gynaecologically minded visitors. There are two main types: Small Grey and Tall beings, neither of which breathe air or ingest food. Their mouths do not move; telepathy is their preferred mode of communication. They appear to have no obvious opposable thumbs and huge ET-like eyes. A third type, half-human, half-reptile, makes an appearance from time to time as does another more glamorous extra-terrestrial with shoulder-length blond hair.

How well-intentioned aliens are is a moot point if we consider the case of 28-year-old mother Myrna Hansen. In the company of her five-year-old son, she was driving her car near Cimarron, New Mexico, when she was dazzled and overwhelmed. The vehicle filled with blinding white light after which she saw five UFOs in a field. When one moved towards her, she came over paralysed and afraid for her son. Eventually she rallied and drove to her destination – surprised to find the 28-mile journey had taken six hours.

Under hypnosis, she revealed that she and her son had been taken to an underground facility which, she believed, was in the vicinity of Roswell. There she had been stripped and a cold object inserted in her vagina. She had witnessed aliens operating on a cow that was still alive – 'They're pulling it apart' – and an underground cavern through which a river flowed. She was also shown a room with a humanoid figure floating in vat of reddish liquid which she connected with the tissues removed from animals. After her abduction experience, Myrna became serious ill with a vaginal infection that her doctor was unable to identify; she only survived, he said, because he gave her massive doses of gamma globulin to boost her immune system.

Dr Jaques Vallee finds prototypes for the saucers and their occupants in the folklore of several cultures, like the shape-shifting elves and fairy folk with their magical appurtenances and power of vanishing. The aliens may be 'an advanced race from the future' attempting to guide our civilisation or, alternatively, occupants of a parallel universe, 'another dimension where there are other human races living, and where we may go at our expense'. Perhaps the creatures are only half-human and need cross-breeding in order to maintain contact with earth people?

It is an enigma why psychologists are so baffled and fascinated by these surgical dreamscapes with sci-fi trappings. It is rather as if anxieties over procedures like smear tests have become mysteriously entangled with the 'alien' scenarios of television and film. This is further complicated by much of the evidence emerging under hypnosis: problems arise in establishing a criterion by which one can separate direct experience from more imaginative material 'blowing loose' during a trance state.

Men in Black

How different are the Small Greys, Tall Beings and 'angels' of today from the apparitions and spirits of the Middle Ages and later? Are they none other than traditional ghosts and ghouls but with the garnishings of technology? That the mind tends to dress its fears in contemporary garb is borne out in the accounts of MIBs – 'men in black' – who persecute those who appear too knowledgeable about UFOs. These sinister figures invariably wear black ties, black suits, black shoes and socks – but their shirts are often an immaculate, gleaming white. Sometimes they wear wrap-around shades that shield their eyes, which may be slanted and oriental. Occasionally a witness throws in an arrestingly incongruous detail – one MIB was described as wearing a bright lipstick! Like any medieval inquisitor, they bully, harass and threaten, and leave only after exacting a vow of absolute silence.

They were first identified by Albert Bender, head of the International Flying Saucer Bureau, an organisation based in Connecticut and formed in 1952 but closed down not long after. Previously Bender had made the claim, 'I know what saucers are.' This proved to be unwise, for before he had time to make a disclosure, he had a most startling visitation. While lying down in his bedroom recovering from a spell of dizziness, three shadowy figures marched in, dressed in black clothes. They looked like clergymen and wore Homburg-style hats which made their faces and expressions shadowy. The eyes of the figures began to glow like flashlight bulbs. 'They seemed to burn into my very soul,' he recalled, 'as the pains above my eyes became almost unbearable. It was then I sensed that they were conveying a message to me by telepathy.'

The visitors told him that he had better keep his knowledge under lock and key. Their demeanours were sufficiently scary to cow him into compliance although, paradoxically enough, he was not so terrified as to be unable to produce two books about the experience: the first, *They Knew Too Much About Flying Saucers*, by his colleague Gray Barker, the second, *Flying Saucers and the Three Men* by himself.

Waco

Visions of UFOs, MIBs and angels are the stuff of millennial cults which, as we have seen, lean heavily on the prophetic books of the Bible. One might have thought, more than five centuries after the meteoric blaze-outs of Thomas Muntzer and John of Leyden, that such fervid superstitions could be no longer be seriously reawakened. But old dogmas constantly throw out new leaves, and in April 1993, after enduring a 51-day siege, the cult compound called Ranch Apocalypse went up in flames, killing the self-appointed Messiah, David Koresh, and around eighty of his disciples.

David Vernon Koresh (1959–93) started life as the illegitimate son of a fourteen-year-old girl. An only child, he had grown up dyslexic, ultra-sensitive, terrified of rejection and prone to violent outbursts, until he reached his early twenties and turned to a loving freestyle Christianity. His personal magnetism and fluent knowledge of the Bible impressed many, and soon he drew a circle of converts around him, forming his own community of Branch Davidians at Mount Carmel, near Waco, Texas. But as his charisma grew, so did his tendency to interpret his childish tantrums and sexual demands as directives from God. He was bending Christianity in order to take pleasure and power where and when it suited him.

'If you are a Branch Davidian,' an article on the cult began, 'Christ lives on a threadbare piece of land ten miles east of Waco called Mount Carmel. He has dimples, claims a ninth-grade education, married his legal wife when she was fourteen, enjoys a beer now and then, plays a mean guitar, reportedly packs a Glock 9mm and keeps an arsenal of military assault rifles, and willingly admits that he is a sinner without equal.'

The article went on to deal with allegations of child abuse perpetrated by 'The Sinful Messiah', as Koresh called himself, for whereas Christ had been 'sinless', it was his role to explore sin more thoroughly before cleansing himself. Aware of the net of the FBI closing in, the last days of the Waco community were punctuated by Koresh's apocalyptic rants. In rapidly connected, metaphoric style, he would shout out passages from Prophets and Revelation; they were seemingly inspired, yet not always clear in their meaning. But more and more during these outbursts he would refer to the coming end, to Armageddon, the symbolical battlefield, where the armies of good and evil were destined to engage in a final conflict. Violent storms, Koresh maintained, were signs from God, as was the Californian earthquake – expressions of anger that some of his followers had not obeyed his will. During one of his lectures, he claimed that God had the right to demand the deaths of those who spurned his message – 'if today you are not willing to kill for the Message, or in turn to die for it, then you are not worthy of it and will go to Hell and be severely punished by God'.

Among his last communications to the FBI, written on lavender notepaper and sent out during the siege, was the following:

I offer you my wisdom. I offer you my sealed secrets. How dare you turn away My invitations to mercy. Who are you fighting against? The law is Mine, the Truth is Mine. I AM your God and you will bow under my feet. I AM your life and your death. I am the spirit of the prophets and the Author of their testimonies. Do you think you have the power to stop My will? My seven thunders are to be revealed. Do you want me to laugh at your pending torments? Do you want Me to pull the heavens back and show you My anger? Fear Me, for I have you in my snare. I forewarn you the Lake Waco area of Old Mount Carmel will be terribly shaken. The waters of the lake will be emptied through the broken dam.

In keeping with the blood and fury of his vision, Koresh's charred body was discovered in the communications room of Ranch Apocalypse. He had died from a single gunshot wound through the centre of his forehead and out through the back of his skull. 'It is not among the more frequently encountered suicide wounds,' commented Dr Cyril Welcht, an independent pathologist.

FEAR IN THE CITY

Living in towns, illuminated at night and guarded by police, diminished (for a time) the fear of violence, while prosperity and the welfare state reduced the number of those who feared famine, homelessness, illness, unemployment, old age. Nevertheless the present generation spends far more money insuring itself against those fears than ever its ancestors paid churches or magicians for protection.

(*An Intimate History of Humanity*, Theodore Zeldin, 1994)

Koresh was essentially a child of America, of urbanisation and social expectation. In a sense he was highly ambitious, a 'right man' determined to achieve dominance and mastery over the lives of others. His followers started to morbidly fear him – he seemed to own and direct their lives. But such a feeling is not unique to criminal messiahs – an overbearing or ruthless employer can wield similar power. Most people have been visited with the apprehension (which may tip over into full-scale panic or breakdown) that they can no longer cope with the demands of their job.

'In the office in which I work,' begins *Something Happened* by Joseph Heller, 'there are five people of whom I'm afraid. Each of these five people is afraid of four people (excluding overlaps), for a total of twenty, and each of these twenty people is afraid of six people, making a total of one hundred and twenty people who are feared by at least one person. Each of these one hundred and twenty people is afraid of the other one hundred and nineteen, and all of these one hundred and forty-five people are afraid of the twelve men at the top who have helped found and build the company and now own and direct it.'

As the Heller extract emphasises, employment operates through a network of tension. The pressure to maintain a job and compete with others does not create the same order of sensation as shrinking fear or pure terror because it is often tinged with mild elation. There are huge social rewards for working hard as well as concomitant dangers. But as a job may come to define a man, demarcating his social status, mobility and the type of woman he attracts, losing it can seem like a symbolic stripping – an expulsion from Eden into a Hell of indirection. That is why any boss or figure of authority can loom into a nightmare demon.

And businesses themselves are intimately entangled with fear – fear that revolves around the notion of risk. The latter is a kind of quantified fear – an assessment of potential loss – strained through computers and pocket calculators. In moving men and women about and promoting products, there is an element of gamble and adventure. Implicit in business risk is the idea of future territory about to be colonised or conquered. Without it there would be no tension, no excitement, and success or profit would matter less.

Amygdala

There is a line where excitement or frisson merges into the starker emotion of undiluted fear; this is entirely natural as situations develop and take on a more ominous character. Recently, with sophisticated brain-imaging techniques, it has become easy to observe how physiologically close are excitement, fear and curiosity, the main difference being the psychological interpretation. The brain's alarm system is the amygdala which, if stimulated, sets a chemical bell ringing, but its response is modified by the 'operator' in the frontal cortex.

Although part of the primitive brain, the amygdala is a sophisticated button, producing three definable responses: a feeling of panic and a desire to run, an uprush of rage or violent indignation and a floaty or 'oceanic' feeling that is pleasurable. So, to put it crudely, three survival strategies – panic, aggression and appeasement – are squeezed like a triple-switch into a small knob of tissue, enabling a split-second alteration of mood. If an assailant is not disarmed by the sweetness of a smile, he might be mollified by sight of a pair of feet running away. What if flight is impossible? Then a further stimulus produces a bunching of muscles and physical assertiveness. Intelligent activity is taking place at the same time between instinctive and thinking parts. Rapid messages are flashed to the frontal cortex; the thinking part of the brain weighs and mediates the pros and cons: 'He's far too big too fight – better smile or offer him money. On the other hand, he's very fat – perhaps I might outrun him!' But often the field of reaction is restricted. If you're in fear of your boss or a creditor, it is not always tactful to dash out of his office screaming. After consulting the frontal cortex, the amygdala might persuade you to grin or grovel amicably. If the boss's manner is kind, you may relax and come over warm and dizzy. But what if, however, subsequent to apology, he humiliates you further? You may well redden with rage and make him the offer of your fists.

Naturally city life often triggers messages of arousal and high tension. Cities contain a motley of types who pose a threat to those intimidated by contrasts of culture and attitude. Even the physical aspect of a metropolis presents a problem. There are high buildings that make people feel insignificant and confined spaces like elevators where they are oppressed by the closeness of others – 'Oh God, these people are taking my air away from me!' Even parks, usually comforting places, become threatening at night, with trees obscuring the view and providing shelter for rapists and robbers. In such locales, people have to learn to cope with fear. One method is to hide it by never looking afraid or as if you do not know where you are going. Another ruse is to feign mild insanity. 'Sometimes I've acted as if I'm a bit mad,' admitted one London resident, 'because you don't tend to approach people if they look a bit loopy, so I talk to myself or something, or whistle or sing. If I just act a bit loopy, people might think I'm strange and leave me alone.' A New Yorker proffered the following observation: 'One thing about New York is that you're always told never to look anybody straight in the eyes because you don't want to provoke somebody. I tend to wear sunglasses on the subway because I can observe them without them seeing me, and it's this kind of incognito costume I wear.'

This fear of 'another looking at you' transfers to traits like being fanatically house-proud. A stare implies judgement or disapproval and an untidy house may be seen as a symbol of a careless or 'undressed' mind. But are such manifestations mere shadow play? Do they mask an overwhelming primal fear that infuses all phenomena? When, on seeing a damp stain on the carpet, a housewife breaks down in heavy sobbing – is she lamenting the prosaic evidence that confronts her? Or has that tiny circle of wetness become saturate with the horror and glory of existence? The small worry is channelling a larger one. So one must always pause and allow for such outbursts. We are all harassed passengers aboard a vessel whose destination – if, indeed, there is one – awaits disclosure.

No One Is Immune

No doubt, in this third millennium, mankind will continue to be beset by fears, crazes and swirling panics. The twentieth century has proven a repository of mob violence, racial holocaust, mass bigotry and collective suicide. More recently, we have had startling UFO rumours, food scares and successive waves of 'diabolic' and 'divine' happenings. Many of these have surged through societies like forest fires and just as inexplicably vanished – as though the whole thing had never taken place. As this book has, I hope, demonstrated, no one is immune to fear or the crowd madness it generates. It can strike any nation, profession or social stratum. The first step in dealing with the phenomenon is to recognise its existence; the second is to suppress any headstrong urge and think long and hard about an issue before embracing or rejecting it.

THE VISION IN THE TOWER

> All human wisdom is summed up in two words – wait and hope.
> (Alexander Dumas the Elder, 1802–70)

The foregoing has been a kind of journey through the badlands of history – a narrative of terror, torture and desecration. Among other things it has shown how, by the political use of fear, the darker side of mankind has so often gained the upper hand; how it can manifest itself in violence against people and animals; how men and women down the ages have been oppressed with a nameless dread or ubiquitous 'fear of nothing' which has assumed various spectral shapes.

In some ways it has been a bleak – but I hope not uninstructive – narrative. Is there any hope at the end, one asks? Is there light behind the primal terror of existence? If fear is the shadow of our apprehension, where is the hidden sun that inspires it? Novelist and dramatist J.B. Priestley wrote in his autobiography, *Rain Upon Godshill*, an account of a dream. He was standing at the top of a tower looking down upon a vast aerial river of birds flying in one direction. He was thrilled and overwhelmed by the sight but then 'the gear was changed' and time started to move faster, and 'I saw generations of birds, watched them break their shells, flutter into life, mate, weaken, falter and die. Wings grew only to crumble; bodies were sleek and then, in a flash, bled and shrivelled; and death struck everywhere at every second. What was the use of all this blind struggle towards life, this eager trying of wings, this hurried mating, this flight and surge, all this gigantic meaningless biological effort? As I stared down, seeming to see every creature's ignoble little history almost at a glance, I felt sick at heart. It would be better if not one of them, if not one of us all, had been born, if the struggle ceased forever. I stood on my tower, still alone, desperately unhappy. But now the gear was changed again and time went faster still, and it was rushing by at such a rate, that the birds could not show any movement, but were like an enormous plain sown with feathers. But along this plain, flickering through the bodies themselves, there now passed a sort of white flame, trembling, dancing, then hurrying on; and as soon as I saw it, I knew that this white flame was life itself, the very quintessence of being; and then it came to me in a rocket-burst of ecstasy, that nothing mattered, nothing could ever matter, because nothing else was real, but this quivering and hurrying lambency of being. Birds, men, or creatures not yet shaped or coloured, all were of no account except so far as this flame of life travelled through them. It left nothing to mourn over behind; what I had thought was tragedy was mere emptiness or a shadow show; for now all real feeling was caught and purified and danced on ecstatically with the white flame of life. I had never felt such deep happiness as I knew at the end of my dream of the tower and the birds, and if I have not kept that happiness with me, as an inner atmosphere and a sanctuary for the heart, that is because I am a weak and foolish man who allows the mad world to come trampling in, destroying every green shoot of wisdom.'

In a sense, Priestley had glimpsed – or thought he had glimpsed – a vision of the *elan vital* behind appearances – a force that contained each individual life, yet collectively amounted to much more than the sum of its parts. While 'containing' compassion, it was essentially vast and impersonal.

It appears that Priestley was undergoing a kind of 'tunnel' experience before he had the dream. During the early part, he was depressed by the swarming profusion of dying birds, the infinite duplication of living forms, but this later gave way to a 'white flame', standing for the unifying principle behind matter, the Spanish *duende* or the dance of Pan. It is perhaps significant that, in the West, mystics see God in the form of a descending ray of white light, while those in the East speak of the spiritual being taking the form of fire. But whatever the terminology, fear is the shadow of this light, this intimate apprehension of mortality that every man and woman must confront in order to find a way through. Each must understand how the 'white flame' will one day absorb and recycle them, and the meaning of the process will be rewritten endlessly by those who come after.

BIBLIOGRAPHY

Panic: the Birth & Spread of Terror

Autobiography of Saint Teresa of Jesus (c. 1562–8), translated by David Lewis

Boardman, John, *The Great God Pan: the Survival of an Image*, Thames & Hudson (1997)

Carus, Dr Paul, *The History of the Devil and the Idea of Evil*, Chicago (1900)

Craze, Richard, *Hell: An Illustrated History of the Netherworld*, Godsfield Press (1996)

Hogg, James, 'The Black-Faced Sheep and Her Ways' from *The Farmer's Life*, JM Dent (1936), pp. 104–9

Hull, John M., *Hellenistic Magic and the Synoptic Tradition*, SCM Press (1974)

Jung, C.G., *Man and His Symbols*, Aldus Books (1964)

Nietzsche, Frederick, *The Birth of Tragedy* (1872), reprinted Doubleday (1956)

Simpson, Professor Keith, *Life & Death: An Illustrated Investigation into the Incredible World of Death*, Galley Press (1979)

Thorpe, Nick, 'The Archaeology of the Undead', *3rd Stone* (April/June 1998), p. 43

The Middle Ages: Theological Nightmares

Bainton, Roland H., *Here I Stand: A Life of Martin Luther*, New American Library (1950)

Baring-Gould, Sabine, *The Book of Werewolves* (1865), Senate reprint (1995), pp. 85–99

Berman, Morris, *Coming To Our Senses*, Unwin Paperback (1989), pp. 63–102, 178–220

Bloch, Marc, *Feudal Society*, Chicago (1961)

Cohn, Norman, *The Pursuit of the Millennium* (1957), Secker & Warburg, pp. 234–51, 271–80

Cooper, J.C., *An Illustrated History of Symbols*, Thames & Hudson (1978)

Davies, Norman, *A History of Europe*, Oxford University Press (1996)

De Lancre, Pierre, *Tableau de l'inconstance des mauvais anges et démons*, Paris (1612)

Frayling, Christopher, *Strange Landscape: A Journey Through the Middle Ages*, BBC (1995)

Kiple, Kenneth E. (ed.), *Plague, Pox and Pestilence: Disease in History*, Weidenfeld & Nicolson (1997)

Nikiforuk, Andrew, *The Fourth Horseman: a short history of plagues, epidemics and other scourges*, Fourth Estate (1992), Chapter 3 'Immortal Blemish' on leprosy, pp. 27–41

Ogilvy, Mrs D., *A Book of Highland Minstrelsy*, Griffin (1860)

Riemer, A.P., *Patterns of Evasion in Shakespeare's Comedies*, Manchester University Press (1980), pp. 165–6

Robbins, Rossell Hope, *An Encyclopaedia of Witchcraft and Demonology*, 6th impression, Spring (1970)

Sale, Kirkpartrick, *The Conquest of Paradise: Christopher Columbus & the Columbian Legacy*, Hodder & Stoughton (1991)

Schmitt, Jean-Claude, *Ghosts of the Middle Ages*, Chicago University Press (1998)

Stoyanov, Yuri, *The Hidden Tradition in Europe: The Secret History of the Medieval Christian Heresy*, Arkana (1994)

Wilson, Colin, *The Occult*, Hodder & Stoughton (1971)

Elizabethans: Disorder in the Kingdom

Brown, Ivor, *Shakespeare*, William Collins (1949)

Deacon, *John Dee: Scientist, Geographer, Astrologer & Secret Agent to Elizabeth I*, Muller (1968)

Donne, John (1572–1631), *Selected Prose*, Penguin (1987)

French, Peter J., *John Dee: The World of an Elizabethan Magus*, RKP (1972)

Machiavelli, Niccolo, *The Prince* (1532), Oxford University Press World Classic

Marlowe, Christopher, *Dr Faustus*, ed. J.D. Dump, Manchester University Press (1962)

Nashe, Thomas (1567–c. 1600), *The Unfortunate Traveller and Other Works*, Penguin (1972)

Pagels, Elaine, *Adam, Eve and the Serpent*, Weidenfeld & Nicolson (1988), p. 89 on St Jerome

Scot, Reginald, *The Discoverie of Witchcraft*, Brome, London (1584)

Tillyard, E.M.W., *The Elizabethan World Picture*, Chatto & Windus (1943)

Restoration & Revolution: Nature & Nothing

Greene, Graham, *Lord Rochester's Monkey*, Bodley Head (1974)

Hobbes, Thomas, *Leviathan* (1651), abridged and edited by J. Plamenatz, Collins (1972)

Lyons, Paddy, *Lord Rochester*, Everyman's Poetry series, JM Dent (1996)

Palmer, Tony, *Charles II: Portrait of an Age*, Cassell (1979)

Ricks, Christopher (ed.), *English Drama to 1710*, Sphere History of Literature in the English Language, Sphere Books (1971)

de Sade, *Selected Writings of De Sade*, selected and translated by Margaret Crosland, Peter Owen (1964)

Thomas, Donald, *The Marquis de Sade*, Allison & Busby (1992)

Wilson, Colin, *A Criminal History of Mankind*, Grafton Books (1985)

The Romantics: Ministry of Fear

Clark, Kenneth, *Civilisation*, BBC/John Murray (1969)

Cohen, Daniel, *The Body Snatchers: The Weird and Horrible Library*, JM Dent & Sons (1977)

Ford, Boris (ed.), *From Donne to Marvell*, Penguin (1956)

Frayling, Christopher, *Nightmare: The Birth of Horror*, BBC (1996)

Lamb, Charles (1775–1834), 'Witches and Other Night Fears' from *Selected Prose*, Penguin (1985)

Quincey, Thomas de, *Confessions of an English Opium Eater* (1821), Wordsworth Classics (1994)

Todd, Ruthven, 'The Reputation of Henry Fuseli', *Horizon: a review of literature and art*, Volume 6 (1942)

Varma, Devendra P., *The Gothic Flame*, Arthur Barker (1957)

Volta, Ornella, *The Vampire: Myth or Reality*, Tandem Books (1965)

Wilson, Rowan, *Vampires: Bloodsuckers from Beyond the Grave*, Parragon (1997)

Victoriana: the Reign of Ghosts

Behrman, S.N., *Conversations with Max*, Hamish Hamilton (1960) pp. 113–16

Butler, Samuel, *The Way of All Flesh* (1903), Modern Library (1998)

Crowley, Aleister, *Confessions of Aleister Crowley*, Jonathan Cape (1969)

Gosse, Edmund, *Father and Son*, Heinemann (1888)

Gosse, Philip, *Omphalos: An Attempt to Untie the Geological Knot*, John Van Voorst (1857)

Huysman, Joris-Karl, *Against Nature* (1884), Oxford University Press (1998)

Inglis, Brian, *Natural and Supernatural: A History of the Paranormal*, Hodder & Stoughton (1977)

Jackson, Kevin (ed.), *The Oxford Book of Money*, Oxford University Press (1995)

Lautréamont, *Maldoror* (1868), translated by Paul Knight, Penguin (1978)

Mackay, Charles (1814–89), *Extraordinary Popular Delusions and the Madness of Crowds*, Wordsworth (1995)

Newman, Paul, *The Meads of Love: A Life of John Harris*, Truran (1995)

Twentieth Century: Thin Ice of Civilisation

Blackwood, Algernon, *Tales of the Uncanny and Supernatural*, Peter Nevill (1949)

Bloom, Clive (ed.), *Creepers: British Horror & Fantasy in the Twentieth Century*, Pluto Press (1993)

Carter, Rita, *Mapping the Mind*, Weidenfeld & Nicolson (1998)

Edwardes, Michael, *The Dark Side of History: Magic in the Making of Man*, Granada (1978)

Guirdham, Arthur, *The Cathars and Reincarnation*, Neville Spearman (1970), pp. 88–9

Hagger, Nicholas, *Overlord: The Triumph of Light*, Element (1995), p. 82

Hastings, Robert J., 'An Examination of the Borley Report', *Proceedings of the Society for Psychical Research*, Volume 55 (March 1969)

Hawken, Paul, *The Magic of Findhorn*, Fontana (1976)

Iverson, Jeffrey, *More Lives Than One*, Souvenir Press (1976)

La Fontaine, Joan, *Speak of the Devil: Tales of Satanic Abuse in Contemporary England*, Cambridge University Press (1998)

Leppard, David, *Fire and Blood: The True Story of David Koresh and the Waco Siege*, Fourth Estate (1993)

Lewis, Peter, *The Fifties*, William Heinemann (1978)

Masters, Anthony, *The Natural History of the Vampire*, Rupert Hart-Davis (1972)

McClure, Kevin, *The Evidence for Visions of the Virgin Mary*, Aquarian Press (1983)

Priestley, J.B., *Rain Upon Godshill*, Heinemann (1939), pp. 304–6

Sinclair, Andrew, *War Like A Wasp: The Lost Decade of the Forties*, Hamish Hamilton (1989), p. 60

Strieber, Whitley, *Communion*, Century Hutchinson (1987)

Tabori, Paul, *Harry Price, Ghost-Hunter*, The Athenaeum Press (1950)

Thomas, D.M., *Alexander Solzhenitsyn: A Century in his Life*, Little, Brown & Company (1998), pp. 84–5

Valentine, Mark, *Arthur Machen*, Seren (1995)

Vansittart, Peter, *In the Fifties*, John Murray (1995)

Warnock, Mary, *Existentialism*, Oxford University Press (1970)

Wilson, Colin, *Alien Dawn*, Virgin Books (1998)

INDEX